DISHING UP® WASHINGTON

DISHING UP® WASHINGTON

150 RECIPES THAT CAPTURE AUTHENTIC REGIONAL FLAVORS

JESS THOMSON

Photography by Lara Ferroni

The mission of Storey Publishing is to serve our customers by
publishing practical information that encourages
personal independence in harmony with the environment.

Edited by Margaret Sutherland and Lisa H. Hiley
Art direction and book design by Cynthia N. McFarland,
      based on a design by Tom Morgan of Blue Design

Cover and interior photography by © Lara Ferroni, except
      for author photograph by © Clare Barboza
Map, pages 10–11, by © Anne Smith

Indexed by Nancy D. Wood
Reprint permissions appear on page 287

Storey Publishing
210 MASS MoCA Way
North Adams, MA 01247
www.storey.com

Printed in China by R.R. Donnelley
10 9 8 7 6 5 4 3 2 1

LIBRARY OF CONGRESS CATALOGING-IN-PUBLICATION DATA

Thomson, Jess.
    Dishing up Washington / Jess Thomson ; photography by
      Lara Ferroni.
        pages cm
    Includes index.
    ISBN 978-1-61212-028-7 (pbk.)
    1. Cooking, American—Pacific Northwest style.
    2. Cooking—Washington (State) I. Title.
TX715.2.P32T556 2012
641.59797—dc23

                                                2012024857

TO WASHINGTON,
for giving me a place I so happily call home

★ ★ ★

ACKNOWLEDGMENTS

FIRST AND FOREMOST, a huge and fragrant bouquet of thanks goes to the chefs and farmers who donated their time and energy. Their hard work has made this state's food scene vibrant, and this book would not have been possible without their generous contributions of information and recipes.

Applause and thanks also go to the entire team at Storey Publishing, who put this gorgeous Dishing Up series together and invited me to be a part of it.

This book would not be what it is without Lara Ferroni, the outstanding photographer I'd wanted to work with for years. Throughout the process, she was a trusted resource for recipe testing and a fabulous travel companion. Lara, this book is as much yours as it is mine, and I thank you for your constant commitment and support. Someday, we'll do a book that's only photos of us with baby animals and you'll be able to use all those outtakes.

Thanks also to my recipe testers: Sarah Collyer, always my go-to gal, as well as Libby Fernau, Carma Burnett, Lauren Schultz, Mary Russell, Lindsay Hill, Carole Mathieson, Marny Lichtenstein, Amy Howe, Allison Howe, Nancy Thomson, Rebekah Denn, Susan Brook, Tami Horner, Hannah Viano, Alida Moore, Tim Collyer, Marc Schermerhorn, and Sarah Wallingford Blohm. And to my tireless reader, Lauren Bedford, for always having time for me.

Laura Russell, you were the best intern a woman could have.

Finally, thanks to my Seattle friends and family, who have dealt with my crazy dinners, my piles of dishes, and my litany of testing complaints. Your friendship and feedback are a crucial part of this process.

And thanks to my husband, Jim, and to our son, Graham, for always being there at the table with me.

contents

FOREWORD BY ETHAN STOWELL

of Anchovies & Olives, How to Cook a Wolf, Staple & Fancy, and Tavolata

I'M A WASHINGTON BOY. I spent cool, dappled summers in Seattle, prowling the dense blackberry thickets that grow like, well, weeds in every Seattle backyard. When we were young, my father did the cooking, gathering us nightly for a big family feast. Even then, you could find incredible food just by walking out the door, even near the city. Lakes are ringed with wild watercress and fern fronds coiled like green snails. Gray beaches and tidal flats offer up oysters, mussels, and clams to those with strong arms and a willingness to dig, not to mention the enormous geoduck, a giant clam that looks much like a small elephant trunk hanging out of a shell. Insane to look at, but incredible to eat — sweet and briny, the flesh nearly crisp.

The same mild, damp weather that gives the Emerald City its name coaxes morels and chanterelles out of the needle-strewn forest floor and urges those tangles of thorny, obnoxious blackberry canes that, one glorious day in August, all seem to burst simultaneously with heavy purple-black fruit as fragrant as it is sweet.

Now that I think about it, it's a place where some of the best food seems to almost bite you back: tender spring nettles that sting, those armored blackberries, aerodynamic razor clams that send up a little see-you squirt in your face as they dive toward the center of the earth, two-and-a-half-pound Dungeness crabs that try to grab you as you haul them out of the crab pot.

That was all there 35 years ago, and still is (nothing will kill blackberries short of an apocalypse), but what's amazing to me is what wasn't. There weren't farmers' markets in every neighborhood, offering handmade goat cheese, and fresh eggs, and new potatoes in shades from blush to bright rose. There were no urban chickens or backyard goats.

Community Supported Agriculture, or CSA, programs, where subscribers pay in advance for produce grown at a certain farm, had not yet caught on. Pike Place Market wasn't the showstopper it is today, a vibrant, working public market where restaurateurs handpick their produce and tourists flock to see salmon fly. (Remember, it's where the very first itty-bitty Starbucks opened its doors in 1971, if that's any indication of how things have grown.)

Back then, if you wanted to buy fresh fish, you went down to the docks. Now, places like Taylor Shellfish offer some of the world's best oysters at trendy storefronts in the most urban pockets of Seattle. Now, instead of the odd forager dropping by a commercial kitchen to offer handpicked nettles or a bagful of buttery chanterelles, it's not uncommon for chefs to be out on the farm, cultivating relationships that benefit both farmer and chef.

We're not as divided as we used to be: city or farm, chef or home cook. And we have come to appreciate anew the gift of food grown, raised, and crafted with care. It's why I love being a chef, and why I'm proud to be a Washington boy.

In *Dishing Up Washington,* Jess Thomson brings together all that is delicious about this state and puts it in your kitchen. The recipes focus on ingredients from farmers' markets and local seafood and butcher shops, often giving a fresh twist to traditional dishes. Many come from well-known restaurants and inns, and I'm pleased to be included in the collection. The recipes are accompanied by profiles of area farmers, restaurateurs, and food purveyors from one end of the state to the other, and enhanced by the lush photography of Lara Ferroni. Whether you're a visitor, a newcomer, or a native like me, this book conveys the essence of Washington's character and the scope of its food scene.

INTRODUCTION

AS FAR AS STATES GO, I'm afraid I can no longer claim objectivity. Since the fall of 2006, when I moved to Seattle, I've developed a bit of a favorite. I'll give you a hint: it's square, mostly, except for a bit of a ruffle along its western edge. It's probably the one that should be called the Big Apple, because it looks like a square state with a big bite taken out. (Only, the bite was put back, the way my son does when he doesn't like something and wants to pretend it never happened.) And well, because 10 to 12 *billion* apples are picked here each year.

Okay, fine. It's Washington. But this state has so much more than the produce that makes it most famous. Here it is in book form — with all the apples, berries, cheeses, cherries, potatoes, people, meats, and seafood that make it great. The 150 recipes in this book explain why food lovers love it here. It's the story of how Bluebird Grain Farms mills all their Washington-grown flours to order, and when saffron grower Jim Robinson knows to harvest his eccentric little crop, and why harvesting razor clams on a cold winter night is harder than it looks, but worth every freezing finger. Its recipes range from soon-to-be weeknight favorites to more time-consuming company dinners.

I wrote *Dishing Up Washington* for the inspired home cook who wants to try something new, re-create a favorite Washington dish, or learn how to use the state's greatest ingredients. My hope is that you'll find something you've never tried — whether it's tasting smelt for the first time, or roasting delicata squash with a cumin-scented caramel, or making pasta studded with Salumi's guanciale — and from there, find inspiration in your own kitchen. Maybe you'll hop in the car and try digging for razor clams or make your way to Walla Walla for a bit of wine tasting. Or you'll come to Seattle, not because you dream of hanging out in the rain for a week, but simply because you want to eat. Of course, this book isn't exhaustive. It's like any big trip — success is sometimes measured not just by the things you see and collect along the way, but also by what you want to see the next time. It's a collection meant to galvanize an obsession with a really great state.

What's that? You don't know where to start? For a dinner party that's as comforting as it is delicious, you might begin with Marinated Goat Cheese with Honey and Hazelnuts (page 28) and Caramelized Onion and Bacon Dip (page 25), then serve Roasted Chicken with Honey-glazed Shallots (page 119), accompanied by Roasted Carrots with Mustard and Dill (page 78), and serve a Seattle Winter Market Salad (page 60) last. For a trip through the state's best restaurants that's sure to impress, start with Saffron Clam Chowder (page 14), from Allium on Orcas Island, then serve Bastille's Roasted Beet Salad (page 72) before Hunter's-style Rabbit with Wild Mushrooms and Tomato, from Spinasse (page 163).

If you're looking for great DIY projects, there's labne for Persian Cucumber Salad (page 71), smoked chocolate chips for Hot Cakes' Original S'mores Cookies (page 232), Fresh-Hopped Ale (page 269), and Homemade Grilled Green Hot Sauce (page 265). There are also simple weeknight recipes that will slide into your favorites list — dishes like Northwest Crab Chowder (page 55), Quickish Pork Posole (page 146), Skagit River Ranch Pot Roast (page 164), Garlic Fries (page 102), Honey–Cottage Cheese Pancakes (page 240) and a Ten-Minute Yogurt Cake (page 234).

I know. I'm getting carried away. But how could I not? Happy cooking.

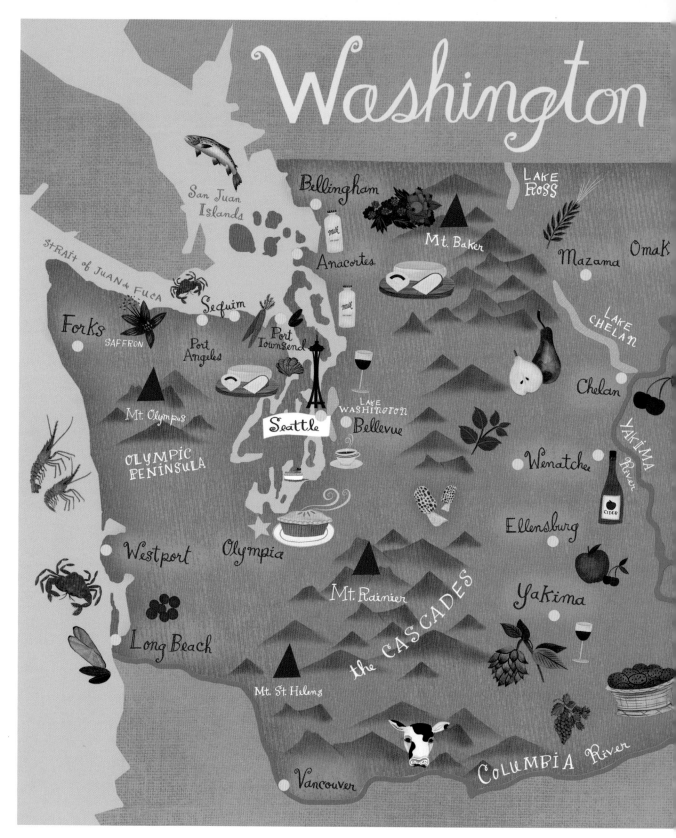

Washington

San Juan Islands

Strait of Juan de Fuca

Forks
SAFFRON

Mt. Olympus

OLYMPIC PENINSULA

Sequim

Port Angeles

Port Townsend

Anacortes

Bellingham

Mt. Baker

LAKE ROSS

Mazama

Omak

LAKE CHELAN

Chelan

YAKIMA River

Seattle

LAKE WASHINGTON

Bellevue

Wenatchee

Ellensburg

Yakima

Westport

Olympia

Mt. Rainier

the CASCADES

Long Beach

Mt. St. Helens

Vancouver

COLUMBIA River

Dishing It Up

IF YOU STAND ATOP SEATTLE'S PHINNEY RIDGE on a clear summer day, near where the windmill sign keeps watch over folks in line for one of Red Mill's famous burgers, you'll see a panorama of what makes Washington food fantastic. Down the hill to the left, just half a block away, is the kind of local farmers' market that Seattleites rely on to feed their families — big, bustling, bursting with produce and pride. In rolling red wagons, toddlers fight tufts of carrot tops and bags of berries for sitting room. Moms munch on thin-crust pizza while Eddie Alvarez, of Alvarez Farms, explains how to peel and cook fresh chickpeas.

With a mild, humid climate in half of the state and a hot, dry climate in the other half, Washington provides good growing conditions for a wide range of crops. In fact, in terms of the number of crops produced, it's second only to California. As a result, the state's food trends are largely driven by what's available in local markets. Look up a little, across Green Lake and toward the Cascade Mountains that sawtooth south toward Mt. Rainier, and you'll see the slopes that provide the same market's freshly foraged mushrooms. Beyond the Cascades, you can imagine the broad, flat plateau that stretches across the rest of the state, where fertile soil and sunny days provide perfect growing conditions for the market's tree fruits.

Let your gaze travel a bit more to the right, and you'll see the Ballard Locks, where fishing vessels coming home from trips up Puget Sound and along the coast patiently wait their turn to dock and unload salmon, halibut, crab, and spot prawns. Beyond the locks, the still-white peaks of the Olympic Mountains tower over the cold waters that produce the nation's tastiest oysters.

It's a killer view, to say the least — and it represents a state whose agricultural wonders make eating here almost absurdly enjoyable all year-round.

I hope you find it as delicious as I do. ★

A Note Before You Start

For the most part, the recipes in this book can be altered to fit your preferences — use walnuts instead of pecans, or red kale in place of green, if that works best for you. With the exception of baking recipes, there's always a little wiggle room. Tinker with the recipes until they fit your taste and your family.

When wine-pairing suggestions are given, they, too, are guidelines. I haven't focused on the state's wine industry, so use my notes as the beginning of your tasting adventure.

To find a listing of all of the restaurants, farms, producers, and events, see the Recipe Contributors and Suppliers on page 274.

SkyCity, the restaurant located 500 feet above the ground in the top of the Seattle Space Needle, rotates a full 360 degrees once every 47 minutes. The turntable, based on railroad technology, runs on a 1½-horsepower motor. Naturally, eating there is called "revolutionary dining."

1
STARTERS

Saffron Clam Chowder

Lisa Nakamura, the chef at Allium Restaurant on Orcas Island, gets her clams from nearby Buck Bay Shellfish or from Jones Family Farms on Lopez Island. Dedicated to sourcing her food locally, she also depends on Phocas Farms on the Olympic Peninsula for her saffron — watching Phocas Farms' owner Jim Robinson pick the saffron out of each tiny crocus flower, there's no question that saffron is worth its price.

1½ pounds Manila clams
1 cup dry white wine
1 sprig fresh thyme
1 garlic clove
2 tablespoons unsalted butter
1 medium onion, chopped
3 stalks celery, cut into ½-inch slices
1 pinch saffron threads (about ½ teaspoon, very loosely packed)
2 fist-sized Yukon Gold potatoes, cut into ½-inch cubes
4 cups heavy cream
1 bay leaf
Salt
Freshly ground black pepper

8 APPETIZER SERVINGS

1. Wash the clams well under cold running water, discarding any with cracked or broken shells. Place the clams in a large wide pot. (The pot should be big enough so the clams are no more than two deep.) Add the wine, thyme, and garlic. Bring to a boil over high heat. Cover the pot, and steam the clams over high heat until they open, about 5 minutes. (If your pot is not big enough to fit them all in two layers, start with half the clams. Use a slotted spoon to remove the first batch of steamed clams, then add the remaining uncooked clams and repeat the process — no need to add more wine or aromatics.)

2. Remove the steamed clams from their shells and discard the shells. Carefully strain the liquid from the pot into a clear narrow container (a glass measuring cup works well) and let the sediment settle to the bottom. Set aside.

3. Melt the butter in a large pot over medium heat. Add the onions and cook, stirring occasionally, until translucent, for 8 to 10 minutes. Add the celery and cook for a few minutes longer, or until the mixture starts to release its aroma. Carefully pour the clam-cooking liquid over the onions and celery, leaving any sediment at the bottom of the container. Add the saffron. Add the potatoes, bring the mixture to a simmer, and let the liquid in the pot reduce by about half.

4. Add the cream and bay leaf, and salt and pepper to taste. Cook for 10 to 15 minutes longer. Stir in the clams and cook until they are warmed through, a minute or two longer. Serve immediately.

THE LOCAL CROKER: GROWING SAFFRON IN WASHINGTON

IN THE 1980s, Olympic Peninsula farmer and gardener Jim Robinson decided his *arroz con pollo* habit was getting a little expensive. The dish required just a pinch of saffron — the dried stigma of a particular species of fall-blossoming crocus flower that ranks as one of the world's priciest spices — but even that was costly enough to convince him to set aside space to plant *Crocus sativus* corms.

Twenty-five years later, Robinson has learned to use Washington's wet climate to his advantage, harvesting saffron in the wee hours of late fall mornings, when his crocuses bloom. He sells it to local restaurants and at farmers' markets for about $30 per gram. Spend a few hours at Phocas Farms with Robinson, who is more hippie than the culinary hipster you might expect, and you'll learn why it fetches such a high price: growing saffron is exceptionally demanding. Saffron corms are sterile, so they only reproduce with the aid of a human helicopter parent willing to lift, separate, and replant the corms every few years. Then there's the actual picking process, which also requires exact timing and precision. Saffron is proof that humans' tendency toward anal-retentiveness has existed for at least three millennia, which is as long as saffron has been cultivated.

Spiced Chardonnay Chicken Liver Mousse

Here, chicken livers are simmered in chardonnay with cinnamon, star anise, allspice, and cloves, then whipped into a spreadable pâté perfect for slathering on crackers or baguette slices. It's easy, and a little work goes a long way — this recipe makes enough for four pots of mousse, each of which should satisfy a crowd of six before dinner. Serve with whole grain mustard, cornichons, and pickled onions, such as Pickled Red Onions with Mustard Seeds (page 268). If that seems like a lot of chicken, this recipe can easily be halved.

2 large shallots, thinly sliced

2 large garlic cloves, peeled and smashed

2 cups dry chardonnay

1 cinnamon stick

1 star anise

3 whole allspice berries

3 whole cloves

3 whole black peppercorns

2 pounds chicken livers, fat and veins trimmed

¾ cup water

1 cup (2 sticks) unsalted butter, softened, cut into 16 chunks

Sea salt

Freshly ground white pepper

NOTE: The mousse can be cooled, then double-wrapped and frozen up to 2 weeks before serving. To serve, thaw for 24 to 48 hours in the refrigerator.

4 (16-OUNCE) RAMEKINS

1. Combine the shallots, garlic, chardonnay, cinnamon stick, star anise, allspice berries, cloves, and peppercorns in a large wide saucepan and bring to a simmer. Cook until the garlic is soft, 5 to 10 minutes. Add the chicken livers and water, bring back to a simmer, then cook until they're barely pink in the center, turning the livers once or twice, about 5 minutes. Remove from heat and let cool for 15 minutes.

2. Transfer the livers and shallot mixture to a food processor, using a slotted spoon and picking out any spices as you see them. Carefully remove the remaining spices, then add the rest of the liquid and shallot mixture. Purée the liver mixture until smooth.

3. With the machine on, add the butter one chunk at a time, and purée until smooth, scraping the sides of the work bowl as necessary. (The mixture will seem thin.) Salt and pepper to taste. Pour the mousse through a fine-mesh strainer into a bowl, then transfer to four large ramekins or bowls. Let the mousse cool to room temperature, then cover with plastic wrap and refrigerate overnight. Serve chilled.

Roasted Fall Mushroom Bruschetta

Nestled into a quiet Seattle neighborhood, the Volunteer Park Cafe is well known for its baked goods — tender scones, kitchen-sink cookies, and moist, fluffy quiche. For a real taste of what chef Ericka Burke and her team can do, hit the café for one of their special Sunday Suppers.

4 cups seasonal mushrooms (chanterelles, oyster, shiitake, or cremini), roughly chopped

½ cup extra-virgin olive oil, plus more for brushing bread and drizzling

¼ cup minced garlic

1 small sweet onion, thinly sliced

¼ cup chopped fresh rosemary

¼ cup chopped fresh Italian parsley

Salt

Freshly ground black pepper

12 pieces of sliced baguette, cut ¼ inch thick diagonally

2 tablespoons chopped fresh chives

¼ cup grated Parmesan cheese

6 SERVINGS

1. Preheat the oven to 375°F.

2. Combine the mushrooms, oil, garlic, onion, rosemary, and parsley in a large bowl. Stir to combine, then salt and pepper to taste. Spread the mushroom mixture in an even layer on a large baking sheet, and roast for 10 to 15 minutes, or until the mushrooms are lightly caramelized.

3. Meanwhile, brush the baguette slices with oil on both sides. Sprinkle lightly with salt. When the mushrooms are done, toast the bread for about 5 minutes, turning once, or until light golden brown on both sides.

4. Arrange the warm baguette toasts on a serving platter. Top with the warm mushroom mixture, drizzle with additional oil, and garnish with chopped chives and Parmesan. Serve immediately.

Simple Smoked Salmon Rillettes
with Dill and Capers

Smoked salmon is the perfect gift to bring home from Washington, but it would be a shame to only use it for topping bagels. Add it to pasta dishes or grilled sandwiches or whip it into an appetizer spread. Like traditional French pork rillettes, this smoked salmon version is rich and smearable. But since it starts with a cooked ingredient, there's much less work involved. Serve with crackers or toast points and a soft, spreadable goat cheese.

8 ounces hot-smoked salmon, drained and skin removed

⅓ cup finely chopped fresh dill

2 tablespoons capers, finely chopped

½ cup (1 stick) unsalted butter, melted

2 tablespoons extra-virgin olive oil

Salt

Freshly ground black pepper

NOTE: You're looking for hot-smoked salmon here — the kind that comes in a fillet, not the kind that is sliced and laid out flat. If you have an abundance of leftover cooked salmon, you could use that instead of the smoked salmon.

4 SERVINGS

1. Combine the salmon, dill, capers, butter, and oil in a food processor, and blend until smooth, like hummus. (The mixture will be thick; you may need to scrape the sides of the bowl.) Salt and pepper to taste. (If your salmon is on the salty side, you probably won't need additional salt.)

2. Transfer the mixture to a small ramekin, cover with plastic wrap, and chill overnight, or until firm.

3. Bring the rillettes to room temperature 2 hours before serving. Spread on crackers or toast points.

Grilled Spot Prawns
with Curried Caramel Dipping Sauce

Spot prawns, the large shrimp found up and down the coasts of the Pacific Northwest and Alaska, are among the more sustainable shellfish. They're known for their sweet flesh, which makes this dipping sauce — a mixture of red curry and coconut milk, simmered down until it caramelizes — a perfect match.

If you'd like, you can substitute Homemade Red Curry Paste (page 137) for the curry paste in this recipe.

2 tablespoons roasted red curry paste

1 (14-ounce) can coconut milk (stirred to blend, if necessary)

2 pounds spot prawns (16–20 count), peeled and deveined, tails removed

6 kaffir lime leaves

¼ cup loosely packed fresh chopped cilantro

¼ cup loosely packed chopped fresh mint, plus 1 tablespoon finely chopped fresh mint

Vegetable or extra-virgin olive oil, for the grill

¼ teaspoon kosher salt

1 tablespoon honey

NOTE: You'll need about three dozen small (4- or 6-inch) skewers for this recipe; soak them in water for about 30 minutes before threading the shrimp on to avoid burning.

8–12 SERVINGS

1. Place the curry paste in a large mixing bowl. Add about a quarter of the coconut milk and whisk until blended. Add the remaining coconut milk, whisk again, then add the prawns, lime leaves, cilantro, and ¼ cup of the chopped mint. Stir to combine and refrigerate, covered, for at least 1 hour and up to 6 hours.

2. Prepare a medium-hot fire (about 450°F) in a gas or charcoal grill. While the grill heats, thread 2 prawns on each skewer, so the skewer goes through each one twice. Reserve the marinade in the bowl. Lightly oil the grill and cook the prawns in batches until just pink and slightly charred, 2 to 3 minutes per side.

3. While the prawns cook, transfer the remaining marinade to a small saucepan. Bring to a boil and cook, stirring occasionally, until the sauce reduces to about a cup and darkens as the coconut milk caramelizes, 5 to 10 minutes. Stir in the salt and the honey, then pour the sauce through a fine-mesh strainer into a bowl.

4. When the prawns are done, brush the sauce onto them on both sides. Sprinkle the prawns with the remaining tablespoon of mint, and serve warm or at room temperature, with extra sauce on the side, if desired.

Geoduck Crudo
with Celery, Lime, Chiles, and Radish

True to Seattle chef and restaurateur Ethan Stowell's style, this gorgeous appetizer is almost painfully simple, relying on bright, fresh flavors and perfect ingredients instead of complicated cooking techniques. Geoduck clams, also known as king clams, are a bit intimidating with their giant, meaty siphons — ask your fishmonger how to clean them.

4 SERVINGS

- 1 geoduck clam, cleaned, split lengthwise and sliced diagonally as thin as possible
- 4 small stalks celery, cut diagonally as thin as possible
- Juice of 2 large limes (about ¼ cup)
- 2 jalapeño peppers, seeded and diced as small as possible
- 8 red radishes, diced as small as possible
- 2 tablespoons finely chopped fresh chives, shaved thin
- ¼ cup extra-virgin olive oil
- Salt
- Freshly ground black pepper

1. Mix the clam, celery, lime juice, jalapeños, radishes, chives, and oil in a bowl, and salt and pepper to taste. Let marinate for about 5 minutes, then arrange the clam mixture on a plate and serve immediately.

ETHAN STOWELL

KNOWN FOR THEIR BRIGHTLY FLAVORED crudos, flawless pastas, Italian-inspired comfort food, and expert waitstaff, chef and restaurateur Ethan Stowell's Seattle restaurants are gaining nationwide acclaim. Although the restaurant that made him famous, Union, has now closed its doors, the James Beard Award nominee and his wine-expert wife, Angela, now have six popular eateries.

My favorite, Staple & Fancy, gets its name from how one orders — either from the more traditional Staple menu, a brief selection of Italian-inspired small plates, pastas, mains, and *contorni*; or from the Fancy menu. The latter instructs diners to hand the menu back to their server, who will coordinate a surprise four-course family-style menu with the kitchen. Go fancy!

Lentil-Pecan Pâté

At Cafe Flora, one of Seattle's best vegetarian restaurants, the chef serves a somewhat less-than-traditional take on pâté with rosemary crackers. A tangle of Pickled Red Onions with Mustard Seeds (page 268) would make a delicious garnish.

ABOUT 4 CUPS

1 cup red lentils

2 cups water

1 bay leaf

1 tablespoon extra-virgin olive oil

1 medium onion, chopped

1 tablespoon chopped garlic

½ teaspoon dried thyme

½ teaspoon ground sage

2 tablespoons mirin

1 teaspoon umeboshi paste

1 tablespoon light miso

½ cup toasted pecan pieces

½ teaspoon kosher salt

½ teaspoon freshly ground black pepper

NOTE: Look for mirin, umeboshi paste, and light miso in the ethnic foods section of a large grocery store, or at an Asian market. If you can't find umeboshi paste, substitute sherry vinegar.

1. Rinse the lentils and put them in a pot with the water and bay leaf. Bring to a boil, then reduce heat and simmer, covered, until the lentils are very soft and most of the water has been absorbed, about 20 minutes. (Add more water if necessary.) Remove the bay leaf and set the lentils aside to cool.

2. Meanwhile, heat the oil in a large skillet over medium heat. When hot, add the onion, and cook, stirring occasionally, until it begins to soften, about 5 minutes. Reduce heat to low and continue cooking, stirring occasionally, until the onion is browned and soft, 15 to 20 minutes. Add the garlic, thyme, and sage, and cook, stirring, for 1 minute, and remove from the heat.

3. Purée the lentils, onion mixture, mirin, umeboshi paste, miso, pecans, salt, and pepper in a food processor until smooth. (Add a bit more water, if the mixture is too thick to blend.) Transfer the mixture to a large bowl or a few small ramekins, and serve warm; or cover, refrigerate, and serve chilled.

Caramelized Onion and Bacon Dip

This is a dip any potato chip would love to call "friend." Inspired by a similar version made at Matt's in the Market, the small, bright restaurant that overlooks the Pike Place Market's main entrance, this dip combines all our savory vices — bacon, cream, good cheese, and caramelized onions — into an appetizer that will bring guests into a huddle.

1 tablespoon extra-virgin olive oil

1 large yellow onion, quartered and thinly sliced with the grain

Salt

Freshly ground black pepper

¼ pound thick-cut slices bacon, diced

1 egg

1 tablespoon heavy cream

½ cup sour cream

½ cup mayonnaise

3 ounces Gruyere cheese, grated (about ¾ cup)

NOTE: The dip can be made ahead, covered with plastic wrap, and chilled overnight before baking.

4 SERVINGS

1. Heat a large heavy skillet over medium heat. When hot, add the oil, then the onions, and salt and pepper to taste. Cook, stirring frequently, until the onions are soft and well browned, 25 to 30 minutes, adjusting the heat as necessary so they don't burn. Set aside to cool.

2. Meanwhile, cook the bacon over medium heat in a separate skillet, until brown but not quite crisp, stirring occasionally, about 10 minutes. Transfer to a paper towel–lined plate and set aside to cool.

3. Preheat the oven to 400°F.

4. Whisk the egg, heavy cream, sour cream, and mayonnaise together in a mixing bowl. Season with additional pepper, then stir in the cooled onions, bacon, and cheese.

5. Transfer the mixture to a small shallow dish (such as a 1-quart casserole dish) or a few small ramekins, and bake for 20 minutes, or until browned and bubbling. Let cool 5 minutes before serving.

Recipe from TOM DOUGLAS, BRAVE HORSE TAVERN

Brave Horse Tavern's Deviled Eggs

Tom Douglas has spent decades building a restaurant empire in Seattle, and each time he opens a new spot, his experience shows. His most recent cluster of restaurants in Seattle's South Lake Union neighborhood includes Brave Horse Tavern, which offers an alluring mix of great beer, hearty fare, and shuffleboard. While the restaurant is most known for its brick-oven pretzels served with sides like smoked peanut butter and bacon spread, I'm a sucker for items on the bar's snack menu, like these deviled eggs. Blended with bacon fat, spicy pepper sauce, and sour cream, this is an egg in evening wear that couldn't get any fancier or be any more delicious — until it's topped with more crisp bacon, diced pasilla peppers, and sweet, tangy pickled green garlic.

PICKLED GARLIC

- 1 cup water
- ⅔ cup apple cider vinegar
- ½ cup sugar
- 1 teaspoon kosher salt
- 1 teaspoon mustard seeds
- 1 bay leaf
- 1 cup chopped green garlic

DEVILED EGGS

- 6 eggs
- 4 thick slices smoked bacon
- 3 tablespoons sour cream
- 2 tablespoons mayonnaise
- 1½ teaspoons Dijon mustard
- 1 teaspoon sambal or other spicy Asian chile sauce
- ¼ teaspoon Tabasco or other hot pepper sauce
- 2 tablespoons finely chopped fresh chives
- ¼ cup diced pasilla or poblano peppers
- 2 tablespoons finely chopped fresh Italian parsley

12 DEVILED EGGS

1. **Make the pickled garlic:** Bring the water, vinegar, sugar, salt, mustard seeds, and bay leaf to a boil in a small saucepan, stirring until the sugar has dissolved completely. Add the garlic, simmer for 5 minutes, then remove the pan from the heat and let cool to room temperature. (The garlic can be made up to 1 week ahead and stored in an airtight container in the refrigerator, in its pickling liquid, until needed.)

2. **Make the deviled eggs:** Place the eggs in a saucepan and add cold water to cover. Bring to a boil over high heat. When the water boils, remove the pan from the heat, cover, and let sit for 12 minutes. Drain the eggs, let cool in a bowl of ice water, and peel.

3. Meanwhile, cook the bacon over medium heat in a large saucepan until crisp, about 10 minutes, turning occasionally. Transfer to a paper towel–lined plate, reserving the bacon fat for the egg filling, and set aside. (Yes, you can eat a piece. The chef accounted for this.)

4. Cut the eggs in half lengthwise, transferring the yolks to a medium bowl and the whites to a serving platter. Add the sour cream, mayonnaise, mustard, sambal, Tabasco, chives, and 1½ teaspoons of the bacon grease. Finely chop the bacon and add about three-quarters of it to the yolk mixture.

5. Just before serving, pile the yolk mixture into the egg whites. Top each egg with some of the leftover bacon, pasilla peppers, parsley, and a few pieces of pickled green garlic, and serve.

NOTE: If you can't find green garlic, substitute a head's worth of peeled garlic cloves, and thinly slice the garlic before adding it to the top of each egg.

Marinated Goat Cheese with Honey and Hazelnuts

Driving onto Marrowstone Island, just off the eastern coast of the Olympic Peninsula, feels like entering Eden. Fields soar in every direction. The bay sparkles. And if you hang a right at the bucolic general store in Nordland, you'll find Mystery Bay Farm, where cheesemaker Rachel Van Laanen turns the rich milk from her small herd of American Alpine goats into tart, creamy chèvre. Although her award-winning goat cheese coated with white pepper and thyme demands center stage on a piece of great bread, the plain version is more adaptable. Here, I marinate it in honey and hazelnut oil, shower it with toasted hazelnuts and serve it with good, crusty bread.

If you can't find hazelnuts or hazelnut oil, simply use any other combination of nuts and oil — walnuts and walnut oil, for example.

1 (4-ounce) log goat cheese
¼ cup hazelnut oil
1½ tablespoons honey
2 tablespoons chopped toasted
   hazelnuts
Sea salt
Freshly ground black pepper

4 APPETIZER SERVINGS

1. Place the goat cheese in a serving dish just a little deeper and wider than the log itself. Pour the oil over the cheese, then drizzle the honey on top. Let sit at room temperature for 1 hour, turning once or twice.

2. Sprinkle the hazelnuts, salt, and pepper on top, and serve spread on bread or crackers.

Recipe from SEAN GILBERT, GILBERT CELLARS

Gilbert Cellars' Bacon-wrapped Dates

The mountain panorama that dominates Gilbert Cellars' downtown Yakima tasting room has a purpose: it reminds sippers that the winery's founders, a family that's been growing grapes in the Yakima Valley for more than a century, wanted the mountains to inspire them to better things. Case in point: Gilbert's tasting room, which combines great wines with fun bites, an educated staff, and chic sustainable furniture, to boot. These simple bacon-wrapped dates, a favorite of one of the owners, are a great pairing for their syrah or Left Bank blend. See page 178 for more on the chemistry behind how bold, fatty flavors make the tannins in a "big" red wine seem softer.

12 slices bacon

12 Medjool or other large dates

2 ounces goat cheese

3 cups Marcona almonds

SPECIAL EQUIPMENT: bamboo toothpicks

MAKES 12

1. Preheat the oven to 400°F.

2. Place the bacon in one layer on a foil-lined baking sheet and bake for 15 to 20 minutes, until cooked but still pliable. Transfer the bacon to a paper towel–lined plate to cool.

3. While the bacon cooks, slice open each date on one side and remove the pits. Fill each date with about ½ teaspoon of goat cheese and an almond or two.

4. When the bacon comes out, increase the oven temperature to 450°F.

5. When the bacon is cool enough to handle, wrap each date in a piece of bacon, tearing off any fatty parts at the end. Secure each bacon piece with a toothpick, if desired. (Bamboo toothpicks can withstand the temperature of the oven without burning.)

6. Transfer the bacon-wrapped dates to a broiling pan and bake for 5 to 10 minutes, or until the bacon is sizzling again. Cool for 1 minute, then serve piping hot next to a bowl of the almonds.

Zucchini Ganoush

If I have one major weakness as a cook — or perhaps more accurately, as an eater — it's that I don't like eggplant. Encase it in a crisp crust and bathe it with marinara, and sure, I'll eat it, but by then it's not really the same eggplant. Ditto for baba ganoush, the Middle Eastern dip made by roasting the vegetable, then puréeing it (most often) with tahini, olive oil, and lemon juice. Inspired by Seattle's Zucchini 500s — farmers' market events where kids transform zucchini into race cars and zoom them down a giant multilaned ramp for prizes — it occurred to me that zucchini, in all their glorious abundance, would make a similarly light, airy, lemony spread I could whip together without facing my shortcomings.

3 small or 1 large zucchini (about ¾ pound), peeled and cut into 1-inch rounds

3 tablespoons plus 1 teaspoon extra-virgin olive oil

1 teaspoon ground cumin

Salt

Freshly ground black pepper

¼ cup pine nuts

Juice of 1 medium lemon (about 3 tablespoons)

1 large garlic clove, peeled and smashed

3 tablespoons tahini

NOTE: You can fancy this dish up by sprinkling a layer of toasted sesame seeds on top before serving.

6 APPETIZER SERVINGS

1. Preheat the oven to 400°F. Line a baking sheet with parchment paper or a silicone baking mat, and set aside.

2. Combine the zucchini pieces with 1 teaspoon of the oil and ½ teaspoon of the cumin, then salt and pepper to taste. Spread the zucchini on the baking sheet in an even layer, and bake for 20 minutes, or until just beginning to brown. Add the pine nuts to the sheet, and bake another few minutes, or until the pine nuts are nicely browned. Let cool for 10 to 15 minutes.

3. Transfer the zucchini and pine nuts to a food processor, along with the remaining oil and cumin, plus the lemon juice, garlic, and tahini. Purée until smooth; salt and pepper to taste; and serve with crudités, pita bread, or crackers.

2
SOUPS

Fall Sausage Minestrone
with Mushrooms and Squash

Use whatever mushrooms look best at your market for this warming stew. For a bit of heat, substitute a spicy Italian sausage for the pork sausage.

1½ pounds pork sausage

3 tablespoons extra-virgin olive oil

2 large onions, chopped

10 stalks celery, chopped

6 large carrots, peeled and chopped

6 large garlic cloves, chopped

1 tablespoon dried oregano

Salt

Freshly ground black pepper

1 (28-ounce) can diced tomatoes

2 quarts chicken broth

1 large delicata squash, halved, seeded, and chopped

2 cans white beans, rinsed and drained, or 2 cups dried white beans, cooked

¾ pound wild mushrooms, (such as chanterelles or porcini), chopped

2 tablespoons chopped fresh Italian parsley

10–12 SERVINGS

1. Heat a large soup pot over medium heat. Add the sausage, crumbling it into the pan, and cook, stirring occasionally, until no longer pink inside, about 10 minutes. Transfer the sausage and most of the fat to a paper towel–lined plate and set aside.

2. Add the oil to the pot, then the onions, and cook, stirring once or twice, until the onions soften, about 10 minutes. Add the celery, carrots, garlic, and oregano; salt and pepper to taste; and cook 10 minutes longer, stirring occasionally.

3. Add the tomatoes, and cook, stirring occasionally, until the tomatoes begin to break down, about 15 minutes. Stir the sausage back in; then add the broth, squash, beans, and mushrooms; and bring the soup to a simmer. Cook until the squash is completely tender, about 10 minutes longer.

4. Add the parsley and season the soup with additional salt and pepper, if needed. Serve piping hot with big chunks of bread for mopping up the juices.

Spring Pea Soup
with Nettle-Sorrel Pesto and Pea Vines

Here's a soup that celebrates the arrival of spring two ways: first, it uses the nettles that signal the arrival of spring in local farmers' markets, and second, it uses peas both in the body of the soup and as a garnish. If you can make it one day and eat it the next, chilled, sitting on a porch with your feet up and your cheeks tilted toward the sun, consider yourself lucky — these two greens love rainy weather.

2 tablespoons extra-virgin olive oil

2 large shallots, thinly sliced

4 cups chicken or vegetable broth
    Kosher salt

1 pound fresh shelled English peas
    (from 3 pounds pea pods)

¼ cup heavy cream

12 small pea vines, torn

¼ cup Nettle-Sorrel Pesto (recipe
    on page 38)

6 SERVINGS

1. Heat the oil in a large soup pot over medium-low heat. When hot, add the shallots, and cook, stirring occasionally, until the shallots are translucent but not browned, about 10 minutes. Add the broth, season with salt, and bring to a simmer. Add the peas and the cream, and return to a strong simmer. Cook until the peas are tender but still bright green, 3 to 5 minutes.

2. Carefully transfer the mixture to a blender or food processor, then purée until extremely smooth. Season to taste with additional salt, if necessary. Ladle the soup immediately into bowls, and garnish each bowl with a little tangle of pea vines and a dollop of the pesto.

Nettle-Sorrel Pesto

Stinging nettles come by their name honestly, but cooking denatures the stinging mechanism of the hairs on their jagged edges. For this recipe, use both the stems (unless they're tough) and the leaves. Use the pesto in the soup on page 37, spread it on sandwiches, or combine it with pasta and a handful of toasted breadcrumbs. For a quick dip, blend ¼ cup of it with 4 ounces softened goat cheese (or to taste), bake for 10 minutes at 350°F in a small ovenproof dish, and serve with crusty bread.

½ pound fresh nettles

2 large garlic cloves, smashed

½ cup toasted pine nuts

½ teaspoon salt

Freshly ground black pepper

Juice of ½ small lemon (about 1 tablespoon)

½ cup chopped fresh sorrel

1¼ cups extra-virgin olive oil

⅓ cup grated Parmesan cheese

NOTE: To toast pine nuts, place them on a baking sheet and toast in a preheated 350°F oven for 5 to 10 minutes, or until brown and fragrant.

1 GENEROUS CUP

1. Bring a large pot of salted water to a simmer. Add the nettles directly from their bag and cook, stirring continuously, for 2 minutes. Dump into a colander to drain. When the nettles are cool enough to handle, wrap them in a clean dish towel and wring out as much moisture as possible. You'll have about 1 cup of cooked, squished nettles.

2. Whirl the garlic, pine nuts, salt, and pepper in a food processor until finely chopped. Add the nettles, breaking them up as you drop them in, and the lemon juice and sorrel, and whirl until finely chopped.

3. With the machine running, add the oil in a slow, steady stream, and process until smooth. Add the Parmesan, pulse briefly, and season to taste with additional salt, pepper, or lemon juice. Store any leftover pesto in a small airtight container in the refrigerator.

COOKING NETTLES

NETTLES ARE WHAT HAPPENS to spinach when it leaves home at 16 and winds up running with the wrong crowd. Scattered throughout the Pacific Northwest, they disguise themselves in parks and valleys as weeds, pricking curious passersby with the thousands of tiny needles embedded on the sunny side of every jagged, emerald green, pear-shaped leaf.

There's a reason they're called "stinging nettles." If you touch them, it hurts! True to lore, though, the numbness caused by the sting only lasts about seven minutes. Learn to cook with *Urtica dioica*, and you might learn to forgive them — that is, if you get stung at all. Taste a great soup or lasagna made with nettles, and you'll start cooking with them every single spring, despite your instinct to expect a certain docility from your leafy greens.

The dirty little secret that foragers and cooks know is this: those little stinging hairs, technically called *trichomes*, are hollow, with a very small tip that breaks off easily. While nettles may seem dangerous while you're strolling through Seattle's Discovery Park with no socks on, they're very easy to tame in the kitchen because heat denatures the sting. All you have to do is cook them in a pot of boiling water.

At the farmers' market or at some grocery stores early each spring, you'll often find nettles in big plastic bags. Resist the temptation to transfer that big tangle of greens into the pot with your hands, and instead upend the bag right over the water, stray bug and all. If you're the type to separate all your greens from their stems first, I won't stop you — just wear tough rubber gloves to handle the nettles directly.

Once tamed, you can treat the nettles like spinach, squeezing them dry and using them for fillings for ravioli or lasagna, for pesto (like the Spring Pea Soup with Nettle-Sorrel Pesto and Pea Vines on page 37), in soups and stews, in enchiladas, or wherever an herbaceous spinach with a hint of mint might be appropriate. They're high in vitamin K, calcium, and iron — and they'll give you a good dose of character, too, if you pick them yourself.

Recipe from MERNA OLSEN, OLSEN FARMS

Olsen Family Potato Soup

Merna Olsen of Olsen Farms in Colville calls Red LaSodas good soup potatoes because they're waxy enough to hold their shape in the soup and they don't lose their flavor when they're cooked. This here is true comfort food.

2 pounds red potatoes (6–8 medium potatoes), peeled and cut into ½-inch cubes

2 large carrots, peeled and diced

1 large stalk celery, thinly sliced

2 quarts cold water

6 tablespoons unsalted butter

1 medium onion, chopped

⅓ cup plus 1 tablespoon unbleached all-purpose flour

1 teaspoon kosher salt

½ teaspoon freshly ground black pepper

1½ cups whole milk

Grated cheddar cheese, for serving (optional)

4–6 SERVINGS

1. Place the potatoes, carrots, and celery in a large pot; add the water; and bring to a boil. Reduce to a simmer and cook until the potatoes are tender, about 20 minutes. Drain the vegetables, reserving both the liquid and the vegetables, and return the empty pot to the stove.

2. Add the butter to the pot, and melt over medium heat. Add the onion, and cook until soft, about 5 minutes. Add the flour, salt, and pepper, and cook, stirring, for 1 minute. Add the milk in a slow, steady stream, stirring as you add it, and cook until the mixture is smooth and thick and bubbling, about 5 minutes.

3. Whisk in 2 cups of the reserved cooking liquid, then stir in the reserved vegetables. Bring the soup back to a simmer, then thin it with additional liquid (about 1 cup) until the soup reaches the desired consistency. Salt and pepper to taste, and serve hot, heaped with cheese, if desired.

FORAGED AND FOUND

IF YOU'VE EVER HAD a mother or a father, or ever took part in a youth outdoors group, or ever saw *Alice in Wonderland*, or have any common sense at all, you know this: it's not wise to put wild mushrooms in your mouth unless you're positive you know they're not poisonous. And in Seattle, if you're not the type to learn your mushrooms, you trust Jeremy Faber, the owner of Foraged and Found Edibles, to do the research for you.

All year long, Faber's farmers' market stand sells mushrooms with names that sound like a food lover's hallucinations: Fried chicken mushrooms. Snowbank mushrooms. Delicious milk caps. There are also morels and porcini and chanterelles, in season, along with lobster and hedgehog and king bolete — enough mushrooms to make a bouquet, if they were all in season at the same time. Seattle chefs also trust Foraged and Found as a source for wild greens, like wood sorrel, licorice fern, stinging nettles, and wild watercress, as well as wild berries like huckleberries, elderberries, and Saskatoon berries.

Next time you're in Seattle, find Foraged and Found at a farmers' market, and take some dried mushrooms home with you — it's a fabulous gift that travels well and doesn't weigh much.

Cream of Corn Soup
with Sautéed Chanterelles

Any amateur mushroom forager will tell you that chanterelles are a favorite because they're fairly easy to identify when they bloom on wooded hillsides each fall. The problem with foraging, though, is that you're not guaranteed a full bag — sometimes, especially early in the season, you come home with only a handful.

Here's a soup that puts fresh chanterelles on a pedestal, even if you only have a few. Simply sautéed in butter, these tiny mushrooms finish off a lovely, smooth corn soup — one so rich it's best served in tiny glasses as an appetizer or fancy intermezzo. If you're going the fancy route, consider straining the soup through a fine-mesh sieve after you blend it.

3 tablespoons unsalted butter

1 large shallot, finely chopped

Kernels from 3 ears fresh corn (about 2 cups), uncooked

1 cup heavy cream

Salt

Freshly ground white pepper

2 ounces tiny, fresh chanterelle mushrooms, halved if larger than a grape

TIP: To cut corn off the cob, first husk the corn. Place it flat on a cutting board, parallel with your knife. Working the long way, cut a few rows of corn off the cob at once, then rotate the corn cob away from the blade, and cut another three or four rows off. Keep cutting until you've worked all the way around the cob.

6–8 SMALL SERVINGS

1. Heat a medium saucepan over medium heat. Add 2 table-spoons of the butter, then the shallots, and cook and stir until soft but not browned, about 10 minutes. Add the corn and cream, and bring the mixture to a strong simmer. Simmer for 2 minutes, watching carefully and removing the pan from the heat if the cream rises to the top, then set aside and let cool for 5 minutes.

2. Carefully transfer the mixture to a blender or food processor, then purée until extremely smooth. Salt and pepper to taste. (The soup can be made ahead up to this point and reheated before serving.)

3. Just before serving, heat a small skillet over high heat. Add the remaining tablespoon of butter, then the mushrooms, and season lightly with salt. Cook, stirring frequently, for 2 minutes. Serve the soup piping hot in small glasses, garnished with the mushrooms.

Cream of Wild Mushroom Stew
with Sage and Sherry

This is more of a smooth soup than a stew, but it has a heartiness that satisfies anyone who's spent the day outdoors. The word "soup" just doesn't do it justice. If you prefer a chunkier soup, chop the mushrooms finely and skip the puréeing step. Try it garnished with the fried sage from the recipe for Grilled Asparagus with Fried Sage and Lemon (page 94), and use any leftovers for The New Tuna Casserole (page 182).

1 ounce dried wild mushrooms

2½ cups boiling water

6 tablespoons unsalted butter

1 medium onion, chopped

1 pound fresh wild mushrooms, chopped

1 tablespoon finely chopped fresh sage

1 cup half-and-half, heavy cream, or whole milk (plus more, if needed)

2 tablespoons sherry

Salt

Freshly ground black pepper

NOTE: If you don't have sherry, substitute 2 teaspoons sherry vinegar.

4 SERVINGS

1. Place the dried mushrooms in a medium bowl and add the water. Set aside and let sit until the mushrooms are soft, about 1 hour.

2. Melt 2 tablespoons of the butter in a large saucepan or soup pot over medium heat. Add the onion, then cook, stirring occasionally, until the onion is soft, about 10 minutes.

3. While the onion cooks, use a slotted spoon to transfer the dried mushrooms from the bowl to a cutting board, leaving any grit at the bottom of the liquid. Chop the mushrooms and add them to the pot along with the fresh mushrooms, sage, and remaining 4 tablespoons butter. Cover and cook until the mushrooms begin to soften, about 5 minutes.

4. Measure 2 cups liquid from the mushroom broth, again leaving any grit at the bottom, and add it to the pot with the half-and-half. Bring the soup to a simmer and cook for 10 minutes.

5. Carefully transfer the mixture to a blender or food processor, then purée until relatively smooth. Return the soup to the pot, and thin the soup with additional half-and-half, if desired. Stir in the sherry, then salt and pepper to taste, and serve warm.

CHEF GONE WILD: MATT COSTELLO

MATT COSTELLO, the chef-owner at The Inn at Langley, on Washington's Whidbey Island, thinks of cooking locally a bit differently than other chefs do. He starts with his restaurant's extensive herb garden, of course, with the usual homegrown suspects like various shades of thyme and fragrant rosemary, and less typical kitchen herbs like angelica, geranium, and lovage.

But when Costello forages for his restaurant's intricate seven-course dinners, he goes wild. He uses local foods to re-create *experiences*. Which means that when you eat there, perhaps at the cozy communal table in front of the restaurant's giant stone fireplace, you shouldn't be surprised if your plate is full of things you've never seen at your local grocery store. You also shouldn't be surprised if his dishes capture a strong sense of time and place, instead of just a flavor.

Take fall, for example: to remember a tromp through the woods, he distills pine needles into a sap that winds up in a fragrant, sticky sauce below a perfectly cooked slice of lamb loin. Because

he's had decades of experience in top-tier Seattle kitchens, he knows just how you'll like that pine sap — it's flavorful without overpowering, and slightly astringent. Like a walk in the fall woods.

Summer might bring berry picking on a country road to your dessert bowl: a pile of grated lemon verbena gel has the appeal of soft grass, with tiny mint, thyme, and anise hyssop flowers dotted across its top. The lavender-honey cream in the bottom of the bowl tastes like the smell of a hot summer day on Whidbey Island, sweet and floral. And those blackberries, poached in red wine? As perfect as the moment they left the bush, only better.

If you're starting to feel intimidated, don't worry — dining at The Inn at Langley is anything but formal. Costello alternates between cooking — often alone, always efficiently — and strolling around the small room, chatting with diners about what he's made, answering questions, and sharing stories.

Tell him yours. Just don't be surprised if it ends up on the menu.

45

Sunchoke Purée
with Sautéed Radishes and Rosemary Oil

Rarely are soups simultaneously creamy and light. But in a small kitchen on Whidbey Island, chef Matt Costello dependably masters anything that goes into a bowl. From smooth corn soups in the heart of summer to this silky, wintery sunchoke purée, Costello's dishes are always fresh, always local, and always interesting. The garnish for this soup is a quick sauté of thinly sliced sunchokes, radishes, and bacon and a drizzle of homemade rosemary oil. It's a fancy presentation, if that's the way you want to think of it, but I just think of it as delicious.

Juice of ½ small lemon (about 1 tablespoon)

3 pounds sunchokes

1 pound Yukon Gold or White Rose potatoes

1 cup plus 1 tablespoon extra-virgin olive oil

1 medium onion, chopped

¾ cup medium-dry white wine

2 quarts chicken broth (homemade, if possible)

1 cup heavy cream

Salt

Freshly ground black pepper

½ cup tightly packed fresh rosemary leaves

¼ pound bacon, finely chopped

4 large radishes, trimmed

NOTE: Sunchokes, also called Jerusalem artichokes, are awfully lumpy. Peel them carefully, but don't fret too much about getting every last bit of skin off.

6 DINNER OR 8 APPETIZER SERVINGS

1. Fill a large bowl with cold water and add the lemon juice. Peel the sunchokes and potatoes, placing them into the water as soon as they're peeled to prevent browning.

2. Heat 1 tablespoon of the oil over medium heat in a large Dutch oven. When hot, add the onion, and cook, stirring occasionally, until the onion is soft, about 10 minutes. Add the wine and simmer for 2 minutes. Chop all but 3 small sunchokes and all of the potatoes into roughly 1-inch pieces, and add them to the pot, along with enough of the broth to cover the vegetables by about an inch. Bring the liquid to a simmer, then reduce heat to medium-low and simmer until the vegetables are completely soft, skimming off any foam that rises to the top, about 45 minutes.

3. Carefully transfer the mixture to a blender or food processor, then purée until completely smooth. Strain through a medium sieve (if desired), and return the soup to the stove over low heat. Stir in the cream, and salt and pepper to taste.

4. Meanwhile, roughly chop about ⅓ cup of the rosemary. Put it in a small saucepan and add ½ cup of the oil. Heat the rosemary and oil over low heat until the rosemary begins to bubble and look crisp, about 3 minutes. Turn off the heat and allow the oil to cool in the pan. When the oil has cooled, strain it, reserving the rosemary oil and discarding the rosemary. Finely chop the remaining rosemary and set aside.

5. Place the remaining ½ cup oil and the chopped bacon in a medium skillet over medium heat. Cook, stirring occasionally, until the bacon is crisp, 8 to 10 minutes. When the bacon has cooked, transfer it to a paper towel–lined plate, reserving 2 tablespoons of the bacon oil for cooking the garnish. (You can use any remaining bacon oil for cooking eggs in the morning.)

6. Just before serving, prepare the garnish for the soup: Heat the bacon oil over medium-high heat in a large skillet. Slice the reserved peeled sunchokes and the radishes about ⅛-inch thick. (A mandolin slicer works best for this.) When the oil shimmers, add the sunchokes to the pan, separating the slices if they're stuck together, and cook for 1 minute, undisturbed. Add the radishes to the pan, and cook, stirring often, until the radishes are translucent, about 1 minute longer. Stir in half the remaining chopped fresh rosemary and the reserved bacon, and stir to combine.

7. To serve, ladle the hot soup into warm bowls. Using a spoon, float some of the radish mixture on top of each serving, then drizzle with some of the rosemary oil and sprinkle with chopped fresh rosemary. Serve immediately.

Spanish-inspired Root Vegetable Stew

Since the day my husband and I lunched at a truck stop somewhere between Toledo and Madrid, Spain, on a chickpea stew flecked with onions and infused with sweet, smoky Spanish paprika, the spice has become an important part of my winter soup pantry. This stew, made with vegetables you'll find at Seattle farmers' markets in February, transports me back to that trip — but it's a lot cheaper than a trans-Atlantic plane ticket.

For a heartier dish, simmer chopped chicken thighs in the stew with the potatoes.

2 tablespoons extra-virgin olive oil

1 medium onion, chopped

1 medium leek, white and light green parts, halved lengthwise and chopped

2 stalks celery, chopped

3 medium carrots, peeled and chopped

2 parsnips, peeled and chopped

2 large garlic cloves, finely chopped

¾ teaspoon good Spanish paprika (*Pimenton de la Vera*)

1 tablespoon chopped fresh oregano

Salt

Freshly ground black pepper

1 tablespoon tomato paste

1 cup dry white wine

4 cups chicken or vegetable broth (homemade, if possible)

3 cups cubed butternut squash (½-inch cubes, from the long part of a 1½-pound squash)

1 large red potato, cut into ½-inch cubes

1 large sweet potato, peeled and cut into ½-inch cubes

1 tablespoon sherry vinegar

4 SERVINGS

1. Heat a large soup pot over medium-high heat. When hot, add the oil; then the onion and leek; and cook, stirring once or twice, until soft, about 10 minutes. Add the celery, carrots, parsnips, garlic, paprika, and oregano; salt and pepper to taste; and cook, stirring occasionally, until the vegetables begin to soften, about 5 minutes.

2. Stir in the tomato paste, then add the wine, stir, bring to a simmer, and cook for 3 minutes, scraping the bottom of the pot with a wooden spoon. Add the broth, squash, potato, and sweet potato. Bring the soup to a simmer and cook, partially covered, until all the vegetables are tender, 15 to 20 minutes. Add 1 tablespoon of the vinegar (or add it to taste), season again with salt and pepper, and serve hot.

Spicy Beef and Lamb Stew
with Emmer and Rye

After making a name for himself at Stumbling Goat Bistro on Phinney Ridge, Seattle chef Seth Caswell opened emmer&rye in an old Victorian house in the Queen Anne neighborhood. Devoted to local foods, like the hearty grains it's named for, emmer&rye's menu is simultaneously sophisticated and comforting. Its signature dishes include a trio of stews made with emmer and rye. This one, with tender beef and lamb seasoned with rosemary, ginger, and chile, makes the ultimate winter supper. Stir in a few handfuls of chopped chard or kale at the end, if you'd like.

For more information on Bluebird Grain Farms, whose emmer farro and rye berries Caswell uses, see Recipe Contributors and Suppliers (page 274). If you can't find farro or rye berries, substitute wheat berries for both.

2 tablespoons finely chopped fresh gingerroot

1 tablespoon chopped fresh rosemary

2 teaspoons grapeseed or other neutral oil

1 teaspoon finely chopped garlic

1 teaspoon red pepper flakes

Salt

Freshly ground black pepper

½ pound grass-fed beef ribeye steak, trimmed and cut into 1-inch pieces

1 pound boneless lamb stew meat from a leg of lamb, trimmed and cut into 1-inch pieces

2 tablespoons extra-virgin olive oil

1 medium onion, finely chopped

1 medium fennel bulb, finely chopped

2 medium carrots, peeled and finely chopped

1 cup emmer farro

1 cup rye berries

½ cup white wine

4 cups vegetable or chicken broth, warmed

1 bay leaf

4 parsley stems

3 sprigs fresh thyme

4 cups beef broth

1 tablespoon unsalted butter

6 SERVINGS

1. Whirl the ginger, rosemary, grapeseed oil, garlic, pepper flakes, and salt and pepper to taste together a food processor until very finely chopped. Set a quarter of the mixture aside for finishing the stew.

2. Place the beef and lamb pieces in a large roasting pan, mix with the remaining ginger-rosemary mixture, and let sit for 45 minutes at room temperature.

3. Preheat the oven to 325°F.

4. Heat a large pot over medium-high heat. Add the olive oil, then the onions, fennel, and carrots; salt and pepper to taste; and cook, stirring often, until the vegetables begin to brown, about 10 minutes. Add the emmer and rye berries and cook until the grains are coated with oil and warmed through, about 1 minute. Add the wine, simmer for 3 minutes, then add the vegetable broth and bring to a simmer.

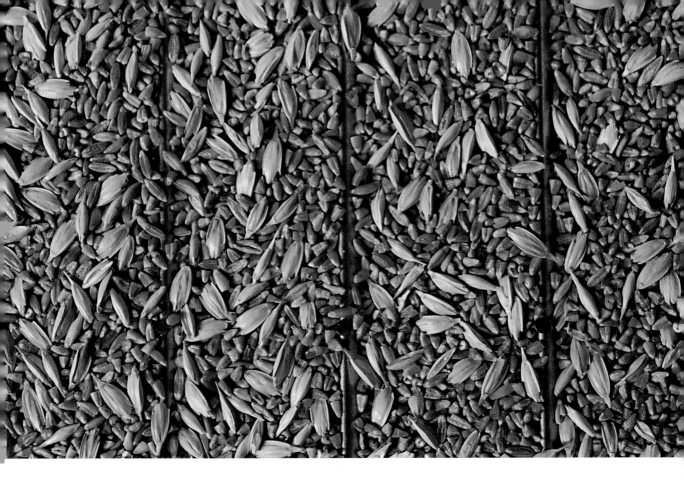

5. Tie the bay leaf, parsley stems, and thyme together with
   twine, and add them to the pot. Salt and pepper to taste
   again, then reduce heat to low and simmer, covered, until the
   grains are tender to the bite but not mushy, 50 to 60 minutes
   (stir once or twice, but not constantly; too much stirring will
   make the grains gummy). Remove the lid and let the grains
   cook until they've completely absorbed the broth, about
   15 minutes longer. Discard the bay leaf, parsley stems, and
   thyme.

6. Meanwhile, roast the meats together, covered, for 20 minutes. Uncover and roast 35 minutes longer, or until the meats
   are both tender and cooked through.

**(The stew can be made up to this point, cooled, and refriger-
ated for up to 3 days before continuing.)**

7. Bring the beef broth to a boil over high heat in a separate pot.
   Pour the beef broth over the grains, and simmer for 10 minutes. Stir in the meats, the reserved ginger-rosemary mixture,
   and the butter. Salt and pepper to taste, and serve hot.

Recipe from JASON FRANEY, CANLIS

Watermelon Gazpacho

Canlis, unequivocally considered Seattle's fanciest restaurant, has a few secrets, and not just the one that magically guides a valet to swing your car around the moment your coat settles back onto your shoulders. Here's another: Although it's known for impeccable service and a flawless combination of timeless, classic food and über-modern cuisine, many of the recipes are actually quite simple, like this savory watermelon gazpacho, made with olive oil and balsamic. Vinegar-sharp and only vaguely sweet, it's garnished with herbs and flowers from the restaurant's garden.

At Canlis, they bake their croutons between two metal baking sheets lined with silicone baking mats, so that they remain perfectly flat, and serve them with a powdered extra-virgin olive oil — a trick achieved with molecular gastronomy that I won't ask you to try at home. I think you'll find this version of the croutons more approachable.

½ small seedless watermelon, diced (about 3 cups), plus more for garnish

2 medium heirloom tomatoes, cored, seeded, and diced (about 3 cups), plus more for garnish

1 medium cucumber, peeled, seeded, and diced (about 1 cup)

2 large shallots, thinly sliced

1 garlic clove, peeled and smashed

¼ cup white balsamic vinegar, plus more for drizzling

1 cup plus 2 tablespoons extra-virgin olive oil, plus more for seasoning

Kosher salt

4-inch section baguette, cut into 1-inch chunks

Foraged flowers, such as borage, nasturtium, chive, parsley, or chervil flowers (optional)

6 SERVINGS

1. Combine the watermelon, tomatoes, cucumber, shallots, and garlic in a large bowl. Whisk ¼ cup of the vinegar and 1 cup of the oil together in a small bowl, then drizzle the vinaigrette over the vegetables, stirring and tossing until well combined. Season the mixture with salt, then squeeze the vegetables with your hands to release the juices. (This is a hands-on experience.) Cover the bowl with plastic wrap, transfer the vegetables to the refrigerator, and marinate overnight or for at least a few hours.

2. While the vegetables marinate, preheat the oven to 300°F. Place the baguette on a baking sheet or a 9- by 13-inch pan, drizzle with the remaining 2 tablespoons oil, and bake for 20 to 25 minutes, tossing occasionally, until golden brown and crunchy. Drain the croutons on paper towels and cool to room temperature.

3. Transfer the soup to a blender or food processor, then purée in batches until very smooth. Transfer to a new bowl (if you'd like to be fancy, you can strain it in, like Canlis does) and season to taste with additional vinegar and salt. Serve cold, garnished with diced tomatoes and watermelon, a few croutons, a drizzle of oil, and a few flower blossoms, if desired.

Northwest Crab Chowder

Let's get something straight: Washington is not Maryland. Here, we do not do crab chowder with tomatoes or lima beans. We don't use Old Bay seasoning. We don't use little crabs, either, because why would we? Here, the rich, flaky meat of big Dungeness crabs — named for the port of Dungeness on the Olympic Peninsula — is enough to fill soups and stews with flavor. This version, which is on the lighter side for a chowder, is the best way to show off our crab season, if you happen to be tired of eating it right out of the shell.

2 tablespoons unsalted butter

1 yellow onion, finely chopped

4 stalks celery, cut into ¼-inch slices

1 tablespoon finely chopped fresh thyme

Salt

Freshly ground black pepper

2 pounds Yukon Gold potatoes (about 7 medium), cut into ½-inch chunks

2 cups whole milk

1 cup heavy cream

1 (15-ounce) can fish broth

1 (8-ounce) bottle clam juice

1½ pounds Dungeness crabmeat, chopped

6 SERVINGS

1. Melt the butter in a large soup pot over medium heat. Add the onions, celery, and thyme; salt and pepper to taste; and cook, stirring, until the vegetables start to soften, about 5 minutes. Add the potatoes, milk, cream, fish broth, and clam juice. Bring the soup to a simmer, and cook until the potatoes are soft, about 10 minutes.

2. Transfer about 2 cups of the vegetables to a food processor or a blender, blend until smooth, and return to the pot. Stir in the crabmeat, cook for 5 minutes longer, and salt and pepper to taste. Serve piping hot.

PIKE PLACE MARKET: THE HISTORY OF AN ICON

FROM FISH AND FARM-FRESH EGGS to coffee and croissants, Seattle's Pike Place Market sells almost everything one could need for a delicious life. Spanning a few city blocks on the edge of downtown, overlooking Elliott Bay, the Market is famous for Rachel, the big bronze piggy bank; for the way the fishmongers at Pike Place Fish lob salmon through the air and across the counter each time someone orders; and for the original Starbucks coffee shop. But the Pike Place Market isn't just a tourist attraction.

As one of the oldest continually operating farmers' markets in the country, the Market initially provided an outlet for farmers to sell directly to consumers, cutting out the middlemen that took so much of growers' profits. Cooks and housewives liked buying directly from the person who grew their food — hence the Market's iconic red sign, which reads Meet the Producer. As more people began shopping there in the '20s and '30s, the Market became a locus of commerce and entertainment.

The market thrived until the end of World War II, when President Franklin D. Roosevelt forced hundreds of thousands of Japanese Americans into internment camps. Many Japanese had grown and sold crops at the Market, and without their hard work the Market languished. Italian immigrant farmers took the place of many Japanese, but during the 1950s, as grocery stores cropped up in Seattle's new suburbs, fewer and fewer people shopped downtown.

In the 1960s, a University of Washington professor named Victor Steinbrueck formed a

group called Friends of the Market, whose mission was to bring the old Market back to life instead of turning it into a more "modern" development. They gathered enough signatures to force a citywide vote, and by a margin of three to one, Seattle voted to keep the Market.

In 1970, the Pike Place Market became one of the state's historic districts, based on the National Historic Preservation Act of 1966. In 1973, the city chartered the Pike Place Market Preservation and Development Authority (PDA), which oversaw the Market's revitalization and worked with the Market Foundation to support a Market-based child-care center, a senior center, and a food bank for low-income families. The Market Foundation is supported by private donations, fund-raisers, and visitors; Rachel the Pig collects upwards of $10,000 each year for the Foundation.

Starbucks opened its first store in 1971, right on Pike Place. Fronted by the original sign (in which, you might notice, the Starbucks mermaid is slightly less modest than she is on Starbucks' cups today), the shop still serves its signature coffees and espressos. Show up on any given afternoon, and you'll find talented buskers singing doo-wop outside for throngs of tourists — proof positive (if 10 million yearly visitors isn't enough) that the Market has once again become the heartbeat of downtown Seattle.

Seattle Shellfish Stew with Sorrel and Couscous

I always use visitors as an excuse to stretch a grocery-shopping trip into an afternoon-long excursion through Seattle. Fish and veggies from the Pike Place Market and a big hunk of guanciale (cured pork jowl) from Salumi Cured Meats inspired this stew, which is a hearty, deeply flavored cross between a San Franciscan cioppino and wonderfully porky braised kale. You could substitute pancetta or thick-cut bacon for the guanciale.

Serve the stew with a simple green salad and good, crusty bread for mopping up the juices.

¼ pound guanciale, cut into ¼-inch cubes

1 large yellow onion, halved and thinly sliced

2 large shallots, halved and thinly sliced

Salt

Freshly ground black pepper

4 large garlic cloves, finely chopped

¼–½ teaspoon red pepper flakes

1 bunch kale (roughly ½ pound), ribs removed and sliced into ¼-inch-thick ribbons

2 cups dry white wine

1 (28-ounce) can diced tomatoes

2 cups chicken broth or water

1 (8-ounce) bottle clam juice

1½ pounds halibut, skin removed, cut into 1-inch cubes

1 pound fresh spot prawns (about 12), deveined

¾ pound Manila clams (about 18), scrubbed clean

¾ pound mussels (about 18), cleaned and debearded

½ pound bay (small) scallops, white tabs removed

Couscous, for serving

¼ cup finely chopped fresh sorrel

1. Heat a large soup pot over medium heat. Add the guanciale and cook until browned and crispy, stirring frequently, about 7 minutes. Use a slotted spoon to transfer the guanciale to a paper towel–lined plate, leaving the grease in the pot, and set aside.

2. Add the onions and the shallots to the pot, salt and pepper to taste, and cook until the onions are soft, stirring occasionally, about 10 minutes. Add the garlic, red pepper, and kale; salt and pepper to taste again; and cook for 10 minutes longer, stirring and turning as the kale on the bottom cooks down.

3. Increase heat to high, add the wine, and simmer for 2 minutes. Add the diced tomatoes, broth, clam juice, and reserved guanciale pieces and reduce to a simmer. Simmer the stew, partially covered, until the kale is soft and the tomatoes begin to break down, about 20 minutes. Salt and pepper to taste.

4. Stir the halibut and the prawns into the stew, cover, and cook for 5 minutes. Add the clams, mussels, and scallops; stir to distribute evenly; and cook, covered, until all the shells have opened, 5 to 10 minutes longer. (Discard any shells that do not open.) Serve the stew piping hot, spooned over couscous in wide, shallow bowls and sprinkled with sorrel.

3 SALADS

Seattle Winter Market Salad

Although the number of farmers' markets decreases during the winter, Seattle boasts three major year-round markets — and there are always relics of seasons past to celebrate. This salad, which combines wintry greens with sweet dried cherries, roasted hazelnuts, and goat cheese, makes the rain a bit more worthwhile. Of course, a drizzle of good market honey or a handful of crisped bacon wouldn't lead you astray, either.

Holmquist Hazelnut Orchards, which grows the long, almond-shaped DuChilly variety of nuts on the western slope of the Cascade Mountains, sells a dry-roasted variety that works perfectly here. The state's restaurants rely on them as a source of locally grown nuts. If you can find them, you won't need to rub the skins off when you toast them because the skins are so thin.

SALAD

- ½ cup raw hazelnuts
- 2 packed cups baby kale (1 bunch), torn
- 2 packed cups arugula
- 1 small head radicchio, thinly sliced
- ½ cup dried cherries, chopped
- 4 ounces goat cheese, crumbled

VINAIGRETTE

- 2 teaspoons Dijon mustard
- ¼ cup sherry vinegar
- Salt
- Freshly ground black pepper
- ½ cup extra-virgin olive oil

6 SERVINGS

1. **Make the salad:** Preheat the oven to 350°F. Roast the nuts on a baking sheet for about 10 minutes, or until the skins begin to darken and peel away from the nuts. (The skins won't peel away much if you use DuChilly hazelnuts.) Rub the nuts in a textured tea towel to remove the skins, roughly chop, and set aside. (Skip this step if you are able to find toasted hazelnuts.)

2. Layer the kale, arugula, radicchio, dried cherries, and goat cheese in a large wide bowl.

3. **Make the vinaigrette:** Whisk the mustard, vinegar, and salt and pepper to taste together in a small bowl. While whisking, add the oil in a slow, steady stream, then whisk until thoroughly incorporated. Just before serving, drizzle the vinaigrette over the salad (you may not need all of it). Toss the hazelnuts with the salad, and serve immediately.

Wood Sorrel, Fava Bean, and Asparagus Salad
with Green Garlic Drizzle

Early each spring, greens that look like overgrown three-leafed clover carpet Washington's forest floors. Wood sorrel, which tastes lemony like sorrel but has a much softer texture, is great for salads. It has been held by some Native American tribes to have aphrodisiac qualities.

Green garlic is immature garlic, often pulled by farmers to thin their garlic crop. It looks like a scallion and tastes somewhere between a scallion and a garlic clove. Use the white and light green parts and save the rest for soup.

½ pound thin asparagus, cut into 1½-inch sections

1 pound whole fava beans, removed from the pods

2 tablespoons finely chopped green garlic

2 tablespoons champagne vinegar

2 teaspoons Dijon mustard

Salt

Freshly ground black pepper

⅓ cup extra-virgin olive oil

¼ pound wood sorrel (about 4 lightly packed cups) or mâche

½ cup shaved Parmesan cheese

4 SERVINGS

1. Fill a medium saucepan with 3 inches of water and bring to a boil. Add the asparagus and shelled fava beans and simmer for 3 minutes, then drain and run under cold water.

2. Transfer the asparagus to a bowl, then peel the thin skin off the fava beans, and add them to the bowl. Set aside to cool.

3. Whisk the green garlic, vinegar, mustard, and salt and pepper to taste together in a bowl. While whisking, add the oil in a slow, steady stream, whisking until combined.

4. Place the sorrel in a salad bowl, and top with the asparagus, fava beans, and Parmesan. Drizzle with the vinaigrette, toss, and serve immediately.

Warm Foraged Mushroom Salad
with Arugula, Fingerling Potatoes, and Bacon

If there's a city that could redefine "airport food," it would be Seattle. But to find it, you'll have to travel about a mile from SeaTac's main terminal. Nestled into a wetlands reserve, Copperleaf Restaurant at Cedarbrook Lodge turns out flawless fancy cuisine using ingredients sourced from within sight — like a mushroom bed that provides about 40 pounds of Brandy Wine mushrooms, which are similar to porcini, each fall. This salad is great with chanterelles, porcini, morels, or anything else you can find fresh at your local farmers' market.

FINGERLING POTATOES

- ½ pound fingerling potatoes, sliced into ½-inch coins
- 1 tablespoon chopped fresh thyme
- 1 tablespoon extra-virgin olive oil
- Kosher salt and ground black pepper

VINAIGRETTE

- ½ cup extra-virgin olive oil
- 4 slices bacon, cut into ¼-inch strips (about ½ cup)
- ½ small red onion, thinly sliced
- 1 small garlic clove, finely chopped
- 1 tablespoon finely chopped fresh Italian parsley
- 1–2 tablespoons sherry vinegar

MUSHROOMS

- 1 tablespoon unsalted butter
- 2 cups wild mushrooms, chopped if large
- 2 medium garlic cloves, finely chopped
- Salt
- Freshly ground black pepper
- ½ cup chicken broth
- 1 tablespoon chopped fresh thyme
- 1 tablespoon sherry vinegar

- 2 cups arugula
- *Fleur du sel*, for serving

2 DINNER OR 4 SIDE SALAD SERVINGS

1. **Make the potatoes:** Preheat the oven to 400°F. Toss the potatoes, thyme, oil, and salt and pepper to taste in a bowl. Transfer to a casserole dish and roast for about 20 minutes, or until golden brown and tender. Set aside, covered with foil to keep warm.

2. **Make the vinaigrette:** Heat the oil in a medium skillet over medium-low heat. Add the bacon and cook until crisp, 6 to 8 minutes. Transfer the bacon and about half the oil to a plate lined with several layers of paper towels. Reduce heat to low, add the onion and garlic to the skillet, and cook, stirring often, until the onions are soft and lightly browned, 3 or 4 minutes. Stir in the parsley and vinegar, and set the pan aside, covered.

3. **Make the mushrooms:** Meanwhile, melt the butter in a large skillet over medium heat. Add the mushrooms and garlic and cook until golden brown, stirring occasionally, for 5 to 10 minutes. Salt and pepper to taste, then add the broth, thyme, and vinegar. Increase heat to high and simmer until all the liquid has evaporated, about 5 minutes longer.

4. Before serving, add the bacon to the onions, reheat the mixture over low heat, then stir in the mushrooms in. Divide the warm potatoes among plates. Top each pile of potatoes with some of the arugula, then some of the mushroom mixture, and serve the salad immediately, garnished with *fleur du sel*.

Caesar Salad
with Roasted Onion, Preserved Lemon, and Bacon

Stand at the entrance to Sleeping Lady Mountain Resort's expansive private vegetable and herb gardens on the outskirts of Leavenworth, and you'll see where it gets its name; up high in the distance, a woman appears to be sunbathing naked along a sun-flecked ridge. She's also apparently keeping a good watch over the gardens, where, since 2009, the resort has grown the produce that complements the meat, dairy, and wine its restaurant sources from the surrounding valleys. Here, chef Kenneth Macdonald, who spent 12 years cooking at the Ritz in London, gives an old-fashioned Caesar salad a twist: it's topped with roasted onion slices, crisp bacon (Zoë's is his favorite brand), and a tiny bit of finely chopped preserved lemon. (For a recipe for Preserved Meyer Lemons, which are a great substitute, see page 258.)

If you want a more substantial meal, consider serving this salad with Roasted Chicken with Honey-glazed Shallots (page 119).

SALAD

- 1 medium red onion, quartered
- 1 tablespoon extra-virgin olive oil
- 4 thick slices nitrate-free bacon
- 4 (1-inch) slices artisanal bread, cut into 1-inch cubes
- 4 tablespoons unsalted butter, melted
- 4 small heads assorted garden lettuce (about ½ pound lettuce leaves total), roughly chopped
- 2 cups shaved Parmesan cheese
- 1 cup loosely packed microgreens or small, soft herbs (such as parsley or chervil)
- 1 teaspoon finely chopped preserved lemon

4 MEAL-SIZED SALADS

1. **Make the salad:** Preheat the oven to 350°F. Place the onion quarters in a small casserole dish, coat with the oil, and roast for 30 minutes, or until soft. Set aside to cool.

2. While the onion roasts, heat a large pan over medium heat. When hot, add the bacon and cook until crisp, about 10 minutes, turning occasionally. Set the bacon aside to drain on a paper towel–lined plate.

3. Increase the oven temperature to 400°F. Place the bread cubes in a large bowl, drizzle the butter on top, and mix (hands work best) until the bread is evenly coated. Transfer the bread to a baking sheet and toast for 10 to 15 minutes, turning once or twice, until golden brown on all sides. Set aside to cool.

DRESSING

1 egg

3 oil- or brine-packed anchovy fillets

1½ teaspoons Dijon mustard

¼ cup fresh herb leaves (such as a mixture of parsley, chives, tarragon, and basil)

1 garlic clove, peeled and smashed

¼ cup champagne vinegar

2 tablespoons shredded Parmesan cheese

½ teaspoon Worcestershire sauce

Juice of ½ small lemon (about 1 tablespoon)

Salt

Freshly ground black pepper

⅔ cup extra-virgin olive oil

4. **Make the dressing:** While the bread toasts, place the egg in a small bowl, add boiling water to cover (just about a cup), and let stand for 10 minutes. (This is called *coddling* the egg; it cooks most of the white outside but not the yolk.)

5. Gently break open the egg, and pour the liquid parts into a blender or food processor, discarding the cooked parts. Add the anchovies, mustard, herbs, garlic, vinegar, shredded Parmesan, Worcestershire, lemon juice, and salt and pepper to taste, and blend well. With the machine running, add the oil in a slow, steady stream, blending until completely smooth.

6. Place the lettuces in a large mixing bowl. Slice and add the onion, then crumble and add the bacon. Add the croutons, shaved Parmesan, microgreens, and preserved lemon. Just before serving, toss the salad with just enough dressing to coat the leaves evenly.

To Market, To Market — Or Not

WHEN ANDREW STOUT FOUNDED Full Circle Farm in the mid-'90s with his wife, Wendy, and a handful of friends, they wanted to grow organic vegetables. "We knew eating organic was our own personal choice, but we also saw it as a growing market for produce," says Andrew. "At the time, our sales conduit of choice was direct marketing — selling directly to customers at farmers' markets or directly to chefs."

In the 1980s, Community Supported Agriculture, or CSA, programs were taking hold in the United States after gaining popularity in the 1970s in Germany and Japan. CSAs were a direct marketing model that allowed a farm to retain its customer

base over the entire length of a growing season. Customers (often called "members") pay in advance for shares of the produce grown at a farm, thereby providing the upfront capital the farm needs at the beginning of a season to remain financially viable. "In traditional food systems, that doesn't happen," explains Stout. "Normally, the farmer doesn't get paid until the end."

When Full Circle Farm opened in 1996, they started with farmers' markets and restaurants. The next year, they started a CSA with 60 members. The pickup site was Stout's driveway, but from the beginning he had big goals. "We started innovating from the get-go, involving bakeries in the area so that we could offer things besides produce," he says. As Full Circle's membership grew, Stout realized that although a CSA program offers farms clear advantages, there are still the pitfalls of traditional farming to navigate.

"In the fall, when your cash flow stops, you can't pay employees so your labor base goes away, and you give your customers away." In effect, CSAs basically give up their customers every year, merely hoping they come back the next season, with no guarantees. This pattern makes the business hard to scale up.

It doesn't take a businessman as shrewd as Stout to realize that these days, when farms stop pulling produce out of the ground, people don't just stop eating. "The wonderful part of food, from a business perspective, is that it's a constant consumable. It's not a durable good that you only buy once in a while," says Stout.

In 2001, Full Circle decided to change their business model to capitalize on the fact that people have to eat. Stout began working with other growers to supplement what his farm could grow with what other people could grow elsewhere. It enabled Full Circle to offer what people bought from the grocery store to supplement their CSA boxes — and offer it weekly, year-round.

Today, they source their produce from their home farm in Carnation, as well as elsewhere in the state, up and down the West Coast, and in some cases from other places in the world. Full Circle still has pickup spots, but in Seattle, they also have delivery options.

"Getting a box of fresh produce at the same time every week becomes a profound experience for people," says Stout. Rather than buying food based on going to the meat counter first, then shopping the rest of a large market, people who receive CSA boxes base their meals on produce. This makes them healthier eaters, which Stout says many people connect with happiness and a strong sense of satisfaction.

In 2012, Full Circle expanded its supply chain further, adding more local foods to their delivery program. If it's starting to sound a lot like your local grocery store, think again — Full Circle's is not an "à la carte" program. In other words, the produce box still anchors the service. You can't just buy meat. And the whole business is still based on providing sustainably produced products, which means Stout now spends much of his time connecting with small business owners, deciding which yogurt, for example, matches the farm's

environmental stewardship ideals. He loves being able to tell the stories other small producers provide.

"Working with Full Circle Farm as a grower has become a part of what I do, instead of the only thing I do," says Stout. "We've chosen a different path from many farms. We really did want to scale up, so we could provide a lot of local food to this marketplace. There are a lot of eaters in this state, and all too often they don't have the choices they're looking for."

And Stout is taking it upon himself to make that change.

Mixed Greens with Apricot-Tomme Toasts

One wet spring day, Catha Link, the cheesemaker at Alpine Lakes Sheep Cheese, invited photographer Lara Ferroni and me into her house for lunch. She bustled about her kitchen, pledging her inability to follow a recipe without skipping steps, dashing in and out of a sunbeam as she prepared this quick salad. Dressed with an orange-inflected balsamic vinaigrette, it relies on grapes and pears for sweetness; for substance, there are thick slabs of baguette spread with homemade apricot jam and blanketed with melted tomme. There in the warmth near her oven, she told us about her farm, and about the life cycle of her sheep, and convinced us, whether she was trying to or not, that getting food from the person who makes it adds a flavor you just can't find in a cheese case.

VINAIGRETTE

- 2 teaspoons Dijon mustard
- Grated zest of 1 small orange
- Salt
- Freshly ground black pepper
- ¼ cup balsamic vinegar
- ¾ cup grapeseed or canola oil

TOASTS

- 12 (½-inch-thick) baguette slices
- Grapeseed or canola oil, for brushing the baguette
- 3 tablespoons apricot jam
- 6 ounces tomme, cut into 12 slices, roughly the same size as the baguette slices (you can also use another semifirm cheese, such as Gruyère, Emmentaler, or fontina)
- 1 teaspoon chopped fresh thyme
- Freshly ground black pepper

SALAD

- 6 ounces mixed greens
- 1 ripe pear, cored and thinly sliced
- 1 cup seedless red grapes, halved
- Tomme, for shaving into the salad

4–6 SERVINGS

1. Preheat the oven to 425°F.

2. **Make the vinaigrette:** Whisk together the mustard, orange zest, salt and pepper to taste, and vinegar in a small bowl. While whisking, add the oil in a slow, steady stream, and whisk until completely blended. Set aside.

3. **Make the toasts:** Place the bread slices on a baking sheet, and brush with the oil. Bake for 5 minutes, or until just beginning to brown. Turn the toasts over. Spread each with a thin layer of jam, then top with a slice of cheese and sprinkle of thyme and pepper. Bake 5 minutes longer, or until the cheese has melted and is just beginning to bubble.

4. **Make the salad:** Meanwhile, place the greens, pear slices, and grapes in a bowl, and drizzle with vinaigrette to taste. (You'll have some left over.) Pile the salad onto plates, and top with shavings of the cheese. Serve immediately, with the hot toasts.

Recipe from MARIA HINES, GOLDEN BEETLE

Persian Cucumber Salad with Labne

At her renowned Seattle restaurant, Tilth, chef Maria Hines made a name for herself cooking New American cuisine with local ingredients — and she did it all with organic food, garnering the restaurant Oregon Tilth's organic certification soon after opening. Next, with the same sustainability goals, she opened Golden Beetle, whose food is inspired by her travels in Turkey, Greece, Lebanon, Egypt, and Israel.

This cucumber salad gets its definitively Persian flavor from mint and orange flower water, which you can find in the ethnic foods section of most large grocery stores, along with labne, a Middle Eastern yogurt cheese. To make your own labne (also spelled lebnah), see the recipe on page 71 — it only takes about 10 minutes of active kitchen time to make.

1 pound Persian or English cucumbers

3 large French breakfast radishes, trimmed

2 teaspoons finely chopped shallots

¼ cup mint leaves, very thinly sliced

¼ teaspoon orange flower water

Juice of ½ small lemon (about 1 tablespoon)

3 tablespoons canola oil

Salt

Freshly ground black pepper

½ cup homemade or store-bought labne

Extra-virgin olive oil, for drizzling

4 SERVINGS

1. Peel the cucumbers and halve lengthwise. (If you're using English cucumbers, scrape the seeds out with a spoon.) Cut the cucumber on the bias into bite-size pieces. Slice the radishes very thinly lengthwise, and place them in a bowl with the cucumbers, shallots, and two-thirds of the mint leaves.

2. Whisk together the orange flower water (add half at a time and taste first, because using too much will make your salad taste soapy), lemon juice, and canola oil in a small bowl. Drizzle the vinaigrette over the vegetables, then salt and pepper to taste, and stir to combine.

3. Pile the vegetables on a large plate, and garnish with dollops of the labne and the reserved mint. Drizzle with olive oil and serve cold or at room temperature.

DIY: Homemade Labne

Labne (also spelled lebnah) is a strained yogurt cheese common to much of the eastern Mediterranean, the Arabian peninsula, and the Middle East. Made at home by straining Greek yogurt through cheesecloth, it's a very simple way to create a flavor and texture not common to many American dinner plates — think extra-thick yogurt with the richness of olive oil and the texture of soft cream cheese.

1 pound (16 ounces) whole milk Greek yogurt

1 tablespoon plus 1 teaspoon extra-virgin olive oil

¾ teaspoon kosher salt

NOTE: Making labne involves only 10 minutes of active preparation, but requires 2 days of draining and standing.

ABOUT 1 CUP

1. Line a colander or strainer with four layers of cheesecloth and place over a pot.
2. Whisk the yogurt, oil, and salt together in a bowl, then pour the mixture into the lined colander. Cover the top with another layer of cheesecloth (stretched over the top, not touching the yogurt) and set aside to drain for 1 day at room temperature.
3. Transfer the setup to the refrigerator and let the mixture hang for 1 day longer in the refrigerator. Remove the cheese from the cheesecloth and serve (or wrap carefully in plastic wrap and refrigerate until ready to use, up to 1 week).

STAR POWER

When **Maria Hines** opened Tilth Restaurant in 2006, after a stint at Earth & Ocean that earned her recognition as one of *Food & Wine* magazine's 10 Best New Chefs, it was the second restaurant in the country to be certified organic. Since then, she's become one of Seattle's superstar chefs. Tilth was named one of the country's 10 best restaurants by the *New York Times* in 2008, and Hines won the James Beard Award for Best Chef Northwest in 2009. Her latest restaurant, Golden Beetle, is known for eastern Mediterranean food, creative cocktails, and décor focused on gorgeous custom-made glass mosaics. ★

Roasted Beet Salad with Pickled Currants, Preserved Lemon, Chèvre, and "Rooftop" Arugula

Head through a door in the back bar of Bastille, the French spot in Seattle's Ballard neighborhood that's my favorite pick for Sunday brunch and people-watching, and you'll meet a set of stairs that leads to nowhere. At least, that's what it seems like, until the chef opens the door onto the restaurant's rooftop garden, which offers a home to gorgeous greens, fragrant (and sometimes unusual) herbs, and happy honeybees.

6 SERVINGS

PICKLED CURRANTS

- ¼ cup dried currants
- ½ cup champagne vinegar
- 2 tablespoons water
- 3 tablespoons sugar
- 3 arbol chiles or bird's-eye chiles

ROASTED BEETS

- 12–14 golf ball–sized beets (about 1½ pounds total), trimmed
- 2 tablespoons extra-virgin olive oil
- 3 sprigs fresh thyme
- ¼ cup white wine
- 1 bay leaf
- 1 teaspoon sea salt
- ½ teaspoon freshly ground black pepper

VINAIGRETTE

- ¼ cup reserved currant liquid
- Juice of ½ small lemon (about 1 tablespoon)
- ⅔–¾ cup extra-virgin olive oil
- Salt
- Freshly ground black pepper

SALAD

- 2 tablespoons thinly sliced preserved lemon rind
- 12 ounces fresh goat cheese
- 3 cups packed arugula (about 3 ounces)

1. Preheat the oven to 400°F.

2. **Make the pickled currants:** Combine the currants, vinegar, water, sugar, and chiles in a small saucepan and bring to a boil. Remove from the heat, set aside, and let the mixture cool for at least 3 hours. Strain the currants, reserving both the currants and the liquid, but discarding the chiles.

3. **Make the beets:** Combine the beets and oil in a bowl, then transfer them to a casserole dish. Add the thyme, wine, bay leaf, salt, and pepper. Cover the beets with foil and roast them for about 1 hour, or until tender all the way through when poked with a skewer.

4. **Make the vinaigrette:** Whisk the reserved currant liquid, lemon juice, oil, and salt and pepper to taste together in a bowl. (Add the lower amount of oil for a spunkier dressing or the higher amount for a more traditional taste.) Set aside.

5. **Make the salad:** Let the beets cool to room temperature, then peel and quarter them. Transfer the beet pieces to a bowl, and add ½ cup of the vinaigrette, the pickled currants, and preserved lemon. Salt and pepper to taste, then set aside to marinate for at least 1 hour, or up to 1 day.

6. To serve, spoon the marinated beets into a bowl and crumble the cheese over them. Lightly dress the arugula with some of the remaining vinaigrette in a separate bowl (you probably won't need it all), and stack it on top of the beets and cheese. Serve immediately.

Roasted Green Bean and Corn Salad
with Crumbled Cheese

Before I moved to Washington, I had a very strict definition of cheeses that didn't come from cows. There was goat cheese, which came in a plastic tube, and feta, which came in a block, and perhaps the occasional crumbly sheep's milk cheese. I knew I loved cheese, but I didn't know just how many varieties could come out of these smaller animals, or how much a sprinkling of said cheese could change the way a simple salad tastes — especially when the cheese is used fresh, instead of aged. This one, made by blasting green beans and corn in a hot oven (or outdoors on a grill pan), tastes different depending on which animal provides the cheese and how old the cheese is — try something different each time.

1 pound green beans, trimmed

Kernels from 1 ear fresh corn, uncooked

1 tablespoon plus 2 teaspoons extra-virgin olive oil

Kosher salt

Freshly ground black pepper

1 tablespoon sherry vinegar

⅓ cup packed roughly chopped fresh Italian parsley

½ cup crumbled fresh cheese (cow's, goat's, or sheep's milk)

NOTE: For a tip on cutting corn off the cob, see page 42.

6 SERVINGS

1. Preheat the oven to 450°F.

2. Toss the green beans, corn kernels, 2 teaspoons of the oil, and salt and pepper to taste until blended in a large casserole dish. Roast for about 20 minutes, or until the ends of the beans begin to brown and shrivel (this doesn't sound sexy, but really, let them brown).

3. Add the remaining tablespoon of oil, plus the vinegar, parsley, and cheese, and transfer to a serving dish. Serve warm or at room temperature.

Wild Salmon with Sweet Corn Salad and Lemon-Herb Vinaigrette

Chef Brian Scheesher was frustrated by shipments of bruised lettuce. Years of working in restaurants taught him that perhaps he was paying too much for things he could grow himself — things like gorgeous heirloom tomatoes, soft lemon verbena, pineapple sage, baby artichokes, purple asparagus, and unblemished baby lettuces. So he opened Trellis in Kirkland, which serves primarily foods grown at his own farm just 6 miles away.

People forget that vegetables change after they're picked, he says, which is why corn must be used as soon as possible after harvest. This salad is a prime example of how growing the ingredients himself makes Scheesher's food great.

CORN SALAD WITH LEMON-HERB VINAIGRETTE

- 3 tablespoons finely chopped fresh Italian parsley
- 3 tablespoons finely chopped fresh basil
- Juice of 1 small lemon (about 2 tablespoons)
- ½ cup extra-virgin olive oil
- 1 medium shallot, finely chopped
- 2 teaspoons capers, finely chopped
- Salt
- Freshly ground black pepper
- Kernels from 4 ears fresh corn, uncooked

SALMON

- 1 tablespoon extra-virgin olive oil
- 4 (6-ounce) fillets wild King salmon

- 4 ounces mixed baby salad greens

NOTE: For a tip on cutting corn off the cob, see page 42.

4 SERVINGS

1. **Make the salad and vinaigrette:** Whisk the parsley, basil, lemon juice, oil, shallot, and capers together in a small bowl. Salt and pepper to taste, fold in the corn, and set aside.

2. **Make the salmon:** Heat a large skillet (or two smaller pans) over medium-high heat. Swirl the oil into the pan(s), then add the salmon, skin side up. Cook until the salmon releases easily from the pan, 3 to 5 minutes on the first side. Turn the salmon skin side down and cook 3 to 5 minutes longer (about 10 minutes total for every 1-inch-thick fish, less for thinner fillets).

3. Divide the salad greens among four plates. Slide a spatula between the flesh and skin of each salmon fillet, and place a piece of salmon next to the greens on each plate. Scoop some of the corn salad on top of the greens and salmon, drizzling some of the extra vinaigrette over the salmon and greens. Serve immediately.

Roasted Carrots with Mustard and Dill

Nash's Organic Produce in Sequim is known for its sweet, crunchy Nantes carrots, which grow particularly well in cool climates and the alluvial soil that covers the northeastern portion of the Olympic Peninsula that Nash's calls home. Roasted, they become even sweeter.

You can cut the tops off the carrots entirely, if you'd like, but I prefer to leave about ¾ inch untrimmed — I like how the little green sprouts look, and they're perfectly edible.

4 SERVINGS

8 medium Nantes or regular carrots (about 1¼ pounds), peeled and halved lengthwise

2 tablespoons extra-virgin olive oil

2 tablespoons whole grain mustard

Salt

Freshly ground black pepper

1 tablespoon finely chopped fresh dill

1. Preheat the oven to 400°F.

2. Mix the carrots, oil, mustard, and salt and pepper to taste together in a casserole dish large enough to hold the carrots in a single layer. Turn the carrots cut sides down, and roast for 25 to 30 minutes, until tender.

3. Sprinkle the dill on top, pile the carrots into a serving dish, and serve immediately.

Warm Split-Farro Salad

At Bluebird Grain Farms, Brooke and Sam Lucy specialize in emmer faro, an ancient grain championed for its nutty flavor and firm texture. It's also used as a dependable, nutrient-packed baking flour. Bluebird sells it whole, cracked, split, or as a flour. Split farro is similar to bulgur wheat and is great in salads like this take on tabbouleh. Serve it warm, or make it up to 2 days ahead, refrigerate it, and let it come to room temperature before serving.

To order split farro directly from Bluebird Grain Farms, see Recipe Contributors and Suppliers (page 274). You can also make a more traditional tabbouleh by substituting bulgur wheat for the farro and cooking it according to the instructions on the package rather than the instructions here for split farro, which takes much longer to cook.

4 SERVINGS

- 1 cup split farro
- 3 cups chicken broth or water
- ¼ teaspoon salt, plus more for seasoning
- 2 tablespoons extra-virgin olive oil
- Juice of 1 small lemon (about 2 tablespoons)
- 1 cup chopped fresh Italian parsley (from 1 medium bunch, stems removed)
- 1 pint grape or cherry tomatoes, halved
- ½ cup finely chopped red onion
- Freshly ground black pepper

1. Combine the farro, broth, and salt in a medium saucepan and bring to a boil over high heat. Reduce heat to low, partially cover, and cook the farro at a simmer, stirring occasionally, until all the water has been absorbed, about 20 minutes.

2. Transfer the farro to a large bowl and let it cool for a few minutes, stirring occasionally. Stir in the oil, lemon juice, parsley, tomatoes, and onion; salt and pepper to taste; and serve.

FRESH FLOUR

MOST HOME BAKERS buy their flour at the grocery store, without thinking much about how it's transformed from amber waves of grain to the stuff in those paper sacks. Very few of us even know people who grind their own flour, let alone do it ourselves. How exactly does the process work?

Flour comes from whole-wheat grains (sometimes called wheat berries), which are the viable seeds at the top of the stalks — 22 per stalk, to be exact. They're oval shaped, like a flattish popcorn kernel with a line drawn down the center. In Winthrop, a hokey, friendly western town with hot, dry summers nestled in the Methow Valley, much of the wheat waving across the ridges each summer belongs to Bluebird Grain Farms. Owners Brooke and Sam Lucy grow wheat, as well as emmer farro, a botanical ancestor of wheat, and sell them as whole grains to be steamed and eaten like rice. Their wheat and emmer are cracked and milled for flour, too, along with the rye they also grow.

Every fall, when the weather is dry, their wheat is harvested with a combine that cuts the stalks away from the ground and threshes the wheat, separating the edible grains from the inedible chaff. The wheat actually cures on the stalks for six weeks before it's harvested, but like other seeds, it can last much longer — literally for generations — if it's stored properly.

In Bluebird Grain's milling room, the berries are separated by size. The largest wheat berries and emmer farro are sold for cooking as a side dish; they're plump and nutty. They cook like rice does, only they're a bit chewier and much more nutritionally complete. They also don't tend to get soggy, like some other grains, which chefs love. The smaller emmer berries are split to make a grain product that cooks more quickly, almost like bulgur wheat, or can be crushed into a multigrain breakfast cereal or ground into flour.

You can use Bluebird Grain Farms' emmer flour or wheat flours as you would any all-purpose flour. For light baked goods, like muffins and cakes, I habitually use half emmer flour and half hard white-wheat flour, both from Bluebird Grain Farms.

Roasted Squash
with Maple-Cumin Caramel

Here's how I cope with my weakness for buying squash: Every October, when the farmers' markets begin bursting with acorn, butternut, spaghetti, and delicata squashes, I give up my mantel. I pile a giant canoe-shaped wooden bowl with orbs of every color, like an edible bouquet of flowers that never wilt. As the fall cools off, I use them one or two at a time, in side dishes like this — simple, warming, and occasionally spicy.

Delicata squash are small yellow or white squash with pretty longitudinal green stripes and a skin that's soft and edible once roasted. You can use bigger squash if you'd like. Just double the sauce and remove the skin first if you're using something with a tough skin like butternut squash.

2 small delicata squash (about 1¼ pounds)

2 tablespoons unsalted butter

2 tablespoons maple syrup or honey

¾ teaspoon ground cumin

¼ teaspoon kosher salt

⅛ teaspoon cayenne pepper (optional)

4 SERVINGS

1. Preheat the oven to 450°F.

2. Cut each squash in half lengthwise, leaving the skin on. Scoop the seeds out (I find an ice cream scoop works best) and cut each half into ½-inch half moons. Set the squash aside.

3. Heat a large ovenproof skillet over medium-high heat. Add the butter, maple syrup, cumin, salt, and cayenne, if using, and cook, stirring occasionally, until the butter has melted. Bring the mixture to a boil, and cook for 1 minute. Remove the pan from the heat and stir in the squash, turning it with tongs so all the pieces get coated in the sauce.

4. Bake the squash for about 20 minutes, or until the squash is tender and the sauce is thick. Transfer the squash to a serving bowl with a slotted spoon, and serve immediately.

Warm Lentil Salad
with Apples and Squash

Each year, Washington farmers harvest over 100 million 40-pound boxes of apples. A good third of those are Red Delicious, that old standby, but each year the popularity of Honeycrisp, Braeburn, and Pink Lady apples — not to mention the heirloom varieties one finds at local farmers' markets, like Gravenstein, Cox's Orange Pippin, and Bramley's Seedling — keeps rising. For this warm salad, look for apples that are equally tart and sweet with a good crunch.

This salad is also a lovely option for a picnic; if you plan to serve it at room temperature, let it cool without the vinegar and stir in the vinegar before serving.

1 tablespoon extra-virgin olive oil

1 medium shallot, finely chopped

2 large stalks celery, finely chopped

Salt

Freshly ground black pepper

2 teaspoons finely chopped fresh thyme

¼ cup dry white wine

2 cups (½-inch) butternut squash cubes

¾ cup brown lentils

2½ cups chicken or vegetable broth

1 medium sweet-tart apple (such as Honeycrisp), cut into ½-inch pieces

2 tablespoons chopped fresh Italian parsley

1 tablespoon champagne vinegar

6 SERVINGS

1. Heat a large saucepan over medium heat. Add the oil, then the shallot and celery, and season with salt, pepper, and thyme. Cook, stirring occasionally, until the vegetables are soft, about 5 minutes.

2. Add the wine, bring the mixture to a simmer, and cook until the liquid is gone, about 5 minutes. Add the squash, lentils, and broth; bring to a simmer; and cook, stirring occasionally, until the lentils are soft and the liquid has been absorbed, 30 to 40 minutes.

3. Stir in the apple, parsley, and vinegar; salt and pepper to taste, and remove from the heat.

4. Let the dish sit for about 5 minutes for the apples to heat through. Transfer the salad to a bowl with a slotted spoon, leaving any residual liquid behind in the pot. Serve hot, warm, or at room temperature.

LENTILS

The Palouse region of eastern Washington and northern Idaho grows more than a third of America's lentils — a fact celebrated each August at the National Lentil Festival, where a giant bowl holds 650 gallons of lentil chili. Celebrate by traveling to Pullman for the festivities, or whip up a dish that brings out their earthy flavor. ★

Recipe from HOLLY SMITH, CAFÉ JUANITA

Spicy Roasted Cauliflower
with Cumin, Lime, and Pine Nuts

Though she's been lauded as one of America's best chefs and was recognized with a James Beard Award in 2008, Holly Smith is perhaps most well known for being creative, spunky, and comforting — both in person and on the plate at her Kirkland restaurant, Café Juanita. This simple *contorni*, made by first sautéing, then roasting, spiced cauliflower florets, is a great example of her northern Italian–inspired cuisine.

1 large head cauliflower (about 1½ pounds), leaves removed and stem trimmed

1 large lime

3 tablespoons cold unsalted butter

1 tablespoon ground cumin

¼ teaspoon cayenne pepper

Salt

Freshly ground black pepper

¼ cup raw pine nuts

4 SERVINGS

1. Bring a large pot of salted water to a boil. Cook the entire head of cauliflower, stem side down, for 4 minutes. While the cauliflower cooks, fill a large bowl with ice water. Transfer the cauliflower directly from the boiling water to the ice water, and let cool for 10 minutes.

2. Preheat the oven to 400°F.

3. Meanwhile, cut the ends off the lime using a small sharp knife. Cut the peel and all of the pith off, and slice between the membranes so you're left with pith-free lime slices (known as "supremes"). Set aside.

4. Cut the florets off the cauliflower, slicing medium and large florets into bite-size pieces. Heat a large heavy skillet over medium-high heat. Add the butter, cumin, cayenne (or more, to taste), and salt, and cook until the butter has melted. Turn the pan to coat it evenly, then add the cauliflower, cut side down wherever possible, and cook until browned, 4 to 5 minutes. Salt and pepper to taste, then stir.

5. Add the lime pieces, then transfer the pan to the oven and roast for 4 to 5 minutes longer, or until the lime is melting and the cauliflower is tender. Stir in the pine nuts, and serve immediately.

Collard Greens
with Apple Cider Vinegar

Here's a winter classic made with ingredients entirely from Washington — local bacon, hearty collard greens, and apple cider vinegar. I buy my vinegar from Rockridge Orchards, where owner Wade Bennett makes his own.

Serve the greens next to Glazed Braised Goat Shanks (page 177) and Camp Fire Grits (page 91).

¼ pound smoked bacon (4 thick slices), chopped into ½-inch pieces

1 bunch collard greens (about ½ pound), cut across ribs into ½-inch strips

2 cups water

2 cups apple cider

¼ cup apple cider vinegar

1 large garlic clove, peeled and smashed

Salt

Freshly ground black pepper

3–4 SERVINGS

1. Heat a large heavy pot over medium heat. Add the bacon and cook, stirring occasionally, until almost crisp, about 10 minutes. Transfer the bacon (and fat) to a paper towel–lined plate, leaving just a sheen of fat in the pan, and set aside.

2. Add the collards, water, apple cider, and vinegar to the pan and bring to a simmer over high heat. Add the reserved bacon and garlic clove, reduce heat to low, and simmer until the greens are soft and the liquid is almost gone, 35 to 40 minutes. Salt and pepper to taste, and serve hot.

El Gaucho's Mashed Potatoes

Think about it: If you're going to find the city's best mashed potatoes, why would you look any further than Seattle's best steakhouse? At El Gaucho, known perhaps as much for its fiery tableside fanfare and killer Caesar salads as it is for flawless tenderloins, they keep their mashers simple — they just add cream and sweet, salted butter. If you'd like, you can garnish the potatoes with chopped fresh Italian parsley or chives.

If you don't have a ricer, mash the potatoes by hand using a potato masher or a large fork.

3 pounds russet potatoes, peeled

¾ cup plus 2 tablespoons heavy cream

6 tablespoons salted butter

1½ teaspoons kosher salt, plus more for seasoning

¼ teaspoon ground white pepper, plus more for seasoning

4–6 SERVINGS

1. Place the potatoes in a large stockpot and add cold water to cover. Bring the water to a boil, and simmer until the potatoes are cooked through and soft in the center when pierced with a skewer, 30 to 40 minutes. Drain the potatoes in a colander, and let the potatoes steam (to cool and dry them out a bit) for about 5 minutes.

2. Meanwhile, heat the cream, butter, salt, and pepper in a small saucepan over medium heat, whisking until the butter is melted. Set aside.

3. Using a hand ricer, rice the potatoes into a large bowl or a stand mixer fitted with the paddle attachment. Beating the potatoes with a spoon (or with the mixer set on medium speed), add the hot cream-butter mixture. Season to taste with additional salt and pepper, and serve hot.

SMALL POTATOES

FACT: IN 2010, WASHINGTON produced more than 8 *billion* pounds of potatoes.

Potato farmer Brent Olsen says Washington is in a potato revolution. In the mid-'90s, when he decided to follow in his grandfather's footsteps and start farming, potatoes meant one thing: big, burly, brown-skinned russets. While Olsen started searching for a crop that he could market year-round from his farm in Colville, his sister was working toward her graduate degree in potato science. Combining her knowledge of potato varieties and his desire to farm, Olsen found a niche growing more unique potato varieties than the market had previously offered — striking Viking Purples, creamy Bintjes, dense German Butterballs, and quartzlike Mountain Roses, to name a few.

Since Olsen started his operation with seven different potato varieties, Olsen Farms has grown in size but maintains the warm family feel that, he thinks, makes their business so successful. These days, Olsen Farms' main goal is to keep their customers happy. They harvest over 20 varieties of potatoes on 25 acres for a yearly total exceeding 400,000 pounds. That might seem like a lot of spuds, but Olsen Farms is small potatoes, so to speak.

Idaho may be more famous for potatoes, but Washington State runs pretty close in potatoes produced. The land here also seems to be more productive — something the Washington Potato Commission attributes to a statewide focus on reducing chemical use and constantly improving sustainable farming practices. According to the commission, if the state's yearly potato crop was packed into 50-pound boxes and laid end to end, it would circle the globe twice. Now *that's* a lot of spuds — the large majority of which are sent to packers to be made into French fries, potato chips, and mashed potatoes. But the best ones, in my humble opinion, are the heritage varieties, which are often tastiest just served plain.

Though it's small, Olsen Farms thrives because of the variety it sells, and because of the culture of dedication Olsen and his family have created not only with customers, but also with his employees. For Olsen Farms to survive at the rate they are growing, Olsen relies on constant feedback from his crew; he says good teamwork is everything in his business. The market purveyors tell him what customers are buying, which allows him to maintain the best-selling products — products that are far more varied than they were even a decade ago. I mean, did your parents get to choose between 20 potato varieties, like you can today at Washington farmers' markets? Revolution, indeed.

Potato Gratin with Dinah's Cheese and Pancetta

At Vashon Island's Kurtwood Farms, owner Kurt Timmermeister makes a bloomy-rind cow's milk cheese called Dinah's Cheese. When it was first released in 2009, Seattle swooned; nowhere in the state is there a farmstead Camembert-style cheese so clearly fit for international fame. In my official opinion, it would be an atrocity to do anything to Dinah's Cheese besides eat it at room temperature at its peak ripeness, when the middle succumbs to a thumb's soft pressure and the inside has the consistency of thick homemade pudding. But should your path cross a certain gooey cheese good enough to make you voluntarily lie prostrate in a busy street, and you promise not to tell anyone that you'd consider putting half a wheel into a simple potato gratin with little bits of pancetta and a glug of cream, read on. This is just the right way to do the wrong thing.

8 SERVINGS

- 2 teaspoons extra-virgin olive oil
- ¾ cup (about 3 ounces) diced pancetta
- 4 medium Yukon Gold potatoes (about 2 pounds), peeled and sliced ⅛ inch thick
- 3 tablespoons unbleached all-purpose flour
- Salt
- Freshly ground black pepper
- 4 ounces not-quite-ripe Camembert-style cheese (about ½ wheel), chilled
- ⅔ cup heavy cream
- ½ cup whole milk
- 1 egg

1. Preheat the oven to 350°F. Coat an 8- by 8-inch (or similar) gratin dish with the oil and set aside.

2. Heat a medium skillet over medium heat. Add the pancetta, and cook, stirring occasionally, until crisp, 6 to 8 minutes. Set aside.

3. Meanwhile, toss the potato slices and flour in a large bowl, using your hands to distribute the flour evenly. Season the potatoes with salt and pepper (the amount of salt you use should depend on how salty your pancetta tastes). Cut the cheese into thin slices. (You can leave the rind on.)

4. Spread one-third of the potatoes along the bottom of the dish, overlapping them as necessary. Scatter one-third of the cooked pancetta over the potatoes, followed by one-third of the cheese, broken up into little bits. Repeat with the remaining ingredients, making two more layers, ending with pancetta and cheese. Whisk the cream, milk, and egg together in a small bowl, then carefully pour the liquid mixture over the potatoes.

5. Cover the gratin tightly with aluminum foil and bake for 30 minutes. Remove the foil, increase the temperature to 400°F, and bake 40 to 45 minutes longer, or until the potatoes are lightly browned on top and a skewer can pierce through the layers easily. Let cool for 10 to 15 minutes before serving.

NASH'S ORGANIC PRODUCE

The carrots at Nash's Organic Produce are easy to fall in love with. Then again, so are the zucchini and onions. At their farm store, off a country road in Sequim, on the Olympic Peninsula, Nash's piles produce high on the tables so you can see, almost at eye level, that something about their farm's soil makes their produce especially bright and beautiful.

Since they began selling at the Port Angeles Farmers Market in 1979, Nash's has grown considerably, creating farm shares for customers to purchase and trucking much of their produce to PCC Natural Markets, a Seattle co-op chain that offers a huge array of local produce. ★

Recipe from MT. TOWNSEND CREAMERY AND JESS THOMSON

Camp Fire Grits

Port Townsend's Mt. Townsend Creamery teamed up with Crimson Cove Smokehouse to create an alder wood– and applewood-smoked version of New Moon, their creamy, buttery, jack-style cheese. The result is great on its own, but even better stirred into grits, like the Creamery does in its shrimp and grits recipe. Serve them anywhere you'd serve mashed potatoes — under stews, alongside roasts, or with roasted vegetables.

4 cups water

1 cup grits or medium-ground cornmeal

4 ounces Camp Fire jack cheese, grated (1 cup)

2 tablespoons heavy cream

Salt

Freshly ground black pepper

NOTE: If you can't find Camp Fire by Mt. Townsend Creamery (see Recipe Contributors and Suppliers, page 274), look for another smoked cheese, such as a cheddar, or substitute regular Monterey jack cheese.

4 SERVINGS

1. Bring the water to a boil in a large saucepan. Add the grits in a slow, steady stream, stirring constantly with a wooden spoon or spatula, then reduce heat to the lowest setting and cook the grits, stirring often, until thick and soft, about 40 minutes.

2. Stir in the cheese, cream, and salt and pepper to taste, then remove the grits from the heat and let sit, covered, for 5 minutes before serving.

Cheesemonger's Creamy Dreamy Mac and Cheese

In 2010, when Sheri LaVigne opened The Calf & Kid, the artisanal cheese shop in Seattle's tony Melrose Market, she filled a hole Seattle might not have known was there. She's now the city's go-to independent cheesemonger, with intricate knowledge of cheeses made across the state and around the globe.

Since LaVigne always has access to a multitude of cheeses (she stocks 80 to 100 at any given time), she's constantly experimenting with new combinations in her macaroni and cheese recipe. So don't feel married to the cheeses below — just remember that if you use washed- or brushed-rind cheeses, you should skim the rinds out of your sauce once all the cheese has melted down. In fact, don't feel married to much about this recipe — you can add more or less milk, for a thicker or creamier macaroni and cheese, and you can skip the crunchy topping, if you'd prefer, serving it hot right off the stove.

1 pound short pasta (such as penne, rigatoni, elbow macaroni, or fusilli)

2 tablespoons unsalted butter

2 tablespoons unbleached all-purpose flour

1¼ cups heavy cream

4 ounces triple-cream cow's milk cheese (such as Domaine du Village, chopped)

4 ounces Brie, chopped

4 ounces Seastack cheese (from Mt. Townsend Creamery), chopped

2 ounces Cambazola cheese, chopped

½ cup panko breadcrumbs

⅓ cup grated Parmesan cheese

4 SERVINGS

1. Preheat the oven to 425°F.

2. Bring a large pot of salted water to a boil for the pasta, and cook the pasta until al dente according to package instructions.

3. Meanwhile, melt the butter in a large saucepan over medium heat. When melted, add the flour, whisk until no lumps remain, and cook, whisking constantly, for about 1 minute. Add the cream in a slow, steady stream, whisking gently, and cook until the mixture comes to a simmer, stirring often. Cook for 2 minutes, stirring, then whisk in the triple-cream cheese, Brie, Seastack, and Cambazola.

4. Drain the pasta, and add it to the pot with the cheese sauce (or mix the two together in a large bowl). Transfer the macaroni and cheese to a casserole dish. Sprinkle with the breadcrumbs, then the Parmesan, and bake for 10 to 15 minutes, or until the Parmesan is golden brown and the sauce bubbles around the edges. Serve hot.

Sheri LaVigne

Recipe from JERRY TRAUNFELD, POPPY

Grilled Asparagus
with Fried Sage and Lemon

Jerry Traunfeld isn't known for cooking within the lines. At The Herbfarm, the no-holds-barred Woodinville restaurant known for exquisitely prepared local foods, hours-long dining experiences, and kitschy décor that would make the most doily-happy grandmother proud, he pioneered the popular use of unusual herbs like anise hyssop and rose geranium.

At Poppy, the restaurant he now spearheads in Seattle's Capitol Hill neighborhood, he's introduced a new style of dining. Based on the traditional Indian *thali*, a large plate with multiple dishes served simultaneously, his food is rich with spice while staying true to Northwestern cuisine. This gorgeous dish works as part of a huge spread that might appear at Poppy but is garnished with sage blossoms, reminiscent of The Herbfarm.

DRESSING

¼ cup extra-virgin olive oil

Juice of 1 medium lemon (about 3 tablespoons)

Grated zest of ½ lemon

¼ teaspoon kosher salt

Freshly ground black pepper

FRIED SAGE

1 cup vegetable or olive oil, for frying

32 whole, medium fresh sage leaves, patted dry

Kosher salt

ASPARAGUS

2 pounds asparagus

1½ tablespoons extra-virgin olive oil

Kosher salt

1 cup thinly shaved Parmesan cheese

Sage blossoms, for garnish (optional)

6 SERVINGS

1. **Make the dressing:** Whisk the oil, lemon juice, lemon zest, salt, and pepper together in a small bowl. Set aside.

2. **Make the fried sage:** Heat the oil in a small saucepan until it reaches 330°F. Drop in the sage leaves and turn them in the oil with a wire skimmer or slotted spoon. Fry for 10 to 15 seconds, then transfer them to a paper towel–lined plate to drain. Do not let the leaves brown. Sprinkle the leaves with salt. (They should crisp when they cool.)

3. **Make the asparagus:** Prepare a medium-hot fire (about 450°F) in a gas or charcoal grill. (Alternatively, the asparagus may be roasted in a 450°F oven for 4 to 8 minutes.) Cut off the bottom quarter of each asparagus spear, or at the point where they turn pale and tough. (If your spears are medium to thick, peel the lower two-thirds of the trimmed spears with a sharp vegetable peeler. Thin spears do not need to be peeled.)

4. Place the asparagus on a platter or baking sheet, and toss with the oil and a sprinkle of salt. Grill the spears, turning occasionally, until they are slightly limp when you hold them from the bottom, 4 to 8 minutes, depending on their thickness. They will continue to cook once you remove them from the grill.

5. Just before serving, toss the asparagus with the dressing in a large bowl. (You can do this when the asparagus is hot, warm, or at room temperature.) Arrange the dressed asparagus on a platter, then garnish with the fried sage leaves, Parmesan shavings, and sage blossoms, if desired, before serving.

Raw Corn Salad with Cotija and Cilantro

If you're of the school that argues summer corn is best simply boiled — maybe buttered and salted if you're feeling sacrilegious — you clearly haven't tried raw corn, cut directly off the cob. Crisp with juice and plump with sugars, each crunched kernel does a little dance on your tongue (but not between your teeth, which is convenient). This simple salad, inspired by *elote,* the Mexican snack of corn on the cob smeared with mayonnaise and sprinkled with Mexican-style cheese and lime juice, makes a great side show for Josh's Pulled Pork Tacos with Smoky Red Cabbage Slaw, Pineapple Salsa (page 156) or Kabocha and Black Bean Tamale Pie (page 110).

Kernels from 6 ears fresh corn

¼ cup roughly chopped fresh cilantro

2 tablespoons mayonnaise

3 tablespoons crumbled cotija or feta cheese

½ teaspoon ancho chile powder

Juice of 1 large lime (about 2 tablespoons)

Kosher salt

NOTE: For a tip on cutting corn off the cob, see page 42.

6 SERVINGS

Combine the corn kernels, cilantro, mayonnaise, cheese, chile powder, lime juice, and salt in a medium bowl and stir to blend. Serve immediately, or cover and refrigerate up to 1 day before serving.

Emmer-Sage Buttermilk Biscuits

At Bluebird Grain Farms in Winthrop, on the eastern slope of the Cascade Mountains, the top of each bin is labeled with a piece of duct tape. On each piece, in sequential order, the owners have written dates, scratching out the previous date each time they add a new one. The numbers are only days apart. They represent when Brooke and Sam Lucy's heritage grains were ground into flour, something they do many times every week, and every single time a customer puts in a large specific order. They wouldn't store milled flour any sooner than your local diner would cook your omelet the night before; they know the products' integrity would suffer. Ditto for all their whole grains, which are stored in the hulls and milled to order.

If you're a biscuit person, incorporating whole grain flours such as emmer flour into the batter makes them a bit more substantial and contributes a great nutty background flavor. Inspired by Bluebird Grain Farm's sage biscuit mix, which they sell in their trademark green bag, these biscuits are great for dinner with Hardware Store Fried Chicken (page 140) or for breakfast.

1½ cups emmer flour

1½ cups unbleached all-purpose flour

2 tablespoons baking powder

2 tablespoons sugar

1½ tablespoons rubbed sage

1 teaspoon salt

1 cup (2 sticks) cold unsalted butter, cut into ½-inch chunks

1¼ cups buttermilk, plus more for brushing

Butter and honey, for serving

8 OR 9 BISCUITS

1. Preheat the oven to 425°F. Line a baking sheet with parchment paper, and set aside.

2. Whisk the emmer flour, all-purpose flour, baking powder, sugar, sage, and salt together in a mixing bowl. Add the butter, and using a large fork or a pastry cutter, cut the butter into the flour until the butter is in pieces the size of small peas.

3. Add the buttermilk, and mix with a fork until no dry spots remain. The dough will be rather wet. (This dough also works well made in a stand mixer fitted with a paddle attachment; blend the butter with the dry ingredients for 30 seconds on low speed, then add the buttermilk in a slow, steady stream, mixing on low until no dry spots remain.)

4. Transfer the dough to a board floured with all-purpose flour, fold it two or three times to help it hold together, and roll with a floured rolling pin into a circle about 1 inch thick and 8 inches across. Dip a 3-inch biscuit cutter (or a glass) in flour, then use it to cut out 6 biscuits, dipping it into the flour again between cuts. (You can make smaller biscuits; just adjust the baking time.) Reroll the dough to make additional biscuits. Brush the flour off the biscuits on both sides.

5. Arrange the biscuits on the baking sheet (they'll rise up, but not out), brush with buttermilk, and bake for 15 to 20 minutes, until puffed and golden brown. Let cool 5 minutes on the baking sheet, then serve warm with butter and honey, if desired.

HOLY TOMATO

Billy Allstot, the founder of Billy's Gardens, is known at Seattle farmers' markets for the rainbows of heirloom tomatoes he brings each summer. Ranging from Yellow Brandywines and Green Zebras to Mortgage Lifters and Paul Robesons, his tomatoes may be the celebrities of the summer market, but they're anything but high maintenance. According to Allstot, no good tomato needs to be put into a salad. It should be eaten out of hand, with the juice dripping down the back of your hand and underneath your elbow.

But if you push him to share a recipe, he'll tell you he starts with excellent ingredients. Slice your large, ripe summer tomatoes moments before serving them, then drizzle with extra-virgin olive oil and a high-quality balsamic vinegar (about twice as much oil as vinegar). Sprinkle with a good flaky sea salt and dig in! ★

Recipe from CAFE LAGO

Cafe Lago's City of Seattle Eggplant

Known for its flawless thin-crusted wood-fired pizzas and housemade pastas, Cafe Lago has been part of Seattle's dining scene since 1990. For rustic Italian food with no frills (unless you count the Parmesan), wander just south of the Montlake bridge, take a seat, and order your favorites. Just don't forget to ask for this eggplant dish on the side. The name is an homage to an appetizer called City of Norwalk Eggplant that the owners had at Pasta Nostra, a restaurant in Norwalk, Connecticut, in 1986.

Use the eggplant with or without the skin, as you prefer.

1 medium eggplant (1 pound)

¾ cup extra-virgin olive oil

5 garlic cloves, peeled and smashed

1 (14.5-ounce) can whole peeled plum tomatoes

1 tablespoon chopped fresh Italian parsley

½ cup balsamic vinegar

½ tablespoon light brown sugar

1 teaspoon sea salt

4 ounces Gorgonzola cheese, thinly sliced

4–6 SERVINGS

1. Prepare a medium-hot fire (about 450°F) in a gas or charcoal grill.

2. Halve the eggplant lengthwise, and cut each half into four or five spears. Brush the spears on all sides with about ¼ cup of the oil, then grill with the lid closed as much as possible, until the spears are well marked and tender, 2 to 3 minutes per side. Transfer the eggplant to a glass or ceramic dish big enough to hold it in a single layer and set aside.

3. Pulse the garlic in a food processor until finely chopped. Add the tomatoes, parsley, vinegar, sugar, salt, and the remaining ½ cup oil, and purée until smooth.

4. Pour the marinade over the eggplant, cover with plastic wrap, and refrigerate for at least 2 hours or up to 3 days. Serve at room temperature with the sliced cheese.

Recipe from JENNY AND ANSON KLOCK, PICNIC

picnic's Kale Salad

It would be fair to call picnic, the little food and wine boutique at the top of Seattle's Phinney Ridge, a blast from the past, even though it opened in 2008. The affable owners, Jenny and Anson Klock, run it the way I imagine my grandmother's cheesemonger did, linking hellos and goodbyes with first names and questions about the kids. But behind the counter, they're all business, slicing artisanal meats and cheeses for the sandwiches and picnic platters people eat in-house while browsing the magazine collection or take for the road, usually with a few bottles from their carefully curated, locally focused wine collection.

This salad, made with raw kale, white beans, and toasted pumpkin seeds, and seasoned with Mama Lil's peppers (a Washington favorite) and the preserved lemons Anson makes and sells at picnic, is great because you can make it ahead and it travels well. If you aren't thinking three months ahead (it takes that long for the preserved lemons to cure), head to picnic for preserved lemons, or find a good homemade variety — the store-bought kind are often far less flavorful.

6 cups (packed) torn kale (a ¾-pound mix of lacinato, green curly, and red kale works best)

2 cups cooked, drained white beans or chickpeas (from 1 cup dry or one 15-ounce can)

¼ cup Mama Lil's or piquillo peppers, finely chopped (see Recipe Contributors and Suppliers, page 274)

¼ cup toasted pumpkin seeds

2 tablespoons finely chopped fresh chives

1 preserved Meyer lemon (page 258)

¾ cup extra-virgin olive oil

¾ cup canola oil

NOTE: When you chop the kale, remove all the ribs and tough pieces — the kale isn't cooked, so it's best if you tear it into soft bite-size pieces.

6 SERVINGS

1. Toss the kale, beans, peppers, pumpkin seeds, and chives together in a large bowl.

2. Rinse the lemon to remove any residual salt, then remove any visible seeds, and whirl it in a food processor or blender with the olive oil and canola oil until completely smooth.

3. Pour about half of the dressing over the salad, and toss very well to combine. This dressing is very powerful — bright, acidic, and salty. Add a bit more vinaigrette to the salad, tasting along the way. (If you don't use all the dressing, save the remainder to use on another salad.) Let the salad sit at least 1 hour at room temperature (or up to 24 hours in the refrigerator) before serving.

Garlic Fries

In my house, it's not exactly a secret: I don't go to see the Seattle Mariners for the baseball. I don't go for the camaraderie, or for the peanuts. I go for the garlic fries from Grounders. I love them precisely because they aren't crisp or crunchy. I love them because they've been bathed with enough garlic to subdue an elephant, and because standing outside the fry stand on the stadium's top level, with a view of Elliot Bay and the Olympic Mountains behind it, I can almost imagine loving baseball.

Here's my version of the stadium standby, made with potatoes roasted in a very hot oven. I like them because they're easy, and because making them means I don't actually have to watch the game. (Sorry. It's the truth.) Serve them the instant they come out, slathered with the garlic butter.

2 medium russet potatoes (1¼ pounds total), peeled (optional) and cut into ½-inch batons

2 tablespoons canola oil

1 teaspoon kosher salt

2 tablespoons salted butter

2 large garlic cloves, finely chopped

4 SERVINGS

1. Preheat the oven to 500°F.

2. Mix the potatoes, oil, and salt together in a large bowl. Transfer the potatoes to a baking sheet, spread them in an even layer, and bake for 20 to 25 minutes, turning once after about 15 minutes, until browned and cooked through.

3. Meanwhile, combine the butter and garlic in a small saucepan and warm over low heat until the butter melts and the garlic softens a bit. When the potatoes are done, reheat the butter if necessary, and drizzle the garlic butter over all the potatoes. Serve immediately.

HIGHEST GROUND

At 6,872 feet, The Summit House, the little bungalow atop Crystal Mountain, is the state's highest restaurant. Take the gondola up on a clear day for one of the best possible views of Mt. Rainier, and you can order my second-favorite garlic fries — in this case, thin, crisp fries with a garlicky aioli. ★

5

MEATLESS MAINS

Yam, Sweet Onion, and Goat Cheese Enchiladas

Walla Walla sweet onions are supposedly mild enough to eat like an apple. I can't claim to have tried them raw, but when they are roasted with yams and rolled into enchiladas with a spicy sauce, they certainly become the star of the plate.

3 large poblano peppers (about 2 pounds total), trimmed, seeded, and chopped

3 small jalapeño peppers, trimmed, seeded, and chopped

2 large sweet onions (such as Walla Walla sweets)

4 large garlic cloves, peeled

¼ cup canola oil

Salt

Freshly ground black pepper

2 large yams (about 2 pounds total)

2 (15-ounce) cans diced fire-roasted tomatoes (with juice)

¼ cup finely chopped fresh cilantro, plus more for garnish

12 (6-inch) corn tortillas

6 ounces goat cheese, crumbled

6 SERVINGS

1. Preheat the broiler to the highest setting.

2. Put the poblano and jalapeño peppers in a sturdy roasting pan. Chop one of the onions, and add it to the pan, along with 2 of the garlic cloves, 2 tablespoons of the oil, and salt and pepper to taste. Stir to combine the ingredients and broil in the upper third of the oven for about 15 minutes, stirring every few minutes, or until the peppers are blackened in spots all over.

3. While the peppers and onions are cooking, peel the yams and cut them into ½-inch cubes. Halve and thinly slice the remaining onion, then chop the remaining 2 garlic cloves. Stir the yams, onion slices, chopped garlic, and remaining 2 table-spoons oil together in a mixing bowl. Transfer the mixture to a parchment-lined baking sheet, spread into an even layer, and salt and pepper to taste.

4. Switch the oven to bake mode, and set it to 400°F. Stir the tomatoes and cilantro into the pepper and onion mixture, so it becomes a sauce.

5. Bake the pepper and onion mixture on the upper rack of the oven and the yam mixture on the lower rack of the oven for 45 minutes, stirring both halfway through cooking, or until the onions are brown, the yams are soft, and the sauce has thickened.

6. Carefully purée the sauce in a food processor or blender, season to taste, and set aside. Wrap the tortillas in a damp hand towel and microwave on high power for 1½ minutes, or until they are soft.

7. Spread about ½ cup of the sauce on the bottom of a 9- by 13-inch (or similar) casserole dish. Working with one tortilla at a time, spread a heaping tablespoon of the sauce on the tortilla, followed by a heaping ¼ cup of the yam and onion mixture. Roll the tortilla up, and place it in the pan seam side down. Repeat with the remaining tortillas, sauce, and filling.

8. Spread the remaining sauce over the top of the enchiladas in an even layer, and scatter the goat cheese evenly on top. Cover the enchiladas with foil. (The enchiladas can be made up to this point, covered with foil, and refrigerated up to 24 hours.)

9. Bake the enchiladas with the foil on for 20 minutes. Remove the foil, bake 5 minutes longer, then serve hot, garnished with additional cilantro.

Fried Tofu and Sesame Soba Salad

Luke Lukoskie, the owner of Island Spring Organics, a tofu producer on Vashon Island, says tofu is best first flash fried, then simmered in your favorite sauce. His technique is simple: You fry naked cubes of tofu for a minute and 45 seconds in 350° oil, then simmer it — in, say, the homemade curry in the Glover Street Chicken Curry Stew (page 136), using fried tofu in place of the chicken. It's also delicious fried and stirred into this simple Japanese-inspired soba noodle salad.

⅓ cup sesame tahini (well stirred)

2 tablespoons dark sesame oil

½ cup boiling water

1 tablespoon grated fresh gingerroot

2 tablespoons low-sodium soy sauce

1 tablespoon rice vinegar

1–2 teaspoons sriracha or similar Asian chile paste (optional)

Canola, grapeseed, or safflower oil, for frying

1 (8.8-ounce or similar) package soba noodles

1 pound tofu, cut into ¾-inch cubes

3 tablespoons toasted sesame seeds

4 SERVINGS

1. Blend the tahini, sesame oil, water, ginger, soy sauce, vinegar, and sriracha, if using, in a large bowl. Set aside.

2. Fill a high-sided saucepan with 2 inches of canola oil and heat over medium-high heat until the oil reaches 350°F on an instant-read thermometer.

3. While the oil is heating, bring a large pot of water to a boil for the noodles, and cook according to the package instructions.

4. When the oil reaches 350°F, add about one-third of the tofu, and fry for 1 minute 45 seconds, turning occasionally with a wire mesh strainer or slotted metal spoon. Transfer the tofu to a paper towel–lined plate to drain, and repeat with the remaining tofu, working in batches and allowing the oil to come back up to 350°F between batches.

5. When the noodles are done, rinse and transfer them to the bowl with the sauce. Add the fried tofu and the sesame seeds, and toss to blend. Serve immediately.

TOFU IN EVERY POT

IN THE EARLY '70s, Luke Lukoskie lived in a macrobiotic commune north of Seattle. "Being macrobiotic, we learned to eat all sorts of tasteless food," says Lukoskie, the founder of Island Spring Organics, a tofu company on Vashon Island. Back then, they'd make tofu occasionally, and in the mid-'70s, after run-ins with *The Book of Tofu* and a piece of equipment suitable for grinding soybeans, he started Island Spring.

"I really went into tofu because I have a Jesus complex," says Lukoskie. "I always felt like I needed to do something to save the world." At 30, after working on an MBA and a PhD in educational psychology at the University of Washington, he decided that if he could teach folks to satisfy their need for protein by eating tofu rather than killing animals, his project might transfer to taming humanity's seeming need to kill other humans — a way to make the world a better place, one pot of food at a time. So he started making tofu on

Vashon, using spring water from a source on the island, with the goal of spreading the word about tofu, then a relatively unknown foodstuff in the United States.

At the time, vegetarianism was gaining a foothold in the Pacific Northwest, and PCC, a Seattle-based food co-op, was looking for a local producer. It was a perfect match; Lukoskie was a tofu evangelist looking for customers interested in buying organically produced food, well before the word "organic" was broadly understood. From its initial $1,200 investment in equipment in 1976, Island Spring has grown from a firm making 300 pounds of tofu per day to a company that produces 7,000 pounds a day, and co-packs for other local firms as well.

It may take another 30 years to get a tofu in every pot, says Lukoskie, but he's ready to keep working on it. After all, it took 2,000 years to get this far.

Egyptian-inspired Chickpeas and Couscous

Although Washington's summer farmers' markets are renowned for their swathes of color, some of the best state-grown produce is available all winter long. Nestled into deep bins, dried chickpeas from the state's eastern farms are almost always available. Here, they're simmered with tomatoes, cumin, coriander, garlic, thyme, and sesame oil in a simple stew inspired by the Egyptian spice mixture called *dukka*. Spice it up with harissa or cayenne pepper, if you'd like. It's delicious with a scoop of labne (page 71).

2 cups (1 pound) dried chickpeas, soaked overnight

4 cups vegetable broth

1 (15-ounce) can diced tomatoes

2½ teaspoons ground cumin

1 teaspoon ground coriander

1 large garlic clove, finely chopped

1 bay leaf

2 teaspoons chopped fresh thyme

Salt

Freshly ground black pepper

¾ teaspoon toasted sesame oil

Israeli couscous, for serving

NOTE: You'll get the best flavor for this recipe if you use freshly ground spices.

4–6 SERVINGS

1. Drain the soaked chickpeas, and combine them in a wide saucepan with the broth and the tomatoes. Bring to a simmer and cook, stirring occasionally, for 30 minutes.

2. Add the cumin, coriander, garlic, bay leaf, and thyme; salt and pepper to taste; and cook until the chickpeas are completely tender, about 30 minutes longer.

3. Remove the bay leaf. Stir in the sesame oil, and serve immediately, over the couscous.

Recipe from TOM DOUGLAS, SERIOUS PIE

Yukon Gold Potato Pizza
with Rosemary and Olive Oil

This pizza, tiled with golden brown rounds of potato and fragrant with rosemary and olive oil, is simple, like most of the offerings at Serious Pie, the Tom Douglas pizzeria in downtown Seattle. Yukon Gold potatoes work best because of their thin skins, creamy texture, and good potato flavor, and because they're not too starchy.

Serious Pie bakes its pizzas directly on the floor of a wood-burning oven, giving them a charred Roman-style crust. If you have a pizza stone, you'll come closer to this effect at home. Slice one pizza up as an appetizer or make two for a main dish.

1 medium Yukon Gold potato (about 8–10 ounces)

2 tablespoons extra-virgin olive oil, plus more for oiling the pan, dough, and crust

1 teaspoon roughly chopped fresh rosemary

Sea salt

Freshly ground black pepper

8 ounces premade pizza dough

Unbleached all-purpose flour, for stretching the dough

3 tablespoons finely grated Pecorino cheese

**1 (11- BY 9-INCH) PIZZA,
SERVES 4 AS AN APPETIZER**

1. Preheat the oven to 450°F.

2. Slice the potatoes about ⅛-inch thick. Put them in a bowl and toss with the oil and ½ teaspoon of the rosemary. Salt and pepper to taste. Spread the potatoes on an oiled baking sheet in a single layer and bake about 12 minutes, until potatoes are cooked through and beginning to brown on the edges. Remove from the oven and set aside.

3. Stretch, pat, and press the pizza dough into an oval about 11 inches by 9 inches (the dough will be thin), flouring the work surface as needed. Place the dough on an oiled baking sheet. Brush the dough with additional oil and sprinkle with ¼ teaspoon of the rosemary. Arrange the potato slices side by side all over the top of the pizza, like you're shingling a house.

4. Bake the pizza 12 to 15 minutes, until both the potatoes and crust are well browned. Remove the pizza from the oven and transfer to a cutting board.

5. Drizzle the pizza with a little oil, sprinkle with salt, the remaining rosemary, and the cheese. Cut the pie into eight pieces and serve immediately.

Kabocha and Black Bean Tamale Pie

I saw you at the farmers' market the other day. You walked right up to that big display of kabocha squash, with their lumpy green skins, and picked one up. I saw you wonder how to cut the thing, and put it right back down. I hate to be Debbie Downer here, but you made the wrong move, sister. Baked in the oven for an hour — uncut, and with the stem on, even — the deep orange flesh of a kabocha squash settles into a smooth, sweet purée. It's perfect for layering into a tamale pie with sautéed onions and peppers and soft black beans, hugged by a crust of masa harina (which requires much less attention than a real pie crust). The big secret, of course, is that this is a vegan dish — but the creaminess of the squash means no one will miss the dairy.

I'll admit that it also tastes delicious with 2 cups of shredded Monterey jack cheese sprinkled over it about 5 minutes before the pie is done. Extra sour cream and salsa won't hurt, either, but for kicks, even if you're not vegan, try it without. You'll never think of squash the same way again.

FILLING

- 1 (2-pound) kabocha squash
- 2 tablespoons extra-virgin olive oil
- 1 medium onion, thinly sliced
- 1 yellow bell pepper, seeded and thinly sliced
- 1 poblano pepper, seeded and thinly sliced
- 2 large garlic cloves, finely chopped
- 2 teaspoons dried oregano
- 1 teaspoon ground cumin
- Salt
- Freshly ground black pepper
- 1 (15-ounce) can black beans, rinsed and drained, or 1 cup dried beans, soaked overnight and cooked until tender
- ½ cup salsa

1 (9-INCH) PIE

1. Preheat the oven to 375°F.

2. **Make the filling:** Place the squash, whole, on a baking sheet lined with aluminum foil, and bake for about 1 hour, or until you can poke through the squash effortlessly with a fork. Set aside to cool.

3. When the squash is done cooking, heat a large skillet over medium heat. Add the oil, then the onion, and cook, stirring, until the onion begins to soften, about 5 minutes. Add the bell pepper and poblano pepper and cook until the onion and pepper are soft and brown, 10 to 15 minutes. Stir in the garlic, oregano, and cumin, and season the vegetables with salt and pepper to taste. Set aside to cool.

4. **Make the crust:** While the vegetables cook, mash the masa harina, water, oil, and salt together with a fork in a large bowl until blended. Cover and set aside for 30 minutes.

CRUST

2 cups masa harina

2 cups hot water

2 tablespoons extra-virgin olive oil

½ teaspoon salt

Extra-virgin olive oil, for greasing the pan and oiling crust

5. When the squash is cool enough to handle, cut it in half with a large knife, and scoop out the seeds with a large spoon or an ice cream scoop. Scoop the flesh into a measuring cup (it should be very soft and smooth); you should have about 2 cups. (You can save the extra for pumpkin pie or just eat it standing there at the counter, like I always do.)

6. Increase the oven temperature to 400°F. Generously grease a 9-inch deep-dish pie pan (or 8- by 8-inch square baking pan, or something similar) with oil, and set aside.

7. Knead the crust dough, then divide it into three roughly equal parts. Combine two of the pieces into a big ball, and roll the dough out between two 12-inch square pieces of waxed paper. (If you're using a pan with a different shape, just roll the dough into roughly the shape of the pan but slightly larger.) Peel one piece of paper off the round of dough and invert the dough into the oiled pie pan. Remove the other piece of paper and press the dough into the corners of the pan.

8. Gently spread about half the mashed squash into the crust, then follow with the vegetables, then the beans, then the salsa, then finally the remaining squash. (It may heap higher than the edge of the pan, which is okay.)

9. Roll the remaining dough out between two fresh sheets of waxed paper, and use the same method to invert the round of dough over the top of the filling. Use your fingers to pinch the edges of the dough together (or use a fork, if you prefer). Use a sharp knife to make a few small vents. Brush the pie with oil, then bake for about 45 minutes, or until the crust is nicely tanned.

10. Let the pie cool for at least 10 minutes (and up to 30) before slicing and serving.

Recipe from THE SAMMIE SHACK AND JESS THOMSON

Chetzamelta Sandwiches

If you stray off the main roads of Port Townsend on the Olympic Peninsula, you might find yourself at a rural intersection anchored by a bright red food truck. It's Wendy Edwards' Sammie Shack, a mobile joint devoted to all things sandwichable. Named to riff on Chetzemoka Park, one of Port Townsend's can't-miss treasures, the "chetzamelta" features Mt. Townsend Creamery's gooey Seastack cheese with fig-balsamic jam and peppery caramelized onions on sourdough from nearby Pane d'Amore bakery. Edwards toasts it until the cheese drips down the sides.

CARAMELIZED ONIONS

1 tablespoon extra-virgin olive oil

1 large onion, thinly sliced

Salt

Freshly ground black pepper

FIG JAM

½ pound dried black mission figs, stems removed and chopped (about 1½ cups)

1 cup balsamic vinegar

½ cup water

Grated zest of 1 orange

SANDWICHES

8 thick slices artisanal sourdough bread

½ pound Mt. Townsend Creamery's Seastack cheese (see Recipe Contributors and Suppliers, page 274), sliced

½ cup (1 stick) salted butter, melted

4 SANDWICHES

1. **Make the onions:** Heat the oil in a large skillet over medium heat. Add the onion, season with salt and plenty of pepper, and cook, stirring occasionally, until the onions are dark golden brown, 30 to 45 minutes.

2. **Meanwhile, make the jam:** Combine the figs, vinegar, water, and orange zest in a small saucepan; bring to a boil; then cook at a low simmer until the figs are tender, about 20 minutes. Transfer the mixture to a food processor, whirl until smooth, then transfer to a bowl.

3. **Make the sandwiches:** Spread half the bread slices with some of the jam. (You won't use all of it.) Divide the cheese slices among the sandwiches, followed by the onions, and then top with the remaining bread slices.

4. Brush the sandwiches on both outer sides with the butter, then toast (two at a time) in a large skillet over medium heat, turning once, until the bread is golden brown on both sides and the cheese has melted, 6 to 8 minutes total. Serve hot.

Recipe from RACHEL YANG, REVEL

Zucchini Pancakes with Blossoms and Basil

Revel's website describes their food as "urban-style Korean comfort food," but unless you've been to the little open-kitchen boîte in Seattle's Fremont neighborhood, the second restaurant from Joule co-owner Rachel Yang, it's hard to know what that means. Visit, and you'll find it means food that tastes like Mom's killer home cooking — only it wasn't your mom, and it wasn't your home, and it most certainly wasn't cooked on your continent. Armed with a rigorous French cooking background and a Korean family history, Yang's food, like these Korean-style zucchini pancakes, is simple but somehow astoundingly different, every single time. And the pancakes themselves are incredibly forgiving.

You can omit the zucchini blossoms, if you can't find them, but they make a gorgeous pattern on the pancake.

1 cup unbleached all-purpose flour

1 teaspoon kosher salt

½ teaspoon baking soda

1 cup water

1 egg, beaten

1 cup grated green zucchini, from 1 medium zucchini (about ½ pound)

¼ cup packed fresh basil, very thinly sliced

3 tablespoons canola oil

4 zucchini blossoms

NOTE: You can reheat the pancakes in the microwave or on the stovetop, but they're best fresh from the pan.

**2–4 SERVINGS OR
6–8 APPETIZER SERVINGS**

1. Whisk the flour, salt, and baking soda together in a medium bowl. Add the water and egg, and whisk until just combined. Add the zucchini and basil, and stir together gently with a spoon.

2. Heat 2 tablespoons of the oil in a small (8- or 9-inch) nonstick pan over medium heat until it shimmers. Add about half the batter (1 heaping cup) and spread it evenly into the pan. Cook until browned on the bottom side, 4 to 5 minutes.

3. While the pancake cooks, break two of the zucchini blossoms apart into distinct petals. Place the petals in a flower pattern on the raw side of the batter, then flip the pancake over with a large spatula. Cook until puffed and evenly browned, 3 to 4 minutes longer. Transfer to a paper towel–lined plate and add the remaining tablespoon of oil to the pan. Repeat with the remaining ingredients.

4. Serve the pancakes piping hot, cut into eight pieces each.

Spinach and Feta Tart with Olive Oil Crust

Many lucky Seattleites get weekly vegetable-box deliveries from Carnation's Full Circle Farm, which grows more than 50 kinds of produce in-season and sources it from other farms along the West Coast when it can't. This tart capitalizes on the inevitable delivery of more spinach than one may envision being able to eat. There are two main advantages to an olive oil crust: it doesn't require chilling time, and it has a savory flavor not normally found in regular crust.

SPINACH-FETA FILLING

- 2 tablespoons extra-virgin olive oil
- 1 garlic clove, finely chopped
- 1 pound baby spinach
- Salt
- Freshly ground black pepper
- 3 eggs
- ¾ cup heavy cream
- 4 ounces crumbled feta cheese

OLIVE OIL CRUST

- 2½ cups unbleached all-purpose flour
- ½ teaspoon kosher salt
- ¼ teaspoon freshly ground black pepper
- ⅓ cup plus 1 tablespoon extra-virgin olive oil
- ⅓ cup water (plus more, if needed)

SPECIAL EQUIPMENT: 9-inch tart pan with removable bottom

6 SERVINGS

1. Preheat the oven to 400°F. Place a 9-inch tart pan with a removable bottom on a baking sheet and set aside.

2. **Make the filling:** Heat a large skillet over medium heat. Add the oil, then the garlic, and cook, stirring, until fragrant, about 30 seconds. Add the spinach, a handful at a time, stirring and adding more, until all the spinach has been added. Season the spinach with salt and pepper to taste, then cook, stirring occasionally, until the spinach leaves have wilted completely and the liquid has evaporated, about 20 minutes.

3. **Make the crust:** Meanwhile, whisk the flour, salt, and pepper together with a fork in a medium bowl. Stir in the oil, mixing until crumbly and evenly moist, then add the water, 1 tablespoon at a time, mixing until no flour remains at the bottom of the bowl. Dump the loose dough into the tart pan. Press the crust into the pan in an even layer with your hands. (You'll have a bit of extra dough, which can be discarded as soon as you have an even layer on the sides and bottom.)

4. Whisk the eggs in the bowl to blend, then stir in the cream, and season the egg mixture with pepper. Spread the spinach on the crust, then carefully pour the egg mixture into the tart shell. (The egg mixture should rise almost to the edge.) Sprinkle the cheese on top, and gently poke it into the egg mixture with your fingers.

5. Bake the tart for 30 to 35 minutes, until puffed and golden. Allow the tart to cool for 10 to 15 minutes before removing from the pan, slicing, and serving.

Gemelli and Cauliflower
with Capers and Goat Cheese

In a lineup of produce beauty queens, cauliflower will always be the runner-up. It doesn't have the sudden springiness of asparagus or the wit of an artichoke, but seared in butter, it's ultrasweet — the perfect partner for tangy goat cheese, tart lemon juice, and salty capers. If you'd like, you can add chopped toasted walnuts, toasted pine nuts, or fine strands of prosciutto, too.

2 heaping cups gemelli, rotini, or similar bite-size pasta

1 tablespoon unsalted butter

1 medium head cauliflower (about 1¼ pounds), cut into bite-size florets

2 garlic cloves, finely chopped

Zest and juice of 1 large lemon (about 3 tablespoons juice)

1 tablespoon chopped fresh oregano

¼–½ cup capers

2 tablespoons extra-virgin olive oil

Salt

Freshly ground black pepper

1 tablespoon chopped fresh Italian parsley

3 ounces crumbled goat cheese

4 SERVINGS

1. Bring a large pot of salted water to a boil for the pasta. Cook it al dente according to package instructions, reserving a cupful of the water toward the end of the cooking time. Drain the pasta.

2. When you add the pasta, start melting the butter in a large sauté pan over medium-high heat. Add the cauliflower, mostly cut sides down, and cook until the florets are all browned on one or two sides, stirring once or twice, about 5 minutes. Add the garlic, lemon zest, lemon juice, and oregano. Cook, stirring, until the pan is dry, 1 or 2 minutes longer.

3. Add the pasta, capers (to taste), oil, salt and pepper to taste, and parsley to the pan. Stir to blend, adding some of the reserved pasta water, if necessary, to loosen the sauce. Serve immediately, in wide bowls, garnished with the goat cheese.

6
POULTRY

Roasted Chicken with Honey-glazed Shallots

Glazed with what can only be described as a honeyed chicken caramel, the shallots that line the pan while this bird roasts emerge as glistening gems — and between their flavor and the time you have to spend to peel them, they seem worth their weight in gold. No one will critique you if you buy prepeeled shallots.

2 pounds whole shallots, peeled

1 tablespoon plus 1 teaspoon extra-virgin olive oil

Salt

Freshly ground black pepper

1 (4–5 pound) whole chicken, trimmed of excess fat

2 tablespoons chopped fresh thyme

Zest and juice of 2 large lemons (about ⅓ cup juice)

¼ cup honey

4 SERVINGS

1. Preheat the oven to 450°F and arrange a rack in the center of the oven.

2. Mix the shallots and 1 tablespoon of the oil together in a large roasting pan. Salt and pepper to taste, then place a wire rack in the pan so the rack sits flat with the shallots surrounding it. Rinse the chicken and pat it dry, then place it on the wire rack, breast side up.

3. Combine the remaining teaspoon of oil, thyme, and lemon zest in a small bowl. Rub the mixture all over the chicken's skin, then season the chicken inside and out with salt and pepper. Tuck the wings behind the chicken's back and tie the legs together with kitchen twine, if desired.

4. Roast the chicken and shallots for 15 minutes. Reduce the oven temperature to 375°F and roast for 50 to 60 minutes longer, or until an instant-read thermometer inserted into the thickest part of the thigh reads 165°F.

5. Carefully transfer the chicken to a serving plate and let rest for 10 minutes. Remove the wire rack. Add the lemon juice and the honey to the shallots, stir to blend, and roast for 15 to 20 minutes longer, or until the shallots are soft and caramelized. Carve the chicken while the shallots are roasting, then serve the chicken with the shallots on top.

Cider-brined Turkey with Rosemary and Thyme

If you show up at the Skagit River Ranch's Ballard Farmers Market booth at 9:45 AM on the Sunday morning before Thanksgiving, you'll be late for your turkey. Judging by the line, which snakes almost a block down the street, the eggs you wanted to include in your stuffing are long since claimed. But when you finally reach the front of the remarkably patient line, well after the market actually opens at 10 AM, there's Eiko Vojkovich, smiling as big as ever, and handing over the 18-pound turkey she promised you two months ago when Thanksgiving still seemed like a mirage. And she wants to know what you'll do with it.

You'll look to one side of her booth, where herbs are already bursting out of someone's basket, and to the other side, where Rockridge Orchards' Honeycrisp apple cider beckons, and you'll know just what to do.

CIDER BRINE

- 1 gallon high-quality apple cider
- 1 cup kosher salt
- ½ cup firmly packed light brown sugar
- 3 garlic cloves, peeled and smashed
- 3 (6-inch sprigs) fresh rosemary, roughly chopped
- 6 (4-inch sprigs) fresh thyme, roughly chopped
- 2 gallons cold water

TURKEY

- 1 (16–18 pound) fresh turkey, giblets removed, patted dry
- Salt
- Freshly ground black pepper
- 2 cups high-quality apple cider
- 1 cup water
- ½ cup (1 stick) unsalted butter, melted
- 2 tablespoons chopped fresh rosemary
- 2 tablespoons chopped fresh thyme

14 SERVINGS, PLUS LEFTOVERS

1. **Make the brine:** Combine the cider, salt, brown sugar, garlic cloves, rosemary, and thyme in a large pot; bring to a simmer; and stir until the salt and sugar have dissolved completely. Add the cold water. (If the pot isn't big enough to hold it all, divide the cider mixture into two pots and add half the water to each.) Let cool to room temperature or set aside overnight in a cold (but not freezing) spot to chill. (Let's not kid ourselves; it won't fit in your refrigerator if you're cooking this for a holiday meal.)

2. **Make the turkey:** Combine the turkey and the brine in a large, clean vessel, making sure the bird is fully submerged, and refrigerate overnight or up to 24 hours.

3. Remove the turkey from the brine, discard the brine, and pat the turkey dry. Let the turkey sit at room temperature for 1 hour.

4. Preheat the oven to 375°F. Season the turkey inside and out with salt and pepper. Tie the legs together with kitchen twine. Place the turkey breast down on a rack in a large roasting pan, and pour the cider and water into the bottom of the pan. Brush the bottom of the turkey with some of the melted butter, sprinkle with about one-third of the rosemary and thyme, and roast for 1 hour.

5. Carefully flip the turkey over using washable oven mitts or a clean kitchen towel. Cover the wing tips with foil if they're looking too brown. Brush the turkey all over with the remaining butter, sprinkle with the remaining rosemary and thyme, and roast another 1½ to 2 hours, basting every 30 minutes, or until an instant-read thermometer inserted into the thickest part of the thigh reads 165°F. (If the turkey is brown enough but the meat hasn't finished cooking, slide a large baking sheet onto a rack set at the very top of the oven or cover the turkey with foil.)

6. Carefully transfer the turkey to a platter, and let rest for 20 to 30 minutes before slicing and serving with the juices. (If desired, you can use the juices to make apple cider gravy.)

NOTE: While the cider brine cools, or before that, if you're smart, figure out what container is big and clean enough to hold both the brine and your turkey but also small enough to fit in your refrigerator. In Seattle, it's typically about 40°F at night around Thanksgiving, which means the entire porch becomes my refrigerator — convenient for me, but not helpful, perhaps, if you're not a Seattleite.

Look for nifty (but pricey) turkey brining bags, or brine the turkey in garbage bags in a clean, lined garbage can with enough ice at the bottom to keep the bird cold. I'd put it in the garage if I were you, but you didn't hear that from me.

SPECIAL EQUIPMENT: a clean container, cooler, trash can, or other container suitable for submerging turkey in brine (that can be kept cold); kitchen twine

❧ *Pair with a crisp, dry hard apple cider, such as Tieton Cider Works' Harmony Reserve.*

THE BACKYARD COOP

WRITTEN IN 2010, Seattle City Council Bill 116907 says that households can keep up to eight chickens (but no roosters) in their backyard. This may sound like esoteric legislation, but in the Emerald City, urban farming is no longer out of the ordinary. Take new coop owners Frank Strack and Michelle Morrison, who live in North Seattle. In 2011, they built an elaborate chicken coop in their backyard because, they say, they like to know where their food comes from. "Well, that and we have a character flaw that has us caring for animals who couldn't care less about us," says Morrison. So they got chickens.

The pair have the trifecta of things you'd expect might prevent a household from starting a chicken coop: big dogs, neighbors, and demanding full-time jobs. Oh, and a thing for cleanliness. But after finding a mentor they trusted at a local coop supply store, they felt they were ready. They learned how to introduce their dogs to the chickens, and the animals get along fine. Their neighbors were overwhelmingly supportive — especially when the promise of free fresh eggs came into play. "The neighbors tell us they like the sounds of the chickens," says Strack. "They cluck at themselves and each other constantly, but they do it pretty quietly."

The couple has learned to fit caring for their "girls" into the time before and after work. And though they initially had a hard time trusting their own sanitation habits with the chickens and eggs, they now feel very sure their eggs are clean and enjoy collecting them from animals they know have been treated well.

So what didn't they have before an intricate structure sprouted up in their backyard a few short weeks after six spring chicks took over the real estate in their bathtub under a red heat lamp? Experience. In the beginning there were surprises — how long the birds would spend in that box in the bathtub, for one thing, and how long it took for them to begin producing eggs, for another. A nicer surprise was that each adult chicken has its own unique personality. Some sing songs after laying eggs, some are better diggers. And Strack and Morrison certainly didn't expect to miss the chickens when they traveled.

"There is huge entertainment value in a creature whose day revolves around simple pleasures like digging," says Strack. "Birds are really funny. They have a completely misplaced sense of self-importance. I challenge you to watch a chicken putter about in the coop for five minutes and not wind up with a huge smile on your face."

Grilled Chicken
with Rodeo City Bar-B-Q Rub

When you slide into a booth upholstered with rodeo-print fabric at Rodeo City Bar-B-Q in Ellensburg, a central Washington town known for its annual Labor Day rodeo, be prepared to saddle up for a big meal. After eating a half rack of St. Louis–style pork ribs with baked beans and macaroni salad, take some time to peruse the rodeo queen photo gallery in the back — you'll certainly feel better afterward about your experience with bad bridesmaids' gowns. Then the next time you're ready for barbecue, make this easy, flavorful grilled chicken, seasoned with one of their house rubs. It's the closest you'll come to getting any of Rodeo City's secret barbecue recipes and a heck of a lot less work.

3 tablespoons paprika

1 tablespoon celery salt

1 tablespoon sugar

1 tablespoon freshly ground black pepper

1½ teaspoons onion powder

1½ teaspoons dry mustard

1 teaspoon grated lemon zest

⅛ teaspoon cayenne pepper

6 large boneless, skinless chicken breasts (about 2½ pounds), trimmed

2 tablespoons vegetable oil

6 SERVINGS

1. Stir the paprika, celery salt, sugar, pepper, onion powder, dry mustard, lemon zest, and cayenne together in a small bowl, using your fingers to break up the lemon zest if necessary.

2. Place the chicken breasts on a platter, sprinkle with the rub on all sides, and cover with plastic wrap. Refrigerate the chicken for at least 12 hours, and up to 24 hours.

3. Brush the chicken with a thin layer of the oil on all sides, and set aside at room temperature. Preheat a gas or charcoal grill to medium-high heat (about 425°F).

4. When the grill is hot, brush the grilling grates clean and grill the chicken over direct heat until cooked through, 10 to 12 minutes, turning once when the chicken releases easily from the cooking grates, after 6 or 7 minutes. Serve the chicken hot.

Recipe from KYLE TWEDE, TWEDE'S CAFÉ

Twede's Special Hot Wings

David Lynch turned Twede's Café into an icon when he filmed *Twin Peaks* in the sleepy mountain town of North Bend and immortalized the diner's cherry pie. But with more than 50 burgers on the menu (his favorite is the chicken teriyaki), owner Kyle Twede is the man who's brought folks back to the café since the television series ended in 1991.

Twede is constantly experimenting. (Adventure comes naturally; he's a science fiction writer on the side.) These hot wings, drizzled with a hot, tea-tinged honey mustard and sprinkled with toasted sesame seeds, are a far cry from cherry pie, but perhaps they'll be your motivation to make a return visit.

Canola oil, for frying

2 eggs

¼ cup water

1 cup breadcrumbs

Salt

Freshly ground black pepper

1½ pounds chicken wings (tips trimmed) or chicken drumettes, or a combination of both

3 tablespoons dry mustard (such as Colman's, or Chinese hot mustard powder)

1½ tablespoons brewed black tea

½ cup honey

2 tablespoons toasted sesame seeds

2–4 SERVINGS

1. Heat 2 inches of oil in a large heavy skillet or Dutch oven until it reaches 325°F on an instant-read thermometer.

2. While the oil heats, whisk the eggs and water together in one bowl, and whisk the breadcrumbs with salt and pepper to taste in another bowl. Working with one piece of chicken at a time, dip it first in the eggs, then in the breadcrumbs, coating it on all sides. Set the coated chicken aside.

3. Whisk the dry mustard and tea in a small bowl until the mixture is thick and smooth. Whisk in the honey.

4. Fry the chicken, turning once halfway through cooking, until golden brown and cooked through, 6 to 8 minutes. (Cook the chicken in two or three batches, taking care not to crowd the pan.) When each batch is done, drain the chicken pieces on a baking rack set over a few layers of paper towels.

5. Drizzle the chicken immediately with the honey mustard and sprinkle with some of the sesame seeds, then turn and repeat on the second side. Serve piping hot.

Chicken Leg Tagine with Lemon, Dates, and Olives

After garnering 25 years of animal-raising experience that included cattle, sheep, goats, pigs, and exotic birds, Jerry and Janelle Stokesberry decided to start a farm business with a focus on poultry and an emphasis on producing self-sufficient, healthy food. Shortly after Stokesberry Sustainable Farm opened in 2004, its place in the Seattle food scene was solidified. Now the couple raises about 800 organic chickens and 100 organic ducks each month and sells dozens of organic eggs. They also keep rabbits, pigs, cattle, and Icelandic sheep.

4–6 SERVINGS

4 large whole chicken legs (thighs and drumsticks connected), or 6 thighs (about 2½ pounds), patted dry with paper towels

Salt

Freshly ground black pepper

1 tablespoon extra-virgin olive oil

1 large onion, quartered and cut into ½-inch slices

3 garlic cloves, peeled and smashed

½ teaspoon ground cumin

½ teaspoon ground cinnamon

½ teaspoon ground ginger

¼ teaspoon ground turmeric

¼ teaspoon ground coriander

10 dates, pitted and chopped

2 cups chicken broth

1 large lemon

1½ cups cracked green olives or unstuffed pitted green olives

2 tablespoons chopped fresh Italian parsley

Couscous, for serving

1. Heat a large heavy lidded pot or a tagine over medium-high heat. Season the chicken pieces on both sides with salt and pepper. Add the oil to the pot, then the chicken, skin side down, and cook until the skin is brown and releases easily from the pan, about 5 minutes. Turn the chicken and cook for 5 minutes longer, then transfer to a plate.

2. Add the onion to the pan, and cook, stirring occasionally and scraping any brown bits off the bottom of the pan, until soft, about 5 minutes. Add the garlic cloves, cumin, cinnamon, ginger, turmeric, and coriander and stir until fragrant, about 1 minute. Add the chopped dates and broth and increase the heat to high. Using a good vegetable peeler, scrape the zest off the lemon in big strips, and add them to the pot, reserving the lemon itself.

3. When the liquid comes to a simmer, reduce heat to its lowest setting, stir in the olives, and slide the chicken pieces in, skin side up. Cover the pot and cook until the chicken meat pulls away from the bones easily, about 30 minutes. (The dish can be made ahead up to this point, either left at room temperature for up to an hour or cooled and refrigerated overnight, then reheated before serving.)

4. Remove the lemon peel pieces, if desired. Stir in the parsley; season to taste with additional salt, pepper, and the juice from the reserved lemon. Serve immediately over couscous.

Recipe from THEIRRY RAUTUREAU, LUC

Seared Duck with White Beans, Fresh Figs, and Huckleberry Gastrique

If there's one word that describes French chef Thierry Rautureau, a man who's also known in Seattle as The Chef in the Hat, it's *force*. After more than two decades running Rover's, the restaurant that gave the fedora-clad chef his reputation for flawless French food, he opened Luc, which brought the flavors of the French countryside to Seattle's Madison Valley neighborhood. This recipe is a house favorite. Soak the beans the night before you plan to serve the duck.

HUCKLEBERRY GASTRIQUE

- 1 (750 mL) bottle port wine
- ½ cup red wine vinegar
- 1 cup black huckleberries (or blackberries, in a pinch)

WHITE BEANS

- 4 thick slices bacon, finely chopped
- 4 tablespoons unsalted butter, plus more if desired
- 1 garlic clove, finely chopped
- ½ cup finely chopped onions
- ¼ cup finely chopped celery
- ¼ cup finely chopped peeled carrots
- 1½ cups dried navy beans, soaked in water overnight
- 4 cups chicken broth
- 1 tablespoon chopped fresh thyme
- 1 tablespoon chopped fresh rosemary

DUCK

- 4 duck breasts (about 1½ pounds total), patted dry
- Salt
- Freshly ground black pepper
- 4 fresh figs, quartered lengthwise

4 SERVINGS

1. **Make the gastrique:** Combine the port and vinegar in a saucepan and bring to a boil. Boil on high heat until the liquid is syrupy, 20 to 25 minutes. Add the huckleberries and cook for 2 minutes longer. Let the gastrique cool to room temperature.

2. **Make the beans:** While the gastrique simmers, cook the bacon over medium heat in a medium skillet until crisp, about 10 minutes, stirring occasionally. Set aside.

3. Melt the butter in a medium saucepan. Add the garlic, cook for 1 minute, then add the cooked bacon, onions, celery, and carrots. Cook for 5 minutes, stirring, then add the beans and broth. Simmer until the beans are cooked through, stirring occasionally, about 45 minutes (depending on the beans). Stir in the thyme and rosemary, and a tablespoon or two of additional butter to taste, if desired. (When the beans are done, you can set them aside to cool until about 15 minutes before you'd like to eat. Reheat them while you cook the duck.)

4. **Make the duck:** Heat a large skillet over medium-low heat. Season the duck on both sides with salt and pepper. Cook the duck breasts, skin side down, until the skin is deep golden brown and most of the fat has been rendered out, 6 to 8 minutes. Turn the duck and roast until it reaches your desired doneness, 5 to 7 minutes longer. Reheat the gastrique over low heat while the duck rests for 3 or 4 minutes, then slice each duck breast into 5 or 6 pieces across the grain.

5. To serve, pile the beans on plates, then top with the duck, gastrique, and figs.

Recipe from CHRIS WEBER, THE HERBFARM

Crisp Spring Chicken with Oysters and Nettle Sauce

When you hear a restaurant is cooking with Washington ingredients, you probably make a lot of concessions without realizing it. You presume the chef is using, say, imported olive oil, or salt and pepper. When The Herbfarm says it's cooking locally, there are no exceptions. The team at The Herbfarm, long considered one of the country's best restaurants, makes nine-course dinners that are always guided by a theme. When that theme is local food, the team goes as far as making salt from local waters.

For this book, chef Chris Weber thought it fitting to write a recipe featuring only ingredients from the Evergreen State. Well, almost — here he uses white pepper. If you can't find nettles (or if you're making this in the summer, winter, or fall), you can substitute spinach. Save the poussin carcasses for making chicken broth, if you can.

---

2 whole poussins (small spring chickens, about 2 pounds each)

Salt

Freshly ground white pepper

2 small Walla Walla onions, finely chopped

1 pound stinging nettles or spinach

¼ cup heavy cream

4 large radishes

½ cup dill leaves, picked into small tips

¼ cup grapeseed oil or other neutral oil

1 cup unbleached all-purpose flour

4 small oysters (such as Hama Hama), shucked and stored in their liquor

🌾 *Pair with a non-oaky semillon– sauvignon blanc blend or another off-dry white wine.*

4 SERVINGS

1. Carve the breasts off the bones of the poussins and separate the legs from the back. Trim the meat off the legs and cut into ½-inch pieces. Season all the meat with salt and pepper and set aside for 30 minutes.

2. Place the onions in a large skillet with a pinch of salt and 2 tablespoons of water. Cover, place the pan over low heat, and cook until tender but not at all browned, 15 to 20 minutes.

3. Bring a large pot of salted water to a boil while the onions cook. Add the nettles and cook until they are almost mush, about 6 minutes. (If you're using spinach, cook for 3 minutes.) Drain the nettles, squeezing out most of the water. (You should have about 1½ cups cooked greens.)

4. Purée the nettles, cooked onions, and cream in a food processor. Salt and pepper to taste. Transfer the nettle sauce to a small pan and keep warm.

5. Slice the radishes as thinly as possible into circles. Toss them with the dill, place the mixture in a bowl, and cover with paper towels dampened with cold water.

NOTE: If you don't want to cut the meat off each leg, you can simplify this recipe. Roast the (whole) legs in an oiled pan in a preheated 450°F oven for 15 minutes, while you make the sauce, then sear them along with the chicken breasts before serving.

6. Heat a large skillet over medium heat. When hot, add 1 tablespoon of the grapeseed oil, then the poussin breasts, skin sides down. Cook until the skin is deeply browned, 4 to 5 minutes, then gently turn the breasts and cook until cooked through, 4 to 5 minutes longer.

7. Meanwhile, heat another large skillet over medium heat. Toss the diced leg meat in the flour and shake off the excess. When the pan is hot, add the remaining 3 tablespoons grapeseed oil, and put the leg pieces in the oil in an even layer. Cook the thigh pieces, stirring occasionally, until browned on all sides, about 6 minutes. Drain off the excess oil and cover to keep warm.

8. Place the oysters and their liquor in a small saucepan and heat over low heat until warm and plumped, about 5 minutes. Set aside and cover to keep warm.

9. To plate, place a few spoonfuls of the nettle sauce in the middle of each plate and spread it around to make a roughly 3-inch-diameter circle. Place some of the chopped leg pieces on the left side of each circle, and place an oyster on top of the thigh meat. Place a chicken breast on the right side of the sauce, and top with a scattering of the radish and dill salad. Serve immediately.

Winter Market Comfort Casserole

It's rare to pair the words "farmers' market" with "casserole," but if a trip through Seattle's early-spring stalls is in your future, pick up some kale and leeks, and look for chicken sausage from Stokesberry Sustainable Farm. You'll fold them all into a baked pasta casserole with goat cheese and Parmesan for a warming, crowd-pleasing meal.

1 pound rigatoni or other short pasta

¼ cup extra-virgin olive oil

1 pound chicken sausage, casings removed

4 tablespoons unsalted butter

¼ cup unbleached all-purpose flour

1 cup heavy cream

1 cup milk

Salt

Freshly ground black pepper

2 (4-ounce) logs goat cheese, crumbled

½ cup grated Parmesan cheese

1 large leek, white and light green parts, chopped into ½-inch half moons

1 small bunch green kale, ribs removed, chopped

1 cup panko breadcrumbs

NOTE: If you'd like, you can split this casserole into two servings. Bake half for dinner, and let the other half cool (just after you add the breadcrumbs). Wrap it in plastic wrap and freeze. Thaw in the refrigerator for 24 hours before baking it, covered with foil, for 30 minutes at 350°F. Remove the foil and bake another 15 minutes at 375°F.

8–10 SERVINGS

1. Bring a large pot of water to a boil for the pasta, and cook until just al dente, about a minute shy of the package instructions. Drain and set aside.

2. Meanwhile, heat a large skillet over medium heat. Add 1 tablespoon of the oil, then crumble the sausage into the skillet and cook until browned on all sides, stirring occasionally, about 10 minutes. Cut the sausage into bite-size pieces and set aside.

3. While the sausage cooks, melt the butter in a medium saucepan over medium heat. Add the flour to the melted butter and cook, stirring, for a minute or so. Slowly whisk in the cream, then the milk, and cook until the mixture simmers and thickens, whisking often, about 5 minutes. Let the sauce simmer for 1 to 2 minutes, then salt and pepper to taste, and stir in one of the goat cheese logs and the Parmesan. Set aside.

4. Add an additional tablespoon of oil to the pan the sausages were cooked in. Add the leek and cook over medium heat, stirring occasionally, until it begins to brown. Add the kale and cook, stirring, until bright green, about 5 minutes longer. Salt and pepper to taste.

5. Preheat the oven to 400°F.

6. Gently stir the cooked pasta, sauce, sausage, leeks, and kale together in a large bowl. Transfer the mixture to a 9- by 13-inch baking pan, and crumble the remaining log of goat cheese over the top.

7. Blend the breadcrumbs with the remaining 2 tablespoons oil in a small bowl until the breadcrumbs are evenly moistened. Sprinkle the breadcrumbs evenly over the pasta. (The dish may be made ahead up to this point, refrigerated, and baked a few hours later.)

8. Bake for 10 to 15 minutes (about 10 minutes longer if the casserole was refrigerated), or until the sauce is bubbling and the breadcrumbs are toasted. Serve hot.

Recipe from ZOI ANTONITSAS, MADISON PARK CONSERVATORY

Roasted Cornish Game Hens
with Parsnips and Bergamot-poached Prunes

The sign that hangs over Madison Park Conservatory in Seattle's Madison Park neighborhood might rattle new diners, with its large black bird showing all the bones in white, like a cartoon X-ray of your Christmas dinner (when it was still flying). Regardless of your ornithology background, you'll soon realize that the restaurant's chefs do poultry as well as they do far less typical dishes. (They're famous for their beef tongue preparations.) Take this game hen, which is topped with prunes simmered slowly with shallots, citrus peels, and Earl Grey tea.

This is a rich meal whose fancy presentation belies the (relatively little) effort required; chef Zoi Antonitsas likes to serve it with a simple, crunchy salad. Double or triple the recipe for more people.

PRUNES

10 dried prunes

2 large shallots, sliced into ¼-inch rings

1 cup good white wine

2 cups water

2 tablespoons sugar

5 sprigs fresh thyme

2 bay leaves

5 whole black peppercorns

2 Earl Grey tea bags, tags removed (or 2 teaspoons loose-leaf tea)

1 orange

1 lemon

2 SERVINGS

1. **Make the prunes:** Place the prunes, shallots, wine, water, and sugar in a small nonreactive saucepan. Place the thyme, bay leaves, peppercorns, and tea bags on a 12-inch square of cheesecloth. Using a vegetable peeler, peel about half of the orange's and lemon's skin off in long, thin strips, and add the peels to the cheesecloth. (Eat the orange, because dinner's still an hour away; quarter the lemon lengthwise and save the wedges to stuff into the hens.) Fold the cheesecloth up and around the contents, tie tightly with a piece of kitchen twine, and add the little pouch to the prunes.

2. Bring the mixture to a simmer, then cook at a gentle simmer, uncovered, until the water and wine have reduced by about half, about 30 minutes. Cover the prune mixture and set aside to steep while the hens roast, about 1 hour.

PARSNIPS AND HENS

½ cup (1 stick) unsalted butter, softened and cut into pieces

1 head garlic, cut in half horizontally

1 small yellow onion, cut into 8 pieces

2 medium parsnips (about ¾ pound), peeled and cut into 1-inch pieces

Kosher salt

Freshly ground black pepper

2 tablespoons chopped fresh thyme

2 Cornish game hens (about 1½ pounds each), rinsed and dried well

1 cup chicken broth (preferably homemade)

Lemon wedges, for serving

Chopped parsley or chives, for serving

SPECIAL EQUIPMENT: 12-inch square cheesecloth, kitchen twine

❧ *Pair with a single Rhone-varietal wine from Syncline Wine Cellars, such as their marsanne.*

3. **Make the parsnips and hens:** Preheat the oven to 425°F. Rub a casserole dish large enough to fit both birds (such as a 9- by 13-inch pan) with 2 tablespoons of the butter. Add the garlic to the pan, peeling off any stray papery husks without really peeling the garlic, then add the onion and parsnips. Season with salt, pepper, and thyme, and dot with about half the remaining butter.

4. Season the hens inside and out with salt and pepper, stuff the reserved quartered lemons into the hens' cavities, and tie the legs together with kitchen twine. Place the hens, breast up, on top of the vegetables, and, using your fingers, push as much butter as possible under the skin, lifting it up gently from the head and tail end.

5. Place the pan on the middle rack of the oven and roast, undisturbed, for 35 minutes. Gently baste the hens with the juices from the bottom of the pan, rotate the pan 180 degrees, and roast 20 to 40 minutes longer (depending on the size of the hens, about 30 minutes for 1½-pounders), until the juices run clear when you pierce the thigh with a knife.

6. Remove the hens from the oven, add the chicken broth to the pan, and use a wooden spoon to scrape the sides and bottom of the pan, pulling up any brown bits clinging to the pan. Transfer the vegetables and birds to a serving platter (or individual serving plates), tent with foil, and allow the birds to rest for 15 minutes.

7. While the hens rest, discard the cheesecloth package used to cook the prunes, and reheat the prunes over low heat. Meanwhile, pour the juices from the baking pan into a small saucepan, bring to a simmer, then cover and keep warm until ready to serve. (For a thicker sauce, bring it to a boil for a few minutes. For a thinner sauce, add water or lemon juice.)

8. To serve, use a slotted spoon to set the prunes next to the warm hens. Serve the hens warm (and still whole), with the sauce on the side. Garnish with lemon wedges and parsley or chives, if desired.

Roasted Chicken and Garlic
with Herbed Dijon Smear

If there's one thing shopping at a farmers' market can teach you, it's that food tastes different when it's grown on a small scale. Take the humble chicken: pastured on sweet grasses and grains instead of chicken feed, the meat tastes slightly different from bird to bird and packs more flavor. Accompanied by toasty roasted garlic and lemony pan juices, this basic chicken roast puts the chicken flavor at the center of the plate.

If you don't want to break down a whole chicken, use whatever combination of bone-in chicken breasts and thighs you prefer.

2 heads garlic

2 tablespoons plus 2 teaspoons extra-virgin olive oil

2 tablespoons Dijon mustard

2 tablespoons chopped fresh rosemary

1 tablespoon chopped fresh thyme

Kosher salt

Freshly ground black pepper

1 (4–5 pound) whole chicken, rinsed, trimmed, patted dry, and cut into 6 parts

1 lemon, quartered

4 SERVINGS

1. Preheat the oven to 450°F.

2. Cut each head of garlic in half horizontally, leaving the skins on, so that each clove is exposed. Brush the exposed sides with 2 teaspoons of the oil and set aside.

3. Whisk the remaining 2 tablespoons oil with the mustard, rosemary, thyme, and salt and pepper to taste in a small bowl. Add the chicken and lemon pieces, and mix with your hands until all the chicken pieces are coated with the mustard-herb mixture.

4. Arrange the chicken pieces, skin side up, in a roasting pan just large enough to fit them. Add the lemon quarters and the garlic (cut sides up) and roast for 30 to 40 minutes, or until the chicken skin is crisp and browned and the meat is cooked through.

5. Serve the chicken and garlic on a platter with the hot lemons for squeezing over each piece.

Simple Baked Chicken
with Real Paprika

If there's one thing Charlie Bodony, the owner of Some Like It Hott, wants people to know about paprika, it's this: paprika comes from chiles. Every summer, Bodony grows chile peppers — jalapeños, habañeros, poblanos, pimentes d'espelette, and enough brightly hued hybrids to make your head spin — in a 1,200-square-foot cold frame in his backyard in Port Townsend. When the chiles are ripe, he smokes each variety separately over freshly felled alder wood, then dehydrates and pulverizes them. The chile powders are then blended into his various paprikas, which he coddles like children. The mildest version, made with poblanos, is deeply smoky and spicy. As Bodony says, "You can buy paprika that's not spicy, but why?" And in the kitchen, his paprika is glorious — sprinkle it over chicken and bake it in a hot oven, and you've got a quick, easy meal with more flavor than you might expect from a single spice. (My husband calls it the new Shake 'n Bake.)

4 bone-in chicken breasts
  (3–4 pounds total)
2 teaspoons extra-virgin olive oil
2 teaspoons real paprika
½ teaspoon kosher salt

NOTE: If you don't have access to Some Like It Hott (see Recipe Contributors and Suppliers, page 274), substitute a smoky Spanish *Pimenton de la Vera*.

4 SERVINGS

1. Preheat the oven to 450°F.

2. Pat the chicken breasts dry, then rub them on all sides with the oil. Place them in a casserole dish, skin side up, and season with the paprika and salt, rubbing a portion of the seasonings under the skin of each breast.

3. Bake for 25 to 35 minutes, or until the skin is crisp and the chicken is cooked through. Serve immediately.

Glover Street Chicken Curry Stew

Ebullient, ever-smiling owner Molly Patterson is the force behind the kitchen at Glover Street Market, the small (but packed) health food store and café in tiny Twisp. (They advertise carrying "pretty good groceries," but I think they should go with the slogan "better selection than the fancy store around the corner from you in Seattle.") Come in for a piece of fruit before a hike, and you may find yourself taking a seat to try a freshly squeezed juice or this spicy curry stew. Piled with yams, sweet potatoes, cauliflower, broccoli, and chopped chicken breast (or make it without the meat, if you prefer), it's best served, like Patterson does, over emmer from Bluebird Grain Farms (page 96).

2 (14-ounce) cans coconut milk

¼–½ cup Homemade Red Curry Paste (recipe at right)

2 cups vegetable or chicken broth

2 medium red potatoes (about 1 pound total), diced

1 medium yam (¾ pound), diced

1 medium sweet potato (¾ pound), diced

1 small head cauliflower, cut into florets (about 2 cups florets)

1 small head broccoli, cut into florets (about 2 cups florets)

2 tomatoes, chopped

1 pound boneless, skinless chicken breasts, trimmed and cut into 1-inch pieces

1 lime, cut into 8 wedges

Emmer or brown rice, for serving

1 cup loosely packed chopped fresh basil

🍃 *Pair with Kung Fu Girl Reisling from Charles Smith Wines.*

6 SERVINGS, PLUS EXTRA CURRY PASTE

1. Combine the coconut milk, curry paste (to taste), and broth in a large saucepan and bring to a simmer over high heat. Add the potatoes, yam, and sweet potato, and cook until the vegetables are just soft enough to poke with a fork, about 10 minutes.

2. Add the cauliflower, broccoli, tomatoes, chicken, and four of the lime wedges, and cook, stirring occasionally, until the broccoli is tender crisp, about 5 minutes.

3. Serve the stew over the emmer, garnished with the remaining lime wedges and the basil.

Homemade Red Curry Paste

½ cup dried wakame seaweed

¼ cup boiling water

½ cup coriander seeds

3 tablespoons cumin seeds

¼–½ cup red pepper flakes

6 stalks lemongrass, white parts only, chopped

1 cup chopped shallots

½ cup chopped gingerroot

¼ cup chopped garlic

12 lime leaves (sometimes sold as kaffir lime leaves)

3 tablespoons kosher salt

⅓ cup vegetable oil

ABOUT 3 CUPS

1. Whirl the seaweed in a food processor until finely ground. Combine the seaweed and boiling water in a small bowl and set aside to soften for about 20 minutes.

2. Put the coriander and cumin seeds in a small skillet and place over medium heat. Cook, shaking the pan frequently, until the spices are lightly toasted and fragrant. Transfer the spices and pepper flakes (more or less, depending on how spicy you like your curry) to the food processor (or a spice grinder, if you have one) and whirl until finely ground. Add the seaweed and water, along with the lemongrass, shallots, ginger, garlic, lime leaves, and salt, to the food processor, and grind into a smooth paste. (If you used a spice grinder for the spices, add the spices to the mixture in the food processor as well.)

3. With the machine running, add the oil in a slow, steady stream, stopping to scrape any large pieces down from the side of the work bowl when necessary. When the paste is smooth, transfer it to a few jars, seal, and keep refrigerated for up to 1 month, or freeze in ziplock bags for up to 6 months.

Recipe from ERIC AND SOPHIE BANH, MONSOON RESTAURANTS

Saigon Chicken Salad

This summery Vietnamese salad has lots of parts, but because Seattle-area Vietnamese restaurant maven Eric Banh lets us start with a store-bought rotisserie chicken, it comes together fast. If you'd prefer, poach a whole chicken and use the meat from that instead.

4 SERVINGS

NUOC CHAM

- ½ cup lukewarm water
- ¼ cup sugar
- ¼ cup fish sauce (such as 3 Crabs brand)
- ¼ cup white vinegar
- 2 teaspoons lime juice
- 1–2 Thai chiles, finely chopped
- 1 garlic clove, finely chopped

FRIED SCALLIONS

- ½ cup canola oil
- ½ cup chopped scallions (from 1 small bunch)
- ¼ teaspoon kosher salt

CARAMELIZED SHALLOTS AND SHALLOT OIL

- 1 cup canola oil
- ¼ pound shallots, peeled and sliced ¼ inch thick, slices separated

SALAD

- 6 cups finely shredded green cabbage
- 1 medium carrot, peeled and shredded
- ½ small red onion, thinly sliced
- ¼ cup roughly chopped fresh mint
- ¼ cup roughly chopped fresh Thai basil
- ¼ cup roughly chopped fresh cilantro
- 3 cups shredded rotisserie chicken
- 3 tablespoons coarsely chopped unsalted peanuts

1. **Make the nuoc cham:** Stir together the water and sugar in a large bowl until the sugar has dissolved. Add the fish sauce, vinegar, lime juice, chiles, and garlic, and set aside.

2. **Make the fried scallions:** Heat the oil in a small skillet over high heat until it begins to smoke. Remove the pan from the heat and let the oil cool for 3 minutes. Add the scallions and the salt, and stir gently for 1 minute. Transfer the scallions to a paper towel–lined plate with a slotted spoon or small strainer, and set the oil aside to cool.

3. **Make the shallots and shallot oil:** Heat the oil over medium-high heat until it reaches 300°F on an instant-read thermometer. Add the shallots and cook, stirring, until caramelized to a golden brown, about 3 minutes. Transfer the shallots to a paper towel–lined plate with a slotted spoon or small strainer, and set the oil aside to cool.

4. **Make the salad:** Combine the cabbage, carrot, onion, mint, basil, cilantro, and chicken in a large salad bowl. Add the fried scallions along with ¼ cup of the shallot oil and ½ cup of the nuoc cham. Stir to combine, then season to taste with additional shallot oil and nuoc cham. Top the salad with the caramelized shallots and the peanuts. Serve immediately.

NOTE: Use any leftover scallion and shallot oil for frying fish or in vinaigrettes.

❧ *Pair with a pinot gris from Ross Andrew Winery.*

MONSOON: ERIC AND SOPHIE BANH

When they opened Monsoon on Seattle's Capitol Hill, siblings Eric and Sophie Banh didn't have any intention of becoming the city's go-to upscale Vietnamese restaurateurs. But since opening Baguette Box, a Vietnamese sandwich shop with two locations, plus Monsoon East, across Lake Washington in Bellevue, and the noodle shop Ba Bar (ba means "father" in Vietnamese), they've become just that. At Monsoon, now-hallmark dishes like caramelized claypot catfish, bo la lot (flank steak wrapped in la lot leaves and grilled), and stuffed grilled squid bring people back again and again. But to me, the Banhs do nothing as well as they do chicken. From the deep-fried drunken chicken sandwich at Baguette Box to the sautéed lemongrass chicken at Monsoon to the pho ga (Vietnamese chicken noodle soup) at Ba Bar, their poultry dishes are dependably excellent.

Hardware Store Fried Chicken

At the center of Vashon Island's town center is a century-old building on the National Register of Historic Places. Its roots as a hardware store are visible in its colorful, slightly kitschy stained-glass windows that read "Guns & Ammunition" and "Wood-Burning Stoves," among other things. Now reborn as a restaurant, it serves a combination of modern and more classic American cuisine.

4 LARGE SERVINGS

4 cups buttermilk

¼ cup paprika

1 tablespoon plus 2 teaspoons garlic powder

1½ teaspoons kosher salt

1½ teaspoons freshly ground black pepper

4 large chicken breasts (about 2½–3 pounds total)

2 cups unbleached all-purpose flour

1 tablespoon onion powder

1 gallon canola oil, for frying

NOTE: The chicken should marinate for at least 4 hours and preferably overnight.

1. Mix the buttermilk, 1 tablespoon of the paprika, 2 teaspoons of the garlic powder, and 1 teaspoon each of the salt and pepper together. Marinate the chicken in the buttermilk mixture for at least 4 hours, or overnight.

2. Mix the flour, the remaining 3 tablespoons paprika, remaining tablespoon garlic powder, and remaining ½ teaspoon each of salt and pepper, and the onion powder together in a large bowl. Set aside.

3. Preheat the oven to 450°F.

4. Set a large Dutch oven (or other wide high-sided pot) over medium-high heat. Pour in enough oil to bring it about 3 inches up the side of the pan. Heat the oil until it reaches 375°F on a deep-frying thermometer. When the oil is fully heated, take one of the chicken breasts out of the buttermilk mixture, let most of the buttermilk drip off, then coat it well in the flour mixture. Make sure every inch is covered, then shake the chicken breast to remove any excess flour. Repeat with the remaining breasts.

5. Take a pair of good tongs and carefully put two of the chicken breasts into the hot oil. Cook until the crust is golden brown, only 1 to 2 minutes, carefully turning the chicken once. Transfer the chicken to a pan big enough to hold all the chicken, then repeat with the remaining chicken breasts.

6. Put the pan into the oven and cook 15 to 20 minutes, until an instant-read thermometer inserted into the thickest part of the chicken breast reads 155°F. Serve immediately.

7
PORK

Recipe from DUSTIN CALERY, LA BOUCHERIE

Sea Breeze Farm's Pork Rib Ragu

When La Boucherie's chef Dustin Calery makes his pork rib ragu, he uses tomatoes, milk, oregano, and wine from Sea Breeze Farm, which also provides the pork the Vashon Island restaurant depends on to make authentic European-inspired food. "We do food the same way people have been cooking for 500 years," says Calery. "We have electricity, I guess, but other than that, we're just cooking with the food we have, from where we live."

There's enough to feed a crowd here, but you'll be glad to have any leftovers — the ragu is rich and meaty, with a great fennel bite. It takes a bit of time to remove the pork bones before serving, but it's worth every second.

½ cup extra-virgin olive oil

2 racks pork ribs (about 5½ pounds total), cut into 2 or 3 sections each

4 medium yellow onions, chopped

2 tablespoons kosher salt, plus more for seasoning

1 cup dry red wine

4 (28-ounce) cans fire-roasted tomato purée (or whole tomatoes, blended)

½ cup whole milk

¼ cup finely chopped fresh oregano

3 bay leaves

1 tablespoon freshly ground black pepper, plus more for seasoning

2 tablespoons ground fennel seed, plus more for seasoning

Cooked pasta or polenta, for serving

NOTE: This recipe can be halved, if desired.

❧ *Pair with a wild-fermented red wine from Sweetbread Cellars.*

12 SERVINGS

1. Heat the oil over high heat in your largest heavy-bottomed stock pot (or two smaller Dutch ovens or soup pots) until it just begins to smoke. Add just enough pork ribs to cover the bottom and cook until deep golden brown on both sides, turning once when the ribs release easily from the pot. Transfer the seared ribs to a plate and repeat the process with the remaining ribs until all are browned.

2. Reduce heat to medium and add the onions to the pot (or divide them evenly between two pots). Add the salt, and cook until the onions are translucent, stirring occasionally, about 15 minutes.

3. Add the wine, stirring until almost completely evaporated, then stir in the tomatoes, milk, oregano, bay leaves, pepper, and 1 tablespoon of the fennel seed. Bring the sauce to a simmer, slide the pork ribs back in, and cook over your stove's lowest heat, stirring once or twice, until the meat is just starting to fall off the bone, 3 to 4 hours. (If you've been using two pots, you can combine the contents in a large roasting pan and roast the sauce and pork at 325°F for 3 to 4 hours, stirring occasionally.)

4. Remove the ribs from the sauce, let them cool for about 10 minutes, then pull the meat off the bones by hand, taking care to discard all the bones, cartilage, and connective tissue.

5. Stir the rib meat back into the sauce. Simmer the sauce for 30 minutes longer over low heat, seasoning as needed with the remaining fennel, salt, and pepper. Serve with pasta or polenta.

HOW TO USE A PIG

The walk-in refrigerator at La Boucherie, the restaurant on Vashon Island where chef Dustin Calery turns meats, produce, and dairy from the island's Sea Breeze Farm into dinner, looks like a porcine crime scene. It's a bit shocking if you're not expecting it — buckets of pig trotters here, a whole skull there. But behind the intricately organized bins of pork pieces and parts lies one clear goal: to use the entire animal, every time.

Like many Washington chefs, Calery's clear focus on reducing waste is part of what makes his food delicious. The result is a parade of dishes that use innovative cuts of meats in place of more traditional ones — like this Pork Rib Ragu. ★

Rain Shadow Meats' Italian Sausage & Meatballs

Seattle's Rain Shadow Meats sells a mean Italian sausage. Come to think of it, butcher Russell Flint makes perfect versions of almost any charcuterie product I can think of, from bratwurst and chorizo to chicken liver pâté and headcheese. These meatballs, made with Flint's Italian sausage recipe, are our new house favorite. We serve them over spaghetti or polenta.

I like to kick the meatballs toward the spicy side by increasing the quantity of red pepper flakes in the sausage recipe to about 2 teaspoons.

Rain Shadow Meats' Mild Italian Sausage

2 pounds ground pork shoulder

⅛ pound pork fat, ground or very finely chopped

2 tablespoons dry red wine

1 large garlic clove, chopped so fine it looks puréed

2 teaspoons kosher salt

2 teaspoons finely chopped fresh rosemary

1½ teaspoons dried thyme

1 teaspoon dried oregano

1 teaspoon red pepper flakes

½ teaspoon freshly ground black pepper

½ teaspoon whole fennel seed

½ teaspoon ground fennel seed

Olive oil, for frying

ABOUT 2 POUNDS SAUSAGE

1. Place the ground pork, pork fat, and wine in a large bowl. Stir together the garlic, salt, rosemary, thyme, oregano, pepper flakes, pepper, fennel seed, and ground fennel in a small bowl until evenly blended. Add the garlic mixture to the pork, and mix gently with a wooden spoon (or your hands, my preferred tool) until blended.

2. Use the mixture for making the meatballs (recipe at right) or form the sausage into palm-sized patties about ½ inch thick. Heat a large skillet over medium heat. Add about a tablespoon of olive oil. When the oil is hot, add two or three patties to the pan, and cook until the patties release easily from the pan, about 5 minutes. Turn and cook on the other side until no longer pink in the center, another 3 to 5 minutes. Repeat with the remaining patties, adding more oil as needed. You can also stuff the mixture into sausage casings. Ask your butcher for more information on where to find and how to use casings.

Rain Shadow Meats' Meatballs

20 MEATBALLS

1 cup breadcrumbs or pretzel crumbs

⅓ cup shredded Parmesan cheese

1 egg, blended

1 recipe Rain Shadow Meats' Mild Italian Sausage (recipe at left), or 2 pounds store-bought Italian sausage

2 tablespoons extra-virgin olive oil

4 cups (32 ounces) tomato sauce

Spaghetti or polenta, for serving

1. Stir ½ cup of the breadcrumbs, the Parmesan, and the egg together in a mixing bowl. Add the sausage and mix thoroughly. Working with a small bowl of warm water next to you, roll the meat mixture into 1½-inch balls, dipping your hands into the water occasionally to prevent the meat from sticking to your hands. Roll each ball in the remaining breadcrumbs and refrigerate, covered, until ready to cook, up to 2 days.

2. To cook, heat a large skillet over medium heat. When hot, add the oil, then the meatballs, and cook, turning only when the meatballs release easily from the pan, until browned on all sides, about 20 minutes. Add the tomato sauce and simmer the meatballs until cooked through, turning occasionally, about 15 minutes longer. Serve the meatballs over spaghetti or polenta.

Quickish Pork Posole

The menu at Seattle's La Carta de Oaxaca doesn't read like other menus at Mexican restaurants in the United States. It does list halibut tacos and enchiladas, and both are excellent, but I always go for the soups: house standards are *albondigas* (rich beef meatballs served in a vegetable soup), *caldo de pescado* (fiery fish soup), and posole (pork and hominy stew). Traditionally, posole is made with stock from a pig's head and dried hominy — delicious options, if you have the time and space to simmer both. This much quicker version, made with store-bought chicken broth, has a spice similar to the soup at La Carta, which is marked with ground cumin and cloves.

1 tablespoon canola oil

1 medium yellow onion, chopped

2 large garlic cloves, finely chopped

2 teaspoons ground cumin

1 teaspoon ground chipotle chile powder

1 teaspoon ground pasilla chile powder

¼ teaspoon ground cloves

Salt

Freshly ground black pepper

2 (28-ounce) cans hominy, drained

1 (28-ounce) can diced tomatoes

6 cups chicken broth

4 cups chopped Smoky Slow-Cooked Pulled Pork (recipe at right)

Lime wedges, radish slices, avocado slices, shredded cabbage, and sour cream, for serving

4 SERVINGS

1. Heat a large soup pot over medium heat. Add the oil, then the onion, and cook, stirring occasionally, until the onion is soft, about 10 minutes. Stir in the garlic, cumin, chipotle, pasilla, cloves, and salt and pepper to taste, and cook for 2 minutes. Add the hominy, tomatoes, and broth; bring to a simmer; then cook over low heat for 45 minutes, uncovered.

2. Add the pork and cook for 15 minutes longer, stirring occasionally. Serve hot, garnished with lime wedges, radishes, avocado, cabbage, and sour cream, if desired.

Smoky Slow-Cooked Pulled Pork

Use this simple pulled pork recipe to make a double batch of either Quickish Pork Posole (page 146) or Josh's Pulled Pork Tacos with Smoky Red Cabbage Slaw and Pineapple Salsa (page 156). Or cook the pork on a Sunday and plan to make both recipes later in the week. You can also use it in tacos, soups, and sandwiches.

2 tablespoons canola oil

Salt

Freshly ground black pepper

1 (7–8 pound) bone-in pork shoulder

2 (16-ounce) jars medium salsa

3–5 chipotle peppers en adobo

SPECIAL EQUIPMENT: slow cooker

ABOUT 8 CUPS CHOPPED PULLED PORK

1. Heat the oil in a large heavy pot over medium-high heat. Season the pork generously on all sides with salt and pepper. When the oil shimmers, add the pork and cook until well browned on all sides, about 20 minutes total.

2. Transfer the pork (but not the oil) to a slow cooker. Dump the salsa and chipotle peppers on top, and cook for 10 hours on low heat, turning once halfway through.

3. When the pork is done, transfer it to a large bowl and let cool until it's comfortable to touch. Using your hands or two forks, pull the meat away from the bone and fat, and shred the meat. The pork keeps, covered and refrigerated, for up to 1 week.

Honey-glazed Ham with Apricots, Caramelized Oranges, and Cardamom

On a late summer day, when you arrange the wrapped and frozen parts from a butchered pig on your driveway so you can divvy them up among friends, there's one given: the ham will be picked last. Next time, pretend to be doing those friends a favor and take the ham first. This version of baked ham, drizzled with an apricot-cardamom glaze and layered with caramelized orange slices, makes a pedestrian cut downright glamorous.

½ cup high-quality honey

¾ cup apricot jam

1 teaspoon ground cardamom

1 (roughly 10-pound) fully cooked, bone-in ham, fat trimmed

2 small oranges, cut into ¼-inch slices

10 SERVINGS

1. Preheat the oven to 350°F.

2. Combine the honey, jam, and cardamom in a small saucepan and cook over medium heat, stirring occasionally, until the honey and jam have liquefied.

3. Place the ham in a roasting pan, so the cut side is vertical. Pour the honey mixture over the ham, cover the pan tightly with foil, and bake for 2 hours, brushing the ham with the glaze from the bottom of the pan halfway through.

4. After 2 hours, remove the foil and brush the glaze from the bottom of the pan over the ham again. Shingle the orange slices in rows across the top of the ham. Brush the oranges with the glaze, and bake for 1 hour longer, brushing the oranges and ham with the glaze (and scooting the oranges back onto the ham, if needed) every 15 minutes or so.

5. Let the ham rest 20 minutes, slice, and serve, garnished with the caramelized orange slices.

PLANNING AROUND A PIG

I designed this chapter around using my share of a pig a friend of a friend raised on a hobby farm on the Olympic Peninsula. My part of what was labeled "Pig A" granted me four pounds of bacon, plenty of ground pork, some ribs, a shoulder, a ham, a few packages of chops, two steaks, and a loin. I used the bacon for breakfast, for the most part, and the rest of the cuts for these recipes. ★

Simple Prune-stuffed Grilled Pork Tenderloin

In a pig-wide competition for convenience, the tenderloin wins every time. This slightly fancied-up version, stuffed with prunes infused with red wine and Armagnac, is tied and grilled — but because the typically lean tenderloin is usually butchered with very little fat attached, it requires less trimming than a whole pork roast and cooks in 20 minutes or so.

1 tablespoon plus 2 teaspoons extra-virgin olive oil

1 large shallot, finely chopped

2 tablespoons chopped fresh thyme

Salt

Freshly ground black pepper

1 cup pitted prunes, chopped

1 tablespoon chopped fresh Italian parsley

¾ cup dry red wine

¼ cup Armagnac or Cognac

2 (1-pound) pork tenderloins

NOTE: You can also stuff the pork, return it to the pan you cooked the filling in, and roast it in a preheated 450°F oven for 20 to 25 minutes instead of grilling it.

SPECIAL EQUIPMENT: kitchen twine

🔖 *Pair with a merlot from RiverAerie.*

1. Heat a large skillet over medium heat. Add 2 teaspoons of the oil, then the shallot and 1 tablespoon of the thyme. Season the shallot with salt and pepper, then cook, stirring occasionally, until soft, about 5 minutes. Add the prunes, parsley, wine, and Armagnac; bring to a simmer; and cook until all the liquid has evaporated, 6 to 8 minutes.

2. Prepare a medium fire (about 400°F) in a gas or charcoal grill.

3. Meanwhile, cut each pork tenderloin almost in half the long way using a small, sharp knife, so each one opens like a book. Open one of the tenderloins on a clean work surface. Use the flat side of a meat tenderizer (or the bottom of a small heavy skillet) to pound it into a roughly even ½-inch-thick piece of meat, then repeat with the second tenderloin.

4. Spread half the prune mixture on each of the pork tenderloins, then roll them up from one long end to the other, so the meat looks about like it did before you cut into it, only fatter, and possibly with prunes poking out here and there. (Don't worry if some of them ooze out.) Tie each pork tenderloin closed with kitchen twine so they're tied about every 2 inches, then trim the twine down to the knots. Brush the tied tenderloins with the remaining tablespoon of oil, then season with salt, pepper, and the remaining tablespoon of thyme.

5. Brush the grill's cooking grates clean. Grill the pork tenderloins with the lid closed, turning occasionally, until the pork is evenly browned and the inside measures 140°F with an instant-read thermometer, about 20 minutes. Let the pork rest for 5 minutes, then slice and serve.

Pork Chops with Stone Fruit Salsa

In August, when farmers' markets begin bursting with stone fruits, you can do so much more than eat them out of hand. Stir up chopped apricots, plums, peaches, or cherries with basil, garlic, jalapeños, and lime juice, and you've got the perfect topping for juicy grilled pork chops. I think bone-in chops have the best flavor, but you can use any pork chop — just adjust the cooking time for smaller cuts.

PORK CHOPS

4 **SERVINGS**

- 4 bone-in pork chops (¾-inch thick, about 2–2 ½ pounds total)
- 1 tablespoon extra-virgin olive oil
- 1 tablespoon finely chopped fresh thyme
- Salt
- Freshly ground black pepper
- Juice of ½ large lime (about 1 tablespoon)

STONE FRUIT SALSA

- 4 medium apricots, or ¾ pound other stone fruit, pitted and chopped
- 1 small shallot, finely chopped
- 1 small jalapeño pepper, seeded and finely chopped
- ¼ cup packed chopped fresh basil
- Juice of 1 large lime (about 1 tablespoon)
- 1 garlic clove, finely chopped
- 2 teaspoons extra-virgin olive oil

1. **Make the pork chops:** Place the pork chops on a large plate. Drizzle on both sides with the oil, then rub in the thyme and salt and pepper to taste. Squeeze the lime juice over the pork, and set aside to marinate at room temperature for about 15 minutes.

2. Preheat a medium-hot (350°F to 450°F) gas or charcoal grill.

3. **Make the salsa:** While the grill heats, combine the apricots, shallot, jalapeño, basil, lime juice, garlic, and oil in a medium bowl.

4. When the grill is hot, grill the pork chops over medium-high heat for about 12 minutes, turning once or twice. (The pork should be well marked on both sides but still a bit pink in the center.)

5. Transfer the pork to a serving plate and let rest for a few minutes before serving, mounded with the salsa.

The Second-Best Cuban Sandwich

Paseo, the Cuban food joint with outposts in Fremont and Ballard, is a sandwich institution; the line habitually snakes down the street from the moment the door opens. This version of their famous grilled pork sandwich, made with pork chops and my own marinade (theirs is a secret, of course), will stand in when you can't procure the original.

4 boneless pork chops (¾ inch thick, about 1½–2 pounds total), trimmed

⅓ cup extra-virgin olive oil

⅓ cup orange juice

Juice of 1 large lime (about 2 tablespoons)

4 garlic cloves, finely chopped

1 tablespoon dried oregano

1 teaspoon ground cumin

1–2 teaspoons adobo sauce, from 1 can of chipotle en adobo

1 soft baguette, cut into 4 equal sandwich sections, each halved lengthwise

1 large red or yellow onion, cut into ½-inch rings

4 tablespoons unsalted butter, melted

½ cup Homemade Garlic Aioli (page 199), or mayonnaise mixed with 2 teaspoons finely chopped garlic

½ cup drained pickled jalapeño peppers

8 leaves romaine lettuce

12 sprigs fresh cilantro

4 SANDWICHES

1. Place the pork chops in a single layer in a casserole dish. Whisk the oil, orange juice, lime juice, garlic, oregano, cumin, and adobo sauce together, and pour the mixture over the pork. Cover and marinate, refrigerated, for 1 hour.

2. Prepare a medium fire (350°F to 400°F) in a gas or charcoal grill.

3. Brush the cut sides of the baguettes and both sides of the onion slices with the butter, and set aside.

4. When the grill is hot, brush the cooking grates clean. Grill the pork and onions (reserve the marinade), covered, until the pork releases easily from the grates, about 5 minutes. Turn the pork and the onions, and grill until the pork is cooked through, 2 to 3 minutes longer.

5. While the pork cooks, transfer the leftover marinade to a small saucepan. Bring to a vigorous boil over high heat, boil for 3 to 4 minutes, until thickened slightly, then set aside to cool. Transfer the pork to a cutting board (leave the onions on the grill), let the chops rest for a few minutes, then cut them into thin slices across the grain. Add the baguettes to the grill, buttered sides down, and grill for 1 to 2 minutes, until toasted. Remove the bread and onions from the grill.

6. Mix the marinade with the aioli, then spread some on the toasted side of each baguette piece. Arrange the jalapeños and romaine leaves on the bottom baguette pieces. Top each with a few cilantro sprigs, a pile of grilled pork, and a pile of grilled onions. Drizzle with any remaining aioli, assemble, and serve immediately.

THE SEATTLE BATALIS

WHEN GINA BATALI SMILES, all warm and friendly, it hits you like a bear hug. You'd tell her your darkest secrets if she asked, but when you walk into her Pioneer Square shop, Salumi, you'll have something else on the brain: salami. Lots of it.

When her father, Armandino Batali, opened Salumi in 2000 after a 31-year career at Boeing, he wanted to revitalize the older kinds of cured meats that had made Europe's 2,000-year-old salami-making traditions so special. He started curing all parts of the pig, making everything from coppa (cured pork shoulder) and guanciale (cured pork jowl) to pancetta (cured pork belly) and various types of salami.

Today, the family sells their meats to wholesale and retail outlets and operates a tiny lunch-only take-out restaurant that Gina calls "the biggest little hole in the wall in the world." They serve meat platters, various sandwiches (I love the meatball sandwich), and occasional hot plate specials, like gnocchi or Spaghetti with Guanciale alla Armandino (page 154), which gets its sweetness from tomato paste. Tuesdays through Fridays, when Salumi is open, you'll find a line snaking out the door and sometimes around the corner — and the wait is worth every moment.

Now that Armandino and his wife, Marilyn (also parents to superstar chef Mario Batali), have retired, Gina and her husband, Brian, are in charge of continuing to create a great domestic artisanal product in a niche where really excellent products traditionally came from abroad. And they're succeeding.

A NOTE ON STORING SALAMI: All salami is shelf stable. Gina Batali recommends storing it at room temperature, because refrigerating dry-cured salamis (like Salumi's) actually increases the water content inside the meat, increasing the chances of bacterial growth.

Gina Batali

Spaghetti
with Guanciale alla Armandino

When Armandino Batali opened Salumi Cured Meats, Seattle's salami haven, his plan was to revitalize older cuts of meat and reinstate an aging method that relies more on time and patience than "modern" meat-making methods (read: chemicals). Take his guanciale, or cured pork jowl. In practice, it's used much like bacon, only a pig's cheek typically has more fat than its belly. The flavor of guanciale tends to be nuttier than bacon, and the jowl isn't usually smoked — just salted and peppered and left to hang in just the right conditions for 70 days. The spaghetti in this casual pasta dish, perfect for a weekend lunch, soaks up the guanciale's flavor. It's not hard to see why Salumi simply can't make enough of the stuff.

1 pound high-quality spaghetti or other pasta

⅓ cup extra-virgin olive oil

½ pound guanciale, cut into ⅛-inch pieces

1 red onion, diced

⅓ cup plus 3 tablespoons white wine

3 tablespoons tomato paste

Salt

Freshly ground black pepper

Red pepper flakes (optional)

Grated Pecorino cheese, for garnish

NOTE: It's important to use high-quality pasta (the kind that soaks up sauces well) for this dish.

🖚 *Pair with a syrah from Gramercy Cellars.*

6 SERVINGS

1. Bring a large pot of salted water to a boil for the pasta. Cook the pasta until al dente according to the package instructions. Drain the pasta.

2. Meanwhile, heat the oil in a large skillet over medium heat. Add the guanciale and cook until lightly browned, 8 to 10 minutes. Add the onion and cook until soft, 2 to 3 minutes longer. (If the pasta isn't done yet, remove the pan from the heat and set aside until the pasta is done.)

3. Whisk 3 tablespoons of the wine together with the tomato paste and add the mixture to the pan with the remaining ⅓ cup wine. Add the salt, pepper, and pepper flakes to taste, if using; bring to a simmer; and cook at a strong simmer, until the liquid has almost evaporated, about 4 minutes.

4. Add the drained pasta, and toss to coat the pasta with the sauce. Serve immediately, with the grated Pecorino.

Pork-stuffed Baby Pepper Gratin

Late each summer, my farmers' market explodes with color as the organic peppers grown at Alvarez Farms in Mabton ripen. The Alvarez family's peppers and chiles are one of my go-to sources for great homemade salsas and sauces. I ask Eddie Alvarez, whose face beams with produce pride, which chiles are best for what I'm cooking, but all the "pepper guys," as a friend calls them, know their peppers well.

You can alter the spiciness of this dish by replacing the mild bell peppers with hotter peppers. If you'd like, serve them with marinara over pasta.

1 pound ground pork
2 tablespoons extra-virgin olive oil
1 medium onion, finely chopped
3 garlic cloves, finely chopped
½ pound cremini mushrooms, trimmed and finely chopped
1½ tablespoons chopped fresh rosemary, or 1½ teaspoons dried rosemary
1 tablespoon chopped fresh thyme, or 1 teaspoon dried thyme
Salt
Freshly ground black pepper
2 tablespoons balsamic vinegar
2 eggs, blended
½ cup panko breadcrumbs
¾ cup grated Parmesan cheese
1½ pounds thumb-sized mild or spicy peppers (about 2 dozen)

6 SERVINGS

1. Heat a large skillet over medium-high heat. When hot, add the pork and cook until browned through, stirring occasionally, about 10 minutes. Transfer the meat to a paper towel–lined plate and drain the pan.

2. Add 1 tablespoon of the oil to the pan, then add the onion and cook, stirring occasionally, until the onion begins to soften, about 5 minutes. Add the garlic, mushrooms, rosemary, thyme, and salt and pepper to taste, and cook, stirring, until the onions are brown, about 10 minutes longer. Stir in the vinegar, then transfer the mushroom mixture to a bowl.

3. Stir in the reserved pork and salt and pepper to taste. Stir in the eggs, breadcrumbs, and ½ cup of the Parmesan.

4. Preheat the oven to 450°F. Use the remaining tablespoon oil to grease an 8- by 8-inch (or similar) baking pan and set aside.

5. Cut the tops off of each pepper with a small, sharp knife and pull out any little seeds. When the stuffing is done, use your fingers or a small spoon to fill each pepper with about 1 tablespoon of the stuffing. Crowd the stuffed peppers into the pan, cut ends up, and sprinkle the tops with the remaining ¼ cup Parmesan. (The peppers can be assembled up to this point, covered, and refrigerated up to 1 day.)

6. Bake the peppers on the middle rack for 20 minutes, or until the peppers are soft and the Parmesan is toasted. Serve hot or at room temperature.

Josh's Pulled Pork Tacos
with Smoky Red Cabbage Slaw and Pineapple Salsa

Every family has its favorite taco recipe. Some start with packets of red spice and store-bought taco shells, like mine did when I was a kid. Now, somehow, the same family gathers around soft corn tacos stuffed with pork shoulder braised in a slow cooker with salsa (and not much else) until it falls apart into moist, tender clumps. The tacos require a topping with sweet-bright heat, like the pineapple salsa my brother Josh uses, to balance the smokiness of the chipotle peppers in the pork and the slaw. They require a brother making fun of a sister for chopping too slowly, or a sister making fun of a brother because he owns a slow cooker that fought in the War of 1812. They require messy hands, and a sloppy pile of dishes, and the inevitable argument over whether the salsa should include garlic. But before dinnertime, they don't require much more effort than those packets did, which is why we keep making them.

12 corn tortillas, warmed

4 cups Smoky Slow-Cooked Pulled Pork (page 147), reheated

Smoky Red Cabbage Slaw (recipe below)

Pineapple Salsa (recipe at right)

4 SERVINGS

Place three tortillas on each of four plates. Divide the pork among the tortillas, then top with slaw and salsa and serve.

Smoky Red Cabbage Slaw

½ small red cabbage, finely shredded

Juice of 1 large lime (about 2 tablespoons)

1 tablespoon sour cream

1–3 teaspoons adobo sauce, from 1 can of chipotle en adobo

Salt

Freshly ground black pepper

ABOUT 4 CUPS

Mix the cabbage, lime juice, sour cream, adobo sauce, and salt and pepper to taste in a medium bowl to blend, and set aside until ready to serve.

Pineapple Salsa

1 cup finely chopped fresh
  pineapple

¼ cup finely chopped red onion

¼ cup chopped fresh cilantro

2 small jalapeño peppers, seeded
  and finely chopped

Juice of 1 large lime (about
  2 tablespoons)

Salt

Freshly ground black pepper

ABOUT 2 CUPS

Mix the pineapple, onion, cilantro, jalapeños, lime juice, and salt
and pepper to taste in a medium bowl to blend, and set aside
until ready to serve.

Soy-braised Pork Belly
with Star Anise and Orange

Seattle's International District claims to be the only community in America where Chinese, Japanese, Filipino, Vietnamese, and Southeast Asians live and work in a combined ethnic neighborhood. Although some corners are clearly more Hmong, such as 12th and Jackson, and others are more Cambodian or Thai, the area is a hotbed of culture, especially when it comes to food.

Beyond a trip to Uwajimaya, the neighborhood's giant pan-Asian grocery store, it's hard to take much of the International District home with you unless it's in your belly. But whether you go in search of dim sum or pho or Szechuan noodles, or to visit one of the neighborhood's great museums, you'll always go home remembering the heady, hearty smells. This pork belly, braised in soy sauce with star anise and fat strips of orange peel, is a way to bring the suppertime smell of one of my favorite "ID" dinners home.

2 teaspoons canola oil

1 (2-pound) pork belly

1 medium sweet onion, peeled and cut into ½-inch slices

3 garlic cloves, finely chopped

1 tablespoon finely chopped fresh gingerroot

2 (3-inch) strips orange zest

2 whole star anise

⅛–½ teaspoon red pepper flakes

¼ cup shaohsing rice wine or sherry vinegar

1 cup low-sodium soy sauce

4 cups chicken broth

Rice and steamed vegetables, for serving

NOTE: You can trim the skin from your pork belly or not, as you prefer.

4 SERVINGS

1. Heat the oil in a large Dutch oven over medium-high heat on the stove. Cut the pork belly into 4 square-ish pieces; their shape will depend on the shape of your pork belly. (The pieces may seem small; this is a rich dish.) Add the pork to the pot and cook until well browned on all sides, turning occasionally, about 20 minutes total. Transfer to a plate and set aside.

2. Reduce heat to medium-low. Add the onion, garlic, ginger, orange zest, star anise, and pepper flakes to the pot. Cook, stirring often, until the onions are shiny and the garlic is toasted, about 8 minutes. Add the rice wine to the pan and simmer until no liquid remains at the bottom of the pan, about 1 minute. Add the soy sauce, broth, and reserved pork, and bring the mixture to a strong simmer.

3. Cook the pork at a strong simmer, covered, adjusting the heat as necessary, until completely tender when poked with a fork, 3 to 4 hours. Remove the star anise. (Optional: Transfer the pork to a plate, strain the sauce, and return it to the pot with the pork.)

4. Serve the pork over rice and steamed vegetables, with as much of the sauce on the side as you'd like.

RED MEATS
& GAME

Tenderloin Steaks
with Syrah-glazed Wild Mushrooms

Desert Wind Winery is the Yakima Valley's foray into the Napafication of Washington wine. Part Southwestern-inspired relaxation haven and part tasting room, this four-room inn in Prosser is hidden above what's arguably the valley's only destination restaurant, MOJAVE. You won't find tour buses, but MOJAVE offers well-executed comfort food (like this steak), adobe architecture, huge rooms with warming fireplaces, and Desert Wind wines worth writing home about — not to mention access to the entire Prosser winemaking area.

Serve the steaks with sautéed greens.

4 (8-ounce) beef tenderloin steaks, trimmed

Salt

Freshly ground black pepper

2 tablespoons extra-virgin olive oil

1 medium yellow onion, chopped

2 cups mixed wild mushrooms (such as porcini, chanterelles, and cremini), trimmed and chopped

½ cup syrah (such as Desert Wind syrah)

½ cup beef broth

2 tablespoons unsalted butter

🔊 *Pair with a syrah from Desert Wind Winery.*

4 SERVINGS

1. Preheat the oven to 325°F.

2. Season the steaks generously on both sides with salt and pepper. Heat the oil in a large skillet over high heat. When the oil shimmers, add the steaks and cook until well browned on both sides, about 2 minutes per side. (The meat will release easily from the pan when it's done searing.)

3. Transfer the steaks to a baking sheet and roast in the oven until the steaks are done to your preference, about 10 minutes for rare or 15 minutes for medium. When the steaks are done, remove the pan from the oven and let the steaks rest until the mushrooms are ready.

4. Meanwhile, add the onion and mushrooms to the hot skillet, salt and pepper to taste, and cook, stirring frequently, until the onion is translucent and the mushrooms are cooked through, 7 to 10 minutes. Carefully add the syrah to the pan, and cook until it has almost evaporated, about 5 minutes. Add the broth and cook, stirring, until the liquid has almost evaporated, about 5 minutes longer.

5. Remove the pan from the heat and stir in the butter. Transfer the steaks to plates, pour the mushroom mixture on top of the steaks, and serve immediately.

Grilled New York Strip and Onions
with Homemade Herb Salt

I like using my version of the housemade salt at Walla Walla's Blue Valley Meats, tinted with lemon zest and chile, on New York strip steaks, but any grillable piece of meat will love it.

4 (8-ounce) steaks, such as New York strips

1 large Walla Walla sweet onion, cut into ½-inch rounds

2 tablespoons extra-virgin olive oil

2 tablespoons kosher salt

½ teaspoon dried oregano

½ teaspoon dried thyme

¼ teaspoon dried dill

Grated zest of 1 small lemon

Pinch red pepper flakes (optional)

4 SERVINGS

1. Prepare a hot fire (about 500°F) in a gas or charcoal grill.

2. Brush the steaks and onions with the oil and set aside. Mix the salt, oregano, thyme, dill, lemon zest, and pepper flakes, if using, in a small bowl, then sprinkle the mixture onto the steaks and onions on both sides. (You will probably have some leftover herb salt, unless you choose to use enormous steaks.)

3. Brush the grill's cooking grates clean. Grill the steaks over high heat, with the lid closed as much as possible, for 4 to 6 minutes for medium-rare, turning the steaks one time when they release easily from the grates. Grill the onions at the same time, keeping the rings intact, if possible, when you turn them, about when you turn the steaks. (If the rings start to burn, transfer them to a cooler part of your grill.) Let the steaks rest for 5 minutes, then serve hot, with the onions.

BLUE VALLEY MEATS

Since the summer of 2011, **Kimi and Christopher Galasso** have run a tiny butcher shop in Walla Walla called Blue Valley Meats. Their experience working as chefs in kitchens across the country means they function as excellent intermediaries between chefs and meat producers, but it's the butchery's old-world feel that makes their shop great. Order a pork roast, and Chris will take the whole loin off the cedar planking in the butcher's case and plunk it down on the cutting board in front of Plexiglas you can lean right up against — don't worry, he's used to people leaning over the glass to show him exactly where they want their meat cut. If you're not the babysitting type, order and then wander over to their salt counter, where you can measure out housemade herb, onion, and chile salts by the ounce, so you only take home as much as you need that night. ★

Recipe from JASON STRATTON, SPINASSE

Hunter's-style Rabbit
with Wild Mushrooms and Tomato

It's fitting that this recipe for *coniglio alla cacciatora*, which combines tender rabbit with foraged mushrooms, canned tomatoes, and hours of half-minded babysitting, matches the style of Italian food you'll find at Seattle's Spinasse — they're both slow, rich, and comforting. Originally, chicken alla cacciatora was prepared with game and the mushrooms gathered in the forest during the hunt; made with rabbit, it's one of Stratton's favorite treatments of the animal.

1 (3–4 pound) fryer rabbit, jointed into 8 pieces

Salt

Freshly ground black pepper

3 tablespoons extra-virgin olive oil

1 pound wild mushrooms such as morels, chanterelles, or porcini, cut into bite-size pieces

¼ pound pancetta, diced

2 medium onions, finely chopped

1 stalk celery, finely chopped

1 carrot, peeled and finely chopped

4 garlic cloves, peeled and smashed

4 bay leaves

1 sprig fresh rosemary, finely chopped

1 (28-ounce) can whole plum tomatoes

2 cups dry white wine

4 cups chicken broth (homemade, if possible)

Good crusty bread, for dipping (optional)

NOTE: Allow for at least 3 hours from start to finish for this recipe, or more, if you have time. Ask your butcher to cut the rabbit into pieces for you, if you don't feel comfortable doing it yourself. You can use cremini mushrooms if you can't find wild ones.

4–6 SERVINGS

1. Heat a large braising pan or Dutch oven with a tight-fitting lid over medium-high heat. Pat the rabbit pieces dry, then season the rabbit with salt and pepper to taste. Add the oil to the pan, then the rabbit, and cook until well browned on all sides, 15 to 20 minutes total, cooking the rabbit in two batches, if necessary. Transfer the rabbit to a plate and set aside.

2. Add the mushrooms to the pan and salt and pepper to taste. Reduce heat to medium-low and cook, stirring occasionally, until the mushrooms have given up their liquid, the liquid has evaporated completely, and the mushrooms have browned, about 30 minutes. (The more slowly you can cook them once the liquid is gone, the better.) Transfer the mushrooms to a bowl and set aside.

3. Add the pancetta, onions, celery, carrot, garlic, bay leaves, and rosemary to the pan. Cook over medium-low heat until the vegetables are well browned, about 20 minutes, stirring occasionally and adding 1 to 2 teaspoons of oil, if needed.

4. Preheat the oven to 300°F. Add the tomatoes and cook, stirring occasionally, until the tomatoes darken in color to a deep brick red, about 20 minutes. Add the white wine and increase the heat to high, bringing the mixture to a simmer. Cook until the liquid is reduced by half, then add the broth and return the rabbit to the pot. Cover the rabbit with parchment paper, then the lid, and braise the rabbit in the oven for 45 minutes.

5. Stir in the mushrooms, and serve the rabbit in its own braising liquid, like a stew, with bread for dipping, if desired.

Skagit River Ranch Pot Roast

Like many farms in Washington, Skagit River Ranch depends on one of the state's mobile slaughtering units for meat processing. On any given day between May and December, you might find owner George Vojkovich out in the pastures, sorting 100 percent grass-fed beef cows for what ends up being, from a novice's perspective, a remarkably clean slaughtering process that essentially takes place in the back of an extremely shiny tractor trailer. After a trip through that trailer, these cows, which have been raised on sea salt and kelp (for vitamins and minerals to keep their immune systems strong) and a variety of grasses and herbs (which give their fat a creamy yellow hue), head to a packaging plant, where they turn into, among other things, chuck roasts — perfect for this pot roast, the Vojkovich family's favorite.

4–6 SERVINGS

- 1 tablespoon kosher salt
- ½ teaspoon freshly ground black pepper
- ½ teaspoon garlic powder
- 1 (2–3 pound) chuck, cross rib, or eye of round roast, patted dry
- 3 tablespoons extra-virgin olive oil
- 1 large onion, chopped
- 2 large tomatoes, quartered, or 1 (15-ounce) can chopped tomatoes
- 2 cups beef broth
- ½ cup dry white wine
- ⅓ cup balsamic vinegar
- 2 bay leaves
- 1½ cups water (or more, if needed)

NOTE: If necessary, you can cook the meat ahead and return it to the strained sauce when the dish is finished. To reheat, bring the sauce to a bare simmer and warm the beef for about 20 minutes, turning once or twice, before serving.

1. Blend the salt, pepper, and garlic powder in a small bowl. Sprinkle the seasoning mixture on all sides of the beef and set aside.

2. Heat a large soup pot or Dutch oven with a tight-fitting lid over medium-high heat. Add the oil. When the oil is hot, add the beef and cook until it is well browned on all sides, turning it only when the meat lifts away from the pan easily, 15 to 20 minutes total. Transfer the beef to a plate and set aside.

3. Reduce heat to medium and cook the onion, stirring and scraping any browned bits off the bottom of the pan as you cook, until the onion begins to soften, about 5 minutes. Add the tomatoes, broth, wine, vinegar, and bay leaves, and bring to a simmer.

4. Return the beef to the pot and add enough water to bring the liquid about three-fourths of the way up the sides of the beef. Reduce heat to its lowest setting, cover the pot, and cook at a bare simmer until the meat is fork-tender, 2½ to 3 hours. (Really, it may take that long. The meat will become tough first, and then relax as the connective tissue turns from collagen into gelatin.)

5. Transfer the roast to a clean platter and cover with foil to keep warm. Bring the liquid to a boil and cook until the sauce has reduced by a bit more than half, 30 to 40 minutes. (You can reduce it longer, if you'd like a thicker sauce.) Strain the sauce, return it to the pot, and add additional salt and pepper to taste, if needed. Serve the roast sliced, with the sauce on top or on the side.

HOME, HOME ON THE RANCH

Even with an address on Utopia Road, farmers **George and Eiko Vojkovich** aren't living the easy life. But if you visit their Skagit River Ranch, you'll see that at least their animals have it good. Each year, they raise and sell 180 pigs, 3,000 broiler chickens, 1,200 layer hens, and 150 head of cattle — and seem to have personal relationships with each one. George will tell you that grass-fed beef like his is higher in omega-3s, vitamin A, vitamin E, and CLA (conjugated linoleic acid); and Eiko will tell you it's what she feels good feeding her family. Their devoted Seattle farmers' market customers will tell you their meats simply taste better. ★

RN74 Beef Bourguignon

Named for the main thoroughfare running through Burgundy, in France, RN74 creates a menu that is nothing if not wine-centric. The dining room is dominated by a giant train station–style departures board, only instead of points of interest, it lists the restaurant's wines that are in most limited supply. Each time someone purchases the last bottle of something, the board goes nuts, clickety-clacking to replace said bottle with another.

Luckily, the restaurant's beef bourguignon is almost always available. Made with boneless short ribs and served with the traditional onions, carrots, and parsleyed potatoes, it's unfailingly tender.

This recipe is a project, so start it 24 hours before serving, if you can, on a day when you have time to babysit your beef. Actually, make that two days — on the first day, call your butcher and ask him to find you six pieces of short ribs from the chuck end that add up to two pounds.

BEEF

6 SERVINGS

¼ cup canola oil

2 pounds boneless short ribs, cut into 6 sections

2 medium yellow onions, quartered

2 carrots, peeled and cut into 2-inch pieces

5 stalks celery, cut into 2-inch pieces

1 head of garlic, cloves peeled and smashed

½ pound thick-cut smoked bacon, cut into 1-inch pieces

12 sprigs fresh thyme

1 bay leaf

Stems from 1 small bunch fresh Italian parsley (save the leaves for the potatoes)

1 (750 mL) bottle cabernet sauvignon

2 quarts veal broth or chicken broth (preferably homemade)

Salt

Freshly ground black pepper

1. **Make the beef:** Heat a large ovenproof pot over medium-high heat. Add the oil. When it begins to smoke, add half of the short ribs (without seasoning) and cook until deeply browned on all sides, turning only when the meat releases easily from the pan, 15 to 20 minutes total. Transfer the meat to a plate, and repeat with the remaining ribs.

2. Preheat the oven to 350°F.

3. Once all the meat has been seared, remove all but about 1 tablespoon of fat from the pan (leaving just enough to coat the bottom). Add the onions, carrots, celery, garlic, and bacon to the pan and cook, stirring occasionally, until they begin to brown, about 10 minutes. Add the thyme, bay leaf, parsley stems, and wine, and bring to a strong simmer, scraping any brown bits off the bottom of the pan with a wooden spoon. Allow the wine to reduce in volume by about half (it should take about 15 minutes), then add the broth and bring back to a simmer. Slide the meat back into the pan, cover tightly with a lid or foil, and cook for about 2 hours, or until it falls apart when you poke it with a fork. (It may take more or less time, depending on the shape of the ribs.)

ACCOMPANIMENTS

- 12 fingerling potatoes (about ¾ pound)
- 1 garlic clove, peeled and smashed
- 4 sprigs fresh thyme

  Kosher salt
- 4 tablespoons unsalted butter
- 1 tablespoon finely chopped fresh Italian parsley, plus more for garnish
- 24 pearl onions, mix of white and red, peeled
- 12 Thumbelina or other small carrots, quartered lengthwise
- 2 cups chicken broth

❧ Pair with a rich, earthy red, like a grenache from Kerloo Cellars or Maison Bleue.

4. Transfer the meat to a small dish, cover with foil, and set aside. Strain the sauce, return it to the pan, and bring to a strong simmer. Cook the sauce until it reduces to the consistency of maple syrup, 45 to 60 minutes longer. (The recipe can be completed up to this step a day or two in advance; store the meat and sauce separately in the refrigerator, and scrape any fat off the sauce before continuing.)

5. Return the meat to the sauce and rewarm over very low heat until heated through, about 20 minutes (or more, if your ingredients were cold). Salt and pepper to taste, if necessary.

6. **Make the accompaniments:** While the meat reheats, place the potatoes in a small saucepan, add cold water to cover, then add the garlic, 2 of the thyme sprigs, and salt to taste. Bring to a boil, then reduce heat to low and cook until tender, 10 to 15 minutes. Drain the potatoes. When they're cool enough to handle, cut them in half lengthwise, then toss with 2 tablespoons of the butter and the parsley.

7. Meanwhile, combine the onions, carrots, broth, remaining 2 sprigs of thyme, remaining 2 tablespoons of butter, and salt to taste in a small pot. Bring to a boil, then reduce heat and simmer over low heat until tender, about 10 minutes.

8. To serve, place a portion of the meat onto each plate, allowing some of the excess glaze to pool onto the plate. Arrange the vegetables next to the meat. Sprinkle with additional chopped parsley, if desired, and serve piping hot.

Buttermilk-battered Corn Dogs

On the dry eastern slopes of the north Cascades, the hills and valleys of northeastern Washington are peppered with the tiniest towns, many of which have faded as the logging industry has moved elsewhere. Take Chesaw: there's a general store and a tavern, and most of the year, it sits quietly in the sunshine. Every summer, though, the town explodes during the annual Fourth of July Chesaw Rodeo. The event is proof that real Western towns still exist — even if only for a day. Go early to get a good seat; the rodeo queens are entertaining, the clowns give out hats and candy, and the cowboys are talented and tough. And grab a bite to eat first thing in the afternoon — the corn dogs (which, if I had to guess, I'd say aren't homemade) sell out early.

Serve this homemade version of a rodeo staple piping hot, with mustard or ketchup.

8 CORN DOGS

Canola oil, for frying
1 cup unbleached all-purpose flour
½ cup cornmeal
½ cup corn flour
2 tablespoons sugar
1 tablespoon baking powder
1 teaspoon kosher salt
1½ cups buttermilk
1 egg
8 hot dogs (beef, turkey, or tofu)
1 tablespoon cornstarch

NOTE: You can use any extra batter to make corn fritters; simply mix the dough with raw corn kernels and drop it by tablespoonfuls into the hot oil. Cook for 3 or 4 minutes, turning once, and then drain on paper towels for a few minutes before serving.

SPECIAL EQUIPMENT: corn dog sticks

1. Add 1 inch of oil to a large saucepan or soup pot and heat over medium heat until it reaches 350°F on an instant-read thermometer.

2. While the oil heats, whisk the flour, cornmeal, corn flour, sugar, baking powder, and salt together in a mixing bowl. Whisk the buttermilk and egg together in a small bowl, and add the liquid ingredients to the dry ingredients, mixing until it forms a thick batter.

3. Blot the hot dogs dry on paper towels, then sprinkle them with the cornstarch. Use your hands to rub the hot dogs on all sides with a thin layer of cornstarch. (You might not use it all.)

4. When the oil is ready, dip three hot dogs into the batter and turn them to coat completely. Pick each hot dog up by its ends with something small and sharp (toothpicks, corn holders, or chopsticks work well, and extended paper clips are fine in a pinch), allowing any excess batter to drip off. Carefully transfer the battered hot dogs to the frying oil and cook until the batter is deep golden brown, turning once or twice, about 3 minutes. Transfer the corn dogs to a cooling rack set over a layer of paper towels to cool for about a minute before inserting a corndog stick and serving.

Roasted Bone Marrow
with Huckleberry and Sweet Onion Mostarda

After amassing a résumé of impressive posts in kitchens across Seattle, chef Brendan McGill opened Hitchcock on Bainbridge Island to cook the food that surrounds him. Using local produce, Puget Sound fish, and meats from in-state ranchers, he highlights the best ingredients he can find — usually simply, always deliciously. This roasted bone marrow, prepared over a few days but requiring very little active time, makes an impressive appetizer or wintry lunch.

Mustard oil is made by pressing the seeds of a mustard plant; you can omit it, if you must, but it adds a hot, pungent flavor to the mostarda that's difficult to achieve with dry mustard alone. Look for it online.

6 (2-inch-tall) pipe-cut marrow bones

1–2 cups kosher salt

Huckleberry and Sweet Onion Mostarda (recipe follows)

Crostini, for serving

Gray sea salt, for serving

6 SERVINGS

1. Cover the bones with ice water and refrigerate for at least 24 hours before preparing. Change the water several times during this period to draw out any blood or impurities.

2. Use a dull knife (a sharp one will snag on the bone and foul the blade, to boot) to scrape down the side of the bone to remove the thin film covering the bones. Once you have removed the film, use a fresh scouring pad to buff the surface.

3. Preheat the oven to 500°F.

4. Place the bones upright in a small casserole dish on a shallow bed of salt, which will absorb the fat that renders out during the roasting process. (How much salt you use will depend on the size of your dish; it should be about ¼-inch thick.) Roast the bones for at least 20 minutes (and up to 40 minutes) or until a thick steel needle or an instant-read thermometer slides effortlessly into the marrow. If it feels at all chalky or grainy, allow the bones to roast until the marrow is tender all the way through.

5. Pick up the bones with tongs, breaking any salt that clings to them off with a fork. Serve immediately with the mostarda, crostini, and a small pile of gray salt.

Huckleberry and Sweet Onion Mostarda

1½ cups sugar

1 cup plus 1 tablespoon water

1 cup fresh or frozen huckleberries (¼ pound)

1 cup finely chopped sweet onion

1½ tablespoons Colman's dry mustard

½ teaspoon mustard oil (optional)

1 tablespoon black mustard seeds

Salt

Freshly ground black pepper

ABOUT 1½ CUPS

1. Combine the sugar and 1 cup of the water in a small saucepan and bring to a boil over high heat, stirring occasionally, until all the sugar has dissolved. Add the huckleberries and the onions, bring to a boil, then reduce to a simmer.

2. While the huckleberries and onions are simmering, combine the mustard powder and remaining tablespoon of water in a small bowl, stirring to form a thin paste. Add the mustard oil, if using, black mustard seeds, and salt and pepper to taste. Stir the mustard mixture into the simmering syrup and cook over medium heat, stirring occasionally, until the mixture is thick and dark, about 30 minutes. Remove from the heat and allow to cool. Serve alongside roasted bone marrow, or refrigerate, covered, up to 1 week, and use as a condiment for meats or as a sandwich spread.

BRENDAN'S BONE TIPS

There are two ways that marrow bones are frequently cut: the pipe cut and the trough cut. The pipe cut is a simple section of beef marrow bone, usually cut to 2 inches high. The trough cut is a 4-inch section that has been cut in half lengthwise so that it sits like a trough filled with marrow. The trough cut is a little more difficult to find but yields more consistent results. It's also easier to eat. The pipe cut is best for people who enjoy using a demitasse spoon to dig out the somewhat hidden lump of marrow within, and ultimately slurp the rest from the bone. In either case, ask for bones that are already well trimmed to cut down on the amount of work you'll have in your own kitchen. ★

Russell Flint

THE MODERN BUTCHER

IF YOU PASS THROUGH THE DOORS to Seattle's Melrose Market on Capitol Hill, don't take too many steps. Turn left right away, where you'll see Rain Shadow Meats' aging room, with housemade salami and prosciutto hanging lazily from the racks. Let your eyes travel to the right and up a little, and you'll see the antique meat-hanging rail, which red-aproned butchers use to transport big carcasses from the walk-in cooler to the butcher's table, where whole animals from sustainable farms and ranches are broken down into primal parts. The meat is then cut to order or made into the charcuterie Seattleites love so much, or their Italian sausage (page 144).

Stroll past the meats, labeled with the farm they came from, picking out the rabbit pâté you'll have for lunch and the pork brisket you've never cooked (two things you didn't plan to buy when you showed up for simple ground beef), and you'll find a bearded, gentle-eyed man with a friendly smile. Meet Russell Flint. He's the modern butcher: always willing to cut something the way your grandmother did, happy to tell you how to cook it, and ready for your special order. If you think he sounds like the old-fashioned butcher, you'd be right — it's not him that's modern, it's you, because you're shopping there again, instead of at the grocery store. (Yes, it's okay to have a crush on him.)

Recipe from MARK FULLER, MAʻONO FRIED CHICKEN & WHISKY

Chicken-fried Veal Sweetbreads

West Seattle's Spring Hill was known for its refined Northwestern fare. But every Monday night, chef Mark Fuller turned the kitchen into a different restaurant — one that offered fried chicken four different ways, plus Hawaiian-style sides like macaroni salad and Spam musubi. The Monday-night version of Spring Hill became so popular that in 2012, the restaurant changed its name to Maʻono Fried Chicken & Whisky, and offered the chicken every night, along with other specialties.

Try these chicken-fried sweetbreads with barbecue, honey, and ranch-style sauces. (To be clear, this isn't the same secret recipe Fuller uses for the chicken.)

1 pound veal sweetbreads

COURT BOUILLON

1 medium yellow onion, sliced

6 large garlic cloves, peeled and smashed

1⅓ cups white vinegar

1⅓ cups water

¼ cup roughly chopped fresh thyme

3 tablespoons kosher salt

2 teaspoons black peppercorns

BATTER

2 cups unbleached all-purpose flour

1 tablespoon onion powder

1 tablespoon freshly ground black pepper

1 tablespoon fine sea salt

1½ teaspoons garlic powder

1 cup buttermilk

½ cup vodka

4 cups canola oil

NOTE: Sweetbreads are actually a young animal's thymus gland, not the pancreas, as is commonly believed. The organ withers with age, so it's important to ask your butcher for *veal* sweetbreads.

4 SERVINGS

1. Soak the sweetbreads in the refrigerator in a bowl of cold water overnight to remove any excess blood.

2. **Make the court bouillon:** Combine the onion, garlic, vinegar, water, thyme, salt, and peppercorns in a large saucepan and bring to a boil over high heat. Reduce to a simmer, cook for 2 minutes, then slide in the sweetbreads and cook until cooked through, turning once or twice, about 20 minutes. Allow the sweetbreads to cool in the poaching liquid.

3. **Make the batter:** While the sweetbreads cool, mix the flour, onion powder, pepper, salt, and garlic powder in a mixing bowl. Stir the buttermilk and vodka together in another bowl.

4. When the sweetbreads have cooled, heat the oil in a medium saucepan to 360°F on an instant-read thermometer.

5. Remove the sweetbreads from the liquid and peel off the thin outer membrane and any bits of spices. The sweetbreads will separate (mostly naturally) into bite-size pieces.

6. When the oil is hot, dredge about a quarter of the sweetbreads first in flour, then in the buttermilk mixture, soaking them for about 30 seconds, then in the flour mixture again, taking care that the sweetbreads are coated thoroughly each time. Fry until golden brown, about 1½ to 2 minutes, then drain briefly on a paper towel–lined plate. Repeat with the remaining sweetbreads and coatings. Serve hot.

Tatanka-style Bison Tacos
with Fiery Garlic Sauce

If you ask Cindy Weiss for an order of her famous bison tacos with the garlic hot sauce on the side, rather than on top of your tacos, she'll give you a good talking-to. I made that mistake once and wondered afterward whether the bullet holes in the windows had something to do with a similar request. The magic of the meal at Tacoma's Tatanka Take-Out is that spicy slather — but it's a secret recipe, of course. This version, which uses Cindy's method of piling cheese between two layers of corn tortillas to keep them together, has my own variation of her sauce. It's still hot and garlicky, and you can serve it however you want.

2 tablespoons canola oil

1 pound ground bison meat

½ teaspoon freshly ground black pepper

½ teaspoon granulated garlic

Kosher salt

16 (6-inch) corn tortillas

8 ounces cheddar cheese, shredded (2 cups)

1 small white onion, finely diced

2 medium tomatoes, chopped

2 cups shredded romaine lettuce

Fiery Garlic Sauce (recipe follows)

4 SERVINGS

1. Heat a large skillet over medium heat. When hot, add 1 tablespoon of the oil, then crumble the meat into the pan. Add the pepper, garlic, and salt to taste. Cook, stirring occasionally and breaking up the meat with a wooden spoon, until cooked through, about 10 minutes.

2. Meanwhile, heat another large skillet over medium-high heat. Brush the skillet with some of the remaining oil, then add two corn tortillas, topping one with 3 tablespoons of the cheese and the other with just 1 tablespoon of cheese. Cook until the cheese is melted, 1 to 2 minutes.

3. Transfer the cheesiest tortilla to a plate, then top with the second tortilla, some of the meat, and some of the onion, tomatoes, lettuce, and garlic sauce. Repeat with the remaining tortillas, serving them piping hot.

Fiery Garlic Sauce

8 large garlic cloves, peeled and smashed

3 tablespoons apple cider vinegar

2 tablespoons Asian chile-garlic sauce (sriracha)

2 teaspoons chunky Thai-style chile sauce

1½ teaspoons sugar

A SCANT ½ CUP

Blend the garlic, vinegar, and chili-garlic sauce in a blender or food processor until smooth. Add the chili sauce and sugar, blend briefly, and transfer to a serving bowl. Store any leftover sauce in an airtight container in the refrigerator for up to 1 month.

Open-Faced Steak and Cheese Sandwiches
with Malt Vinegar Jus

Unlike Philadelphia, Seattle has no hometown sandwich. I would like to nominate the following heretofore completely unfamous mouthful, which starts with a well-stocked pantry. Marinate flank steak in a simple, flavorful mixture of mustards and malt vinegar, grill it, and serve it on a warm sliced baguette topped with a tangy jus and Gouda from Golden Glen Creamery.

1½ pounds flank steak

¼ cup malt vinegar

2 tablespoons whole-grain mustard

1 tablespoon Dijon mustard

2 tablespoons canola oil

½ teaspoon freshly ground black pepper

Kosher salt

½ cup beef or chicken broth

1 soft baguette, cut in half and then halved lengthwise (or 4 hoagie buns, split)

12 ounces Gouda cheese, thinly sliced

4 SANDWICHES

1. Place the flank steak in a casserole dish. Whisk the vinegar, whole grain mustard, Dijon mustard, 1 tablespoon of the oil, and pepper together in a small bowl, and pour the marinade over the steak. Cover with plastic wrap and marinate in the refrigerator for at least 1 hour, and up to 24 hours.

2. Transfer the steak to a plate, leaving as much marinade as possible in the dish. (Reserve the marinade.) Rub the steak with the remaining tablespoon of the oil, then season with salt on both sides.

3. Preheat the oven to 400°F. Line a baking sheet with parchment paper and set aside.

4. Preheat a hot fire (about 500°F) in a gas or charcoal grill. When the grill is hot, brush the grilling grates clean. Grill the steak over direct high heat, keeping the lid closed as much as possible, until cooked to your desired doneness, about 5 minutes for medium-rare, turning one time during cooking. Transfer the steak to a cutting board and let rest for 10 minutes.

5. Transfer the marinade to a small saucepan, stir in the broth, and bring to a boil. Reduce heat and simmer for 5 minutes.

6. Arrange the baguette sections cut side up on the prepared baking sheet. Drizzle the baguettes with the sauce. Slice the steak as thinly as possible, divide the slices (and their juices) among the baguette pieces, and top with the cheese. Bake the open-faced sandwiches for about 5 minutes, or until the cheese is bubbling and the bread is toasted.

Glazed Braised Goat Shanks

Terry Whetham, who owns Quilceda Farm, a goat-meat producer about 40 miles north of Seattle, says there's really not much of a trick to cooking goat. Goat tastes richer than beef but not as gamey as lamb, and the principles for cooking it are about the same as for either — if you have a tough cut of meat, like a shank, cook it long and slow so the meat fibers become meltingly tender. Here, I braise the shanks in the oven, and the marrow melts out of the bones, thickening and enriching the sauce, which reduces to the consistency of honey and is drizzled over the shanks just before serving.

These shanks really put on a show on a dinner plate — the fat melts off and the meat all ends up at one end, for a presentation that will make even the most devout carnivore blush. Serve them with El Gaucho's Mashed Potatoes (page 86) and the Roasted Squash with Maple-Cumin Caramel (page 82) or the Seattle Winter Market Salad (page 60).

4 LARGE SERVINGS

4 (1-pound) goat shanks
2 tablespoons vegetable oil
1 large onion, chopped
5 carrots, peeled and chopped
5 stalks celery, chopped
4 garlic cloves, peeled and smashed
Salt
Freshly ground black pepper
¾ teaspoon dried thyme
1 bay leaf
1½ tablespoons tomato paste
3 cups white wine
2 cups chicken broth

☙ *Pair with a red wine from JM Cellars, such as the 2009 Margaret's Vineyard Estate Red.*

1. Heat a large pot with an ovenproof lid over medium-high heat. Pat the goat shanks dry. Add the oil to the pot, then two of the shanks, and cook until browned on all sides, turning a few times, about 15 minutes total. Transfer the shanks to a plate and repeat with the remaining shanks.

2. While the shanks sear, preheat the oven to 325°F.

3. Add the onion, carrots, celery, and garlic to the pot; salt and pepper to taste; and cook until the vegetables are soft, stirring often, about 10 minutes. Stir in the thyme, bay leaf, and tomato paste; then add the wine and broth; and bring the mixture to a simmer. Slide the seared goat shanks into the pot, cover, and cook for 2 hours, turning once during braising.

4. Transfer the meat to a large platter and tent with foil. Carefully strain the braising liquid, discarding the solids, and return the liquid to the pot. Bring the liquid to a strong simmer over high heat and cook, stirring occasionally, until the liquid has reduced to the consistency of maple syrup, about 15 minutes. Return the shanks to the pan one at a time, rolling them each in the sauce to coat them, and serve hot, drizzled with the remaining sauce.

Why Tannic Wines Pair Best with Rich Food

LAURA RANKIN is the tasting room manager at Gilbert Cellars, one of Yakima's premier wineries. At their downtown Yakima tasting room, they pair their wines with great bites, like the Gilbert Cellars' Bacon-wrapped Dates (page 31), and a dollop of education. Rankin says that when you think about pairing wine with food, one of the most important things to look at is tannin.

Tannins are naturally occurring phenolic compounds found in the skins and seeds of grapes that bind to protein molecules in your mouth. The more tannin a wine has, the more astringency you feel on your palate — it's the same mouthfeel you can get from eating spinach, or if you take a bite of a banana with the strings still attached. But when you eat food with your wine, the fat molecules in the food will attach to the protein molecules in your mouth, preventing the tannins from taking the same spot — and making the wine seem less astringent.

Traditional food and wine pairing rules put lighter proteins and vegetables with white wine and richer, fattier foods with red wine precisely because of this chemistry; richer foods overwhelm the tannins in a lighter wine.

Prime Rib with Cognac-roasted Vegetables and Crunchy Greens

Here's the ultimate company dinner for when you want a pièce de résistance but aren't sure how adventuresome your guests might be: it's a big prime rib roast, surrounded by root vegetables that are roasted right in the beef's drippings, then glazed with cognac as the meat rests. Serve with buttered egg noodles or polenta and a simple green salad.

Bone-in roasts look a bit fancier, and often take a few minutes longer to cook, while boneless roasts are easier to carve. Choose whichever works best for you, and use an instant-read thermometer to judge the meat's doneness.

1 (5-pound) bone-in or boneless prime rib roast (about 3 ribs)

4 large carrots (about 1 pound), peeled and cut into 2-inch sections

1 fennel bulb (¾ pound), cut into 8 sections through the core

1½ pounds small red potatoes, halved if large

6 small shallots, peeled

6 garlic cloves, peeled and smashed

1 tablespoon plus 2 teaspoons chopped fresh thyme

2 tablespoons plus 2 teaspoons extra-virgin olive oil

Salt

Freshly ground black pepper

4 cups chopped winter greens (such as kale, collard greens, or chard, about ¼ pound), ribs removed if large

⅓ cup cognac

8 SERVINGS

1. Remove the roast from the refrigerator and let sit at room temperature for 1 hour while you prepare the vegetables and preheat the oven.

2. Place the carrots, fennel, potatoes, shallots, and garlic in a large roasting pan. Add 2 teaspoons of the thyme, 1 tablespoon of the oil, salt and pepper to taste, and mix the ingredients together. Nestle the roast into the center of the vegetables (bone side down, if using a bone-in roast). Coat it with the 2 teaspoons oil, then sprinkle with the remaining tablespoon of thyme, salt, and plenty of pepper.

3. Preheat the oven to 450°F. When the oven is hot, roast the beef and vegetables for 20 minutes. Reduce the oven temperature to 350°F and roast for 40 minutes longer. Mix the greens with the remaining tablespoon olive oil, nestle them into the vegetables, then cook for 20 to 30 minutes longer (80 to 90 minutes total) or until the inside of the roast reaches 125°F on an instant-read thermometer for rare — the timing will depend on the shape of your roast. (You'll want to cook it to 135°F for medium, or 145°F for well-done meat.)

4. Transfer the roast to a large cutting board and let it rest for 10 minutes. Drizzle the cognac over the vegetables and roast for 10 minutes longer. Cut the meat into thin slices and serve immediately, when the vegetables are piping hot.

A New Way to Eat: Matthew Dillon of Sitka & Spruce and The Corson Building

NAME A NATIONAL AWARD, and there's a good chance Seattle chef Matthew Dillon has won it. And it's no wonder. Besides offering exceptional food that's simultaneously imaginative, simple, and devotedly local, the menu follows a diet Dillon classifies as *integretarianism*: he chooses his food based on integrity, not just of the farmers that grow it, but also of the social constructs it supports. He sources meats from local ranchers, but also buys produce from nonprofits like Seattle Youth Garden Works. His first restaurant, Sitka & Spruce, solidified the habit Seattleites have of dining communally, sharing food and conversation over long tables, because his food gave us something to talk about besides how it tastes.

At Sitka & Spruce, you'll find everything from Cider-battered Puget Sound Silver Smelt with Homemade Garlic Aioli (page 198) to salads topped with locally foraged mushrooms to milk-braised beef tacos — and almost always, if you sit at the long table in the center of the room, you'll find conversation. Since the menu changes almost daily, each experience is different, but the plates are usually shared. Because there's always something to talk about, the line between two dining parties often blurs as the meal proceeds; it's not uncommon to end up sharing dessert with people you've never met.

When Dillon opened The Corson Building, with just three long tables where about 30 people sit together, dining all at once, people started thinking differently about how they define a night out. As the name suggests, The Corson Building is more than a restaurant — it's also part cooking school, part public pantry, part garden, part benefit space, and really, part experiment. And from the moment you walk in, you can tell dinner will be different. "At The Corson Building, you can't think of yourself as a separate party," says Dillon. "All the diners are part of the same experience."

First, there's the little detail that you don't get to decide what to eat. The food just comes. "I'm not a Buddhist by any stretch, but I like to think we take a bit of a Buddhist approach," says Dillon. "If you take away things that diners find comfortable — a host, a menu, and their own private table — you promote a heightened awareness. People talk to each other. And they may actually glean new things from food that they wouldn't get in a regular restaurant situation."

Communal dining isn't for everyone. But if it's for you, grab a glass. At The Corson Building, they don't count how many times the wine is poured, and there's no one waiting for your table. And you'll always, always meet someone new.

The New Tuna Casserole

It isn't that tuna casserole has changed so much since our mothers made it for us, it's that the ingredients that go into it have changed. This version has all the old hallmarks — twisty noodles cooked until just al dente, peas, mushrooms, tuna, cheese . . . except the tuna is sustainable albacore caught by Fishing Vessel *St. Jude* (canned tuna you can buy at Seattle's farmers' markets, among other places), the peas are fresh from the garden, and the mushroom soup is homemade. And those chips on top? Tim's "Cascade Style" potato chips, from Auburn. On a cold late spring night, there's nothing more comforting.

You can use two cans of good-quality condensed mushroom soup if you don't have any homemade soup on hand.

10 ounces (3 cups) short pasta (such as penne or fusilli)

2 cups Cream of Wild Mushroom Stew with Sage and Sherry (page 44)

1 cup fresh or frozen peas

1⅓ cups grated Parmesan cheese

2 (6-ounce) cans water-packed low-sodium albacore tuna, drained and flaked

¼ cup milk or heavy cream

1 cup crushed gourmet potato chips

4 SERVINGS

1. Preheat the oven to 350°F.

2. Bring a large pot of salted water to a boil for the pasta. Cook until not quite tender, about a minute less than what the package calls for for al dente.

3. Drain the pasta, transfer to a large bowl, and stir in the soup, peas, 1 cup of the Parmesan, tuna, and milk.

4. Transfer the mixture to an 8- by 8-inch baking pan (or similar), top with the remaining ⅓ cup Parmesan and the chips, and bake for 30 minutes, or until bubbling. Serve immediately.

Melrose Mussels

If you've cooked mussels outside the Northwest, you've probably operated under the assumption that the bivalves are done cooking when they open. That's not usually the case with Taylor Shellfish Farms' Mediterranean mussels, which are found at restaurants across the state and at Taylor's storefront in Seattle's Melrose Market. Because the mussels are so plump and the shells so thin, Mediterranean mussels typically need to cook a few minutes after the shells open, until you see the meats contract. Some large shells will "glue together" when covered with liquid, causing them to not open even if they're perfectly healthy. As long as the mussels were closed before cooking, pry them open and eat them! And serve them with good, crusty bread for mopping up the juices.

2 tablespoons extra-virgin olive oil

1 medium onion, finely chopped

1 large garlic clove, finely chopped

1 jalapeño or serrano pepper, minced

¼ cup chopped fresh Italian parsley or basil

1 large tomato, chopped

½ cup dry white wine

4 pounds Mediterranean mussels, debearded

NOTE: Mussels attach themselves to their habitat with a series of thick hairs called "byssus threads," or, more commonly, "beards." Although many farmed mussels don't develop large beards, most wild ones do. Just before cooking, discard any mussels that are chipped or that don't close when you tap the shells, then debeard the rest. Use your thumb and first finger to grasp the beard and pull sharply, perpendicular to the mussel.

☙ *Pair with a Columbia River rosé from Syncline Wine Cellars.*

4–6 SERVINGS

1. Heat a large soup pot over medium-high heat. When hot, add the oil, then the onion, and cook, stirring occasionally, until translucent, about 5 minutes. Add the garlic, jalapeño, and 2 tablespoons of the parsley, and cook until the pan seems dry, 3 to 4 minutes.

2. Add the tomato, cook 2 minutes longer, then stir in the wine and bring to a simmer. Add the mussels, cover, and steam until the mussels open, 8 to 10 minutes. Stir in the remaining 2 tablespoons parsley, and serve immediately.

RULED KING SALMON STEAKS

IF YOU GO SHOPPING FOR SALMON with Seattle-based seafood expert Jon Rowley, he might take you to Wild Salmon Seafood Market in my neighborhood, where the fish lounging on ice in the front are often specimens of perfection. Before buying anything, he'll do something you might not feel totally comfortable with: he'll reach out and touch the fish. Not all of them, but most of them. Other customers will probably stare. He's feeling for firmness and freshness — which, in his opinion, are much more important to a salmon dinner than anything you could pile on top of it.

Although Rowley has a very specific way he cooks salmon steaks — he sears them in a hot skillet, then melts the insides just to tender perfection, in a low oven — he's most particular about buying the fish itself. This is a recipe, but it's also a guide, so read it through before you shop. And put a good pinot noir on your list.

First, take a trip to your local fishmonger, one you trust. You can look for king salmon any time of year, but the fat-bellied king salmon from Alaska's legendary Copper River arrive in mid-May to mid-June. They're rich in fat and flavor, and they're usually expensive, which means that when you cook them, you want to let their taste come through as much as possible, capturing every ounce of juice within the skin.

Always buy steaks from a fresh, whole fish. Look for a fish with bright, even scales, with no patches where scales are gone — usually a sign of mistreatment during the catch. Reach out and touch the likeliest prospects. If they're fresh, the surface of the scales should be covered with a bright slime. This is a good kind of slime — it's only present when the fish is fresh, the scales are intact, and the catch has been handled gently and safely. The fish should smell like the sea. If there are a few you like, run your fingers under the belly flap, feeling for thickness — the thicker the belly, the fatter the fish, and the better it will taste.

Ask your fishmonger to cut you a couple 1½-inch steaks. On the page, 1½ inches, cut across the spine, right in the center of the fish, sounds reasonable. But the moment that fishmonger gets his knife out, you might reconsider — 1½ inches makes the equivalent of a Porterhouse of fish; it's a huge, thick slab. If it's from a 25-pound fish, it'll serve 2 people easily. And I don't mean to call your fishmonger's integrity into question, but make sure he's cutting 1½ inches. A quarter inch less will not do. Bring out a tape measure, if you must.

1. Take your fish steaks home. Preheat the oven to 225°F. Heat a large cast-iron skillet over medium-high heat.

2. Season the fish on both sides with salt and freshly ground black pepper. Brush it liberally with olive oil (about 1 tablespoon per steak). When the pan is hot, add the steaks, and cook until the fish is well browned and releases easily from the pan, about 3 minutes. Turn and cook on the second side for 3 minutes longer.

3. Transfer the skillet to the oven and cook the salmon for another 15 minutes, or until you just begin to see albumen (the white stuff) bead at the very edges of the steaks. (If it's really good fish, and you've cooked it just right, you may not see any albumen at all. You can also test the salmon by inserting a small spatula into the rounded edge of a steak, along the backbone — if the meat separates away from the bone easily, it's done.)

4. Serve your fish, with lemon, if you'd like, and eat it slowly. Notice how the texture is consistently moist the entire way through, and say a silent prayer that the extra 2 minutes you cooked it while you were chatting away on the phone doesn't seem to have ruined it. (This method of cooking expensive fish is extremely forgiving.)

Tip: King salmon can vary in color from white to deep red, depending on where they're from. When it comes to salmon, don't use color as an indicator of quality.

Recipe from KEVIN DAVIS, BLUEACRE SEAFOOD

Green Curry Mussels

At Blueacre Seafood, chef Kevin Davis's flagship restaurant in downtown Seattle, the seafood is fresh, sustainably harvested, and reliably interesting. Davis sources his seafood from Taylor Shellfish Farms, which grows mussels, clams, oysters, and geoducks in the bays and inlets of the Puget Sound; the mussels for this dish are always extremely fresh.

For this recipe, you'll need to use full-fat coconut milk, which separates naturally in the can into cream and juice. Serve the mussels with good crusty bread, for soaking up the spicy juices.

3 tablespoons unsalted butter

1 garlic clove, finely chopped

1 teaspoon finely chopped shallot

1 teaspoon finely chopped serrano pepper

1 teaspoon freshly grated gingerroot

½ small leek, white and light green parts only, trimmed and cut into ¼- by 1-inch strips

½ carrot, peeled and cut into ¼- by 1-inch strips

1 teaspoon green Thai curry paste (such as Mae Ploy brand) or 1 tablespoon Homemade Red Curry Paste (page 137)

1 lime

1 (14-ounce) can coconut milk (full-fat, not light), unstirred

2 teaspoons sugar

¾ teaspoon kosher salt

1 pound fresh mussels, rinsed and debearded

¼ cup chopped fresh cilantro

NOTE: For instructions on debearding mussels, see page 183.

☙ Pair with Windfall Winery's Asian pear wine.

6 APPETIZER SERVINGS

1. Melt the butter in a large soup pot with a tight-fitting lid over medium-high heat. As soon as it melts completely, add the garlic, shallot, chile, and ginger, and cook, stirring constantly for about 30 seconds. Add the leeks and carrots, and cook until the carrots are soft, stirring constantly, about 2 minutes. Stir in the curry paste and the juice of half the lime, and cook another 30 seconds or so.

2. Add all of the thick cream from the can of coconut milk, plus about ¼ cup of the coconut juice. (Discard the remaining juice.) Add the sugar and salt, stir, and bring the mixture to a simmer.

3. Add the mussels, cover, and simmer over high heat, stirring once or twice, until all the mussels have opened, 5 to 10 minutes.

4. Squeeze the juice from the remaining lime half over the mussels, stir in the cilantro, and season to taste with additional salt, if necessary. Serve immediately.

Steamed Dungeness Crab Legs
with Preserved Meyer Lemon Aioli

In Washington, during crab season, you'll find (properly licensed) sport crabbers wandering the beaches, preparing to search for dinner just offshore — in boats, with crab pots, or by hand. When I can't convince my husband to don his scuba diving gear to go crabbing in Westport when the fishing town celebrates its yearly crab festival, we buy crabs off the dock there and cook them ourselves.

For this dish, ask your fishmonger to remove the legs from the bodies for you, giving you less prep to take care of in your own kitchen. If you can't find preserved lemons, substitute the grated zest of two large Meyer lemons and an extra pinch of salt.

If you start with cooked crab, steam the crab legs for about 6 minutes instead.

3 pounds raw crab leg sections, from 3 Dungeness crabs

2 cups Homemade Garlic Aioli (page 199) or mayonnaise

1 preserved Meyer lemon, homemade (page 258) or store-bought

NOTE: If you have the patience to crack the crab legs yourself, this aioli makes for a wonderful crab salad. Mix the crabmeat (about 1½ pounds) with aioli to taste, and stir in about ½ cup chopped chives.

Pair with a viognier from àMaurice Cellars.

4–6 SERVINGS

1. Fill a pot large enough to fit all the crab legs (with the lid tightly secured) covered with about 1 inch of water. Bring the water to a rolling boil over high heat. Add the crab legs, cover, and steam until the legs are cooked through, about 12 minutes.

2. While the crab cooks, combine the aioli and the preserved lemon in a food processor or in a blender, and whirl until smooth.

3. Serve the crab legs hot with cracking utensils and the aioli in little bowls for dipping.

RAZOR CLAMMING: IT'S HARDER THAN IT LOOKS

IF YOU SEARCH THE INTERNET for videos of razor clamming, you'll probably find two guys traipsing in the setting springtime sun across firm, glistening sand with full buckets, their steps timed with the crashing surf. They're carrying clam "guns" — special metal, tubular tools most recreational diggers use to catch the flat, oval-shaped West Coast clams — and they look blissfully happy. "We caught our limit, 15 clams, in just under half an hour," one of them reports to the camera. "Now we just have to cook 'em!" They beam and exchange a sprightly high five. Foraging for your own shellfish is clearly just a walk on the beach.

Only, this is not how razor clamming really works. These guys obviously visited Washington's southwest coast, during one of the many yearly clam digs dictated by the Washington Department of Fish and Wildlife, on a day that miraculously matched good weather with daytime low tides. (Since the season runs from October to May, neither are necessarily givens.) Based on my own razor-clamming experience, they came out weeks before, fitted an assortment of razor clams with magnetic attractors, planted them in a bed of fine, pretty sand, then returned with some sort of X-ray sensing device to determine precisely where the clams were planted.

But maybe I'm jaded. When I learned that *Siliqua patula* thrive up and down Washington's eastern shore, I was thrilled by the prospect of digging for them. Razor clams, because they're eaten without their stomachs, have great clam flavor, but neither the weird, sometimes-sandy texture of Manila or littleneck clams nor the leathery siphons of quahogs or cherrystones. They're the boneless, skinless chicken breasts of the shellfish world, with very little work required when it comes to the actual eating, and I perhaps naively expected the digging process to go as easily. These things are four or five inches long. How hard could they be to find?

Well, here's how razor clamming actually works, if you're me: You fight post-Thanksgiving traffic to the Washington coast in freezing rain with a buddy, a dog, and a razor-clamming license, along with your husband's ill-fitting foul-weather gear, a Thermos of coffee, a shovel (no handy clam gun for you!), and lots of flashlights, because on that day, low tide is at 10 PM. You follow around the two small children of a different friend, one who actually knows what he's doing, depending on them to see the telltale clam "show," the signs of life under the sand that you are somehow completely incapable of recognizing. They tell

you to dig, so you dig, but not the way they do online. Actually, you do start out with the shovel but after a foot or so, you collapse to your knees and start heaving sand out in messy handfuls, like you're pawing through a giant vat of 34-degree Cream of Wheat. Then you feel your dog staring at you with her head tilted, wondering who the hell taught you to dig like that.

As soon you feel the tip of the clam, it digs down farther and slightly seaward, so you flatten your chest to the sand and get your whole arm involved, right up to the armpit. Make sure you have your watch on and the sleeves of your fleece a little bit open when you plunge your hand into the liquefied sand, so that millions of hard little particles dive directly *up* your sleeve, where they exfoliate your elbows, and *down* under your watch band and into your good biking gloves.

Then you finally grasp that clam. By then the sand at the surface of the hole has solidified around your bicep and elbow, so pulling your arm out requires significant effort and much grunting. You finally, triumphantly, bring your catch to the surface, which you now realize is much, much warmer than down under the sand. That's one razor clam.

In the end, you dig faster than the clam only about half the time. You accidentally smash some with the shovel, and your friend has to teach you which ones are still okay, and which ones you've really obliterated.

Then, near midnight, on the way to your friend's house to clean the clams and dredge them in flour and fry them up in butter (that part really is as simple as that), when your feet are thawing and your hand has finally stopped bleeding from where you cut it on your own shovel, you have to sing a clam song. There's no particular song; it's not like sailing, where there's a song for the mainsail going up, a song for the anchor, and a song for washing the deck. It could be "The Twelve Days of Christmas," if the season's right. You could start right in the middle: *Six buckets swinging, FIIIIIVE MANGLED CLAMS, four clamming shovels, three cold butts, two new diggers, and a fried clam with a lemon squeeze.*

The next day, someone will ask you how razor clamming went. "Amazing," you'll say, from your warm spot on the couch. And you'll mean it. "Do you want to go with me next weekend?"

For information on recreational razor-clamming seasons, licensing, regulations, and clam cleaning and cooking, visit www.wdfw.wa.gov.

Creamy Razor Clam Linguine
with Parsley and Chives

If you're not up for the adventure of razor clamming (page 190), frozen razor clam meat is frequently available at Wild Salmon Seafood Market or through Pike Place Fish; both fishmongers ship nationwide (see Recipe Contributors and Suppliers, page 274). One 1-pound package frozen clam meat makes about 1½ cups chopped clams.

If you find fresh clams, ask your fishmonger how to clean them.

¼ cup extra-virgin olive oil

3 large garlic cloves, finely chopped

½ teaspoon red pepper flakes

½ cup dry white wine

1 cup heavy cream

¾ pound linguine or other long pasta

1½ cups razor clam meat, chopped into ½-inch pieces

Salt

Freshly ground black pepper

½ cup finely chopped fresh chives

¼ cup finely chopped fresh Italian parsley

½ cup freshly grated Parmesan cheese, plus additional for garnish

4–6 SERVINGS

1. Bring a large pot of salted water to a boil.

2. Heat the oil, garlic, and pepper flakes in a large saucepan over medium heat. Cook, stirring occasionally, until the garlic is tender and begins to sputter, about a minute. Add the wine and cream, bring to a simmer, and cook until the liquid is reduced by half, 8 to 10 minutes.

3. After you add the wine and cream, add the pasta to the boiling water, and cook according to the package instructions. Drain the pasta, but do not rinse.

4. Add the clams to the reduced sauce, salt and pepper to taste, and simmer until the clams are just heated through, 2 to 3 minutes. (They really don't take long to cook.)

5. When the pasta is done, transfer it to the pan with the cream, then add the chives, parsley, and Parmesan. Toss to coat the pasta with the sauce. Transfer the noodles to bowls, spoon the sauce and clams on top, and serve immediately, topped with additional Parmesan, if desired.

Roasted Sockeye
with Warm Orange and Olive Salad

If you haven't lived in Washington, you may not recognize the different salmon varieties the way you intrinsically know the difference in taste between, say, a green apple and a red one. I've learned them well by shopping the coolers at Loki Fish Company's stands in various Seattle farmers' markets; their employees are excellent at describing how each fish tastes. Sockeye salmon have firm, dark red flesh, with a stronger flavor than king, keta, or coho salmon, all of which are also found in markets here. Sockeye dry out easily if you overcook them, which is why I tend to roast big fillets whole, rather than grill them.

1 (2-pound) fillet sockeye salmon (usually a full side of sockeye)

2 tablespoons extra-virgin olive oil

Salt

Freshly ground black pepper

½ medium red onion, thinly sliced with the grain

3 medium oranges

1½ cups firm green olives, pitted and halved

¼ cup roughly chopped fresh Italian parsley

🐟 Pair with a riesling from Chateau Ste. Michelle, such as their Eroica or Cold Creek Rieslings.

4–6 SERVINGS

1. Preheat the oven to 450°F.

2. Place the salmon skin side down in a large roasting pan or on a parchment-lined baking sheet. Rub it with 1 tablespoon of the oil, salt and pepper to taste, and set it aside.

3. Combine the remaining tablespoon oil with the onion in a mixing bowl. Carve the peel and any white pith off the oranges with a small, sharp knife, then cut the oranges into ¼-inch semicircles. Add the oranges, olives, and parsley to the onions, along with any orange juice accumulated on the cutting board, and salt and pepper to taste.

4. Pile the orange mixture on and around the salmon and roast for 15 to 20 minutes, or until the onions are soft and the salmon measures 140°F with an instant-read thermometer in the center. Serve immediately.

Recipe from KATHY CASEY FOOD STUDIOS — LIQUID KITCHEN

Pale Ale Oven-Roasted Clams

Food and cocktail pioneer Kathy Casey has been an important icon of Seattle's food scene for decades. From the quick, healthy food sold at Dish D'Lish — the only place I usually eat at Seattle's SeaTac airport — to the dishes made famous in her newspaper columns to the tips in her cute cookbooks, she's a culinary force. And each one of her recipes makes it clear why; her food is delicious.

With more than two hundred small craft breweries in the Pacific Northwest, beer ends up in a lot of Kathy's dishes. Here, India pale ale adds a slight bitterness that makes for a pleasantly hoppy broth — unequaled for sopping up with lots of crusty bread. She likes to serve the clams directly from the skillet, in the center of the table, for sharing.

2 pounds small Manila clams, rinsed

1 tablespoon finely chopped garlic

⅛-¼ teaspoon red pepper flakes

2 ripe plum tomatoes, chopped (about 1 cup)

1 teaspoon finely chopped fresh rosemary

½ lemon, cut into 4 pieces

¼ cup India pale ale

2 tablespoons unsalted butter, cut into small chunks

1 large sprig fresh rosemary (optional)

2 DINNER OR 4 APPETIZER SERVINGS

1. Preheat the oven to 500°F.

2. Toss the clams, garlic, pepper flakes (to taste), tomatoes, and chopped rosemary in a large bowl. Transfer to a large cast-iron or other ovenproof heavy skillet. Squeeze the lemon pieces over the clams, then drop the pieces into the pan. Pour the beer over the clams and scatter with the butter. Place the rosemary sprig in the center, if using. (Use fresh, healthy rosemary; drier stems will burn while the clams roast.)

3. Roast for 14 to 16 minutes, or until the clams are all open. Remove from the oven, and stir gently with a large spoon. Discard any clams that do not open. Serve in the skillet; set on a hot pad or trivet. (Be sure to wrap the skillet handle with a heavy cloth napkin or pot holder.)

Recipe from MATTHEW DILLON, SITKA & SPRUCE

Cider-battered Puget Sound Silver Smelt
with Homemade Garlic Aioli

Before opening The Corson Building and bar ferd'nand, and before moving Sitka & Spruce, his flagship restaurant, to Melrose Market, Seattle chef Matthew Dillon operated just another strip-mall restaurant. Only, if you could ignore the parking lot, it was never that. It was the anti-strip-mall restaurant. Wherever he's cooking, Dillon focuses on foraged foods and Northwest ingredients, and his menu changes every day. Named for the trees that tower over many of his favorite foraging spots, Sitka & Spruce has always been an incubator — for new cooking ideas, new chefs, and new flavors, like these Puget Sound smelt, dipped in a light apple-cider batter and deep fried.

At Sitka & Spruce, Dillon serves these smelt with fried radishes, made by simply quartering small radishes, dipping them in the batter, and frying for a minute or two, and with grated raw radish seasoned with malt vinegar and salt.

6 SERVINGS

CIDER BATTER

- 2 cups unbleached all-purpose flour
- 2 tablespoons cornstarch
- 2 teaspoons baking powder
- 2 cups ice-cold dry hard apple or pear cider
- Small ice cubes
- Kosher salt

GRATED RADISH

- 2 large radishes, peeled and grated on a Microplane or box grater
- 2 teaspoons malt vinegar
- Kosher salt

SMELT AND FRIED RADISHES

- Vegetable, sunflower, grapeseed, or peanut oil, for frying
- 24 silver smelt, head on, bones intact, gutted, and rinsed
- Kosher salt
- Flaky sea salt
- 10 radishes, greens intact, quartered
- Lemon wedges, for serving

1. **Make the batter:** Stir the flour, cornstarch, and baking powder to blend with a wooden spoon in a medium bowl. Slowly add the cider and four or five ice cubes, stirring only until the mixture coats the spoon — there should still be lumps, which will dissolve eventually. Let the batter rest for 1 hour, stirring once or twice as the ice cubes melt but generally leaving it alone.

2. **Make the aioli:** While the batter rests, make the aioli from the recipe at right.

3. **Make the grated radish:** Mix the radishes, vinegar, and salt together and set aside in a small bowl.

4. **Make the smelt and fried radishes:** Fill a deep-sided pot with 3 inches of oil and heat over medium heat until it reaches 375°F on a deep-frying thermometer.

5. Pat the smelt dry with paper towels. Season inside and out with kosher salt, and season the batter with kosher salt, as well.

6. Dip the smelt in the batter completely, a few at a time — you can cook more than one at a time, but don't crowd the pan. Let some of the batter run off the fish, back into the bowl, then fry until golden and puffed, 2 to 3 minutes, turning once. Drain the fish on a cooling rack set over a few layers of paper towels, and season again with the flaky sea salt.

7. Repeat with the remaining fish, allowing the oil to come back up to 375°F, if necessary, between batches. Between batches of fish, fry a few radishes, dipping them into the batter until golden, 1 to 2 minutes. Serve the fish and fried radishes as soon as possible after frying, with the aioli, grated radish, and lemon wedges.

NOTE: Use your judgment when it comes to fish quantity. Four fish per person is a nice number if the fish are small, like 6 inches each, but for bigger fish, you may only need two or three per person.

☙ Pair with a dry Washington pear cider, like Snowdrift Cider's Perry.

Homemade Garlic Aioli

1 large garlic clove, peeled

Kosher salt

1 egg yolk, from a nice chicken

Juice of 1 small lemon (about 2 tablespoons)

1 cup olive, sunflower, or grapeseed oil, or a blend of the three

ABOUT 2 CUPS

1. Crush the garlic in a large mortar and pestle with a pinch of salt until the garlic forms a smooth paste. Work in the egg yolk and the lemon juice, then add the oil, drop by drop, until about one-third of the oil is used, mashing and mixing to incorporate the oil.

2. Add the remaining oil in a slow, steady stream, switching to a whisk and whisking in the oil a little at a time. (If the mixture seems too thick, add water. If it seems too thin, add oil.) Season the aioli to taste with additional salt and, if necessary, lemon juice. (You can also make the aioli in a food processor or large bowl, if you prefer.)

Mint-crusted Halibut Roast

When fresh halibut hits the markets each spring, the fishmongers' displays boast huge slabs of pearly white fish. You can always grill a halibut steak for an easy weeknight dinner. But for company, try this: Make a quick crust out of breadcrumbs infused with lemon, great olive oil, and plenty of mint, and pat it onto a two-pound slab of halibut. Roast it until the fish barely separates and the crust is golden brown, and serve it as you would a more typical beef or pork roast — it's dinner party food at its simplest, and it cooks just long enough for you to throw the rest of dinner together while it's in the oven.

Serve the roast with Cheesemonger's Creamy Dreamy Mac and Cheese (page 92) or roasted potatoes and a big green salad.

1 (2¼-pound) slab of halibut, cut across the fish (about 4 inches wide by 8 inches long)

1 cup panko breadcrumbs

2 tablespoons extra-virgin olive oil

Salt

Freshly ground black pepper

¼ cup lightly packed, finely chopped fresh mint

Zest and juice of 1 medium lemon (about 3 tablespoons juice)

NOTE: If you can't find a fishmonger that has halibut sides still intact, you can substitute halibut fillets or steaks. Increase the oven temperature to 450°F and roast the fish for 10 to 12 minutes per inch of thickness.

6–8 SERVINGS

1. Preheat the oven to 425°F.

2. Place the halibut in a 9- by 13-inch baking pan (or similar).

3. Combine the breadcrumbs, oil, salt and pepper to taste, mint, and lemon zest and juice in a small bowl, stirring until all the breadcrumbs are evenly moistened. Pat the breadcrumb mixture onto the fish in a roughly even layer (it's fine if some falls off).

4. Roast the fish for 25 to 30 minutes, or until just beginning to flake off easily with a fork at the edges and golden brown on top. Serve warm.

Grilled Salmon with Spring Garden Saag

There is an awkward, pubescent moment in every Seattle garden; it occurs between May and July, when the days are just at their peak length and the excitement over tiny fresh asparagus has died, but the thrill of mature summer tomatoes has yet to begin. In this span of two weeks, the garden *grows*. It's exactly what we wanted it to do, yet when the workhorses of our early summer gardens, the greens, really get down to business, we're often overwhelmed. Here's a great sauce to make when spinach, kale, and arugula threaten to take over every inch of your refrigerator — or any greens, really, as long as they're coming in massive quantities. Inspired by Indian *saag*, a spinach dish often served over *paneer* (Indian cheese), it's delicious on its own, mixed into rice, or draped over a delicately grilled slab of fish, as it is here.

Light coconut milk will work for the recipe, but the flavor will suffer.

4 SERVINGS

1 tablespoon ghee or unsalted butter

1 large garlic clove, finely chopped

1 tablespoon finely chopped fresh gingerroot

¾ pound spinach (regular or baby), chopped

1 medium bunch kale (about ½ pound), ribs removed and chopped

2 (14-ounce) cans coconut milk

Red pepper flakes (optional)

Kosher salt

4 (6-ounce) king salmon fillets (with skin), each about 1 inch thick

1 tablespoon vegetable oil

1. Prepare a medium fire (about 400°F) in a gas or charcoal grill.

2. Heat a large wide pot over medium-high heat. Add the ghee, then the garlic and ginger, and cook, stirring, until the garlic is soft, about 1 minute. Add the spinach and kale and cook until the greens are wilted, stirring frequently, about 5 minutes. Add the coconut milk (water and solids, if the contents have separated), the pepper flakes, if using, and salt. Cover the pot and cook for 10 minutes. Remove the cover and cook, stirring occasionally, until the liquid is almost gone, a few minutes longer. Transfer the greens to a food processor and blend until completely smooth.

3. When the grill is hot, brush the cooking grates clean. Brush the pink side of the salmon with the oil, salt to taste, and place skin side up on the grill. Cook until you can lift the fillets off the grates easily, 6 to 8 minutes, then turn the fish and cook for 2 or 3 minutes longer (for medium-rare), or until they reach your desired doneness.

4. Serve the salmon hot, with the saag draped over the top.

Classic Brasserie Sole
with Brown Butter and Herbs

The bright yellow metal stools at Walla Walla's Brasserie Four give it a schoolhouse feel, and if you stay long enough, you'll learn these things: In the heart of Washington wine country, you can feel confident ordering the $5 glass of house wine. French fries showered with parsley, served in a cone-shaped vessel, are a sure cure for too much wine tasting. A bath in the aroma of a kitchen constantly melting Gruyère is good for every soul. And even here, five hours from the closest ocean, a simple fillet of fish swathed in brown butter and soft herbs can simultaneously satisfy both a wish for fancy food and an earthy desire to eat things prepared as simply as possible.

The fish used for this preparation changes often at Brasserie Four. I had it with Dover sole, but any thin, quick-cooking fillet (like trout or a thin fillet of sockeye salmon) will work. Serve with simple steamed, buttered potatoes.

4 Dover sole fillets (about 1½ pounds total)

Salt

Freshly ground black pepper

6 tablespoons unsalted butter, softened

2 tablespoons chopped fresh Italian parsley

2 tablespoons chopped fresh tarragon, dill, chives, and/or fennel fronds

🍃 *Pair with a chardonnay from Abeja Wines.*

4 SERVINGS

1. Season the fish on one side with the salt and pepper, and set aside.

2. Melt 2 tablespoons of the butter in each of two large skillets over medium-high heat. (If you don't have two skillets, you can make the fish in two batches, wiping the pan out between batches and using 2 tablespoons of the butter for each batch.) As soon as the butter has melted, add two pieces of fish to each skillet. Cook until the fish is opaque throughout, turning gently one time as soon as the fish lifts easily off the pan, 4 to 5 minutes total. Transfer the fish to a serving plate.

3. Add 1 tablespoon of the remaining butter, half the parsley, and half the tarragon to each of the two pans. Swirl the pans until the butter melts and is flecked with brown and the bubbles subside, then pour the herbed brown butter over the fish and serve immediately.

Dill-stuffed Grilled Trout
with Seared Lemon Pan Sauce

If you're not catching your own trout in one of Washington's rivers, lakes, or reservoirs, you can often get them from your local fishmonger for a fraction of the price many larger species fetch. Stuffed with lemon slices and dill, then grilled and topped with a quick stovetop sauce that puts on a pretty face for company, these trout are my go-to fish for summer grilling when salmon prices skyrocket.

4 (12-ounce) whole rainbow trout, cleaned and heads left intact

Salt

Freshly ground black pepper

2 large lemons, halved lengthwise and cut into ¼-inch-thick half moons

8 large fresh dill fronds, plus 2 tablespoons finely chopped fresh dill

2 tablespoons extra-virgin olive oil

5 tablespoons unsalted butter, softened

NOTE: If you have a big grill, you can preheat a heavy-duty skillet over the grates as the fish cooks on the first side, and make the sauce right on the grill.

4 SERVINGS

1. Prepare medium-hot fire (about 450°F) in a gas or charcoal grill.

2. Season each fish inside and out with salt and pepper. Stuff each one with a few lemon slices (using the slices from just one of the lemons for all four fish) and 2 whole dill fronds. Brush each fish on all sides with the oil. Brush the grilling grates clean, then grill the fish for 10 minutes, turning once when the skin releases easily from the grilling grates, after about 5 minutes.

3. After you flip the fish, preheat a large skillet over high heat. Add 1 tablespoon of the butter. When the butter has melted completely, add the lemon slices from the remaining lemon, and cook until the lemons have browned on the underneath side, 2 to 3 minutes. Turn the lemon slices, then add the remaining 4 tablespoons of butter and the chopped fresh dill. Swirl the pan to melt the butter.

4. Transfer the cooked fish to a serving platter, and pour the lemon-dill butter over the fish, lemons and all. Serve immediately.

THE ART OF EATING AN OYSTER

Jon Rowley, an internationally recognized oyster expert and enthusiast, is perhaps Washington's most famous fish lover. His instructions on how to eat an oyster, which follow, have endured for more than 25 years.

THE OYSTER, perhaps more than any other food, is a feast for the senses. Served icy cold on a platter of shaved ice with the oysters glistening in their juices, they need no garnish to attract the eyes and imagination.

To eat an oyster: Forego the fork. Engage the oyster; your fingers have taste buds. If you have been through many oyster seasons, your salivary glands perk up in anticipation when you pick up the cold, damp, rough shell.

As you lift the oyster to your mouth, pause momentarily to breathe in the fresh, clean smell of the sea. Tilt your head back, close your eyes, and slurp in the oyster and its juices. If iced down before serving and if minutes or less off the shucking knife, the oyster is cold and vibrant as an icy gust of wind off the bay on a low winter's tide. Experience the sensation that M. F. K. Fisher, the doyenne of oyster poets, referred to adoringly as the oyster's "strange cold succulence" and what Washington novelist Tom Robbins likens to "French-kissing a mermaid."

Chew the oyster carefully, as your palate is inundated with a variety of distinct successive tastes. First is the sweet taste, which dissipates quickly; then, depending on the growing waters, a unique lineup of flavors — brine, mineral, algal, and various other mollusk flavors on the tip, sides, and finally on the back of your tongue and soft palate. A truly great oyster is characterized by its distinct aftertaste.

Wash down the oyster and invigorate the palate with a brisk, dry, clean-finishing white wine or a malty porter or stout. Take a bite of crusty light rye bread, like the French *pain de seigle*, to neutralize the taste buds, then move on to the next oyster. And the next. And the next.

Raise an oyster to toast a great oyster moment.

10
ENDINGS

Recipe from LINDA YAKUSH, PANE D'AMORE

Baby Orange-Almond Cakes

One fine summer morning, I came home from the farmers' market to find a small paper bag on my front porch. Inside was a note from a friend-to-be, a reader of my blog, named Sarah, who felt that it was her responsibility to introduce me, a Seattleite, to Pane d'Amore, the best bakery in Port Townsend. Truth be told, when I bit into one of these little orange-almond cakes, I might have tried to convince you it's the best bakery in the world, but you know what they say about love being blind. What's true: these little cakes are easy to make, gluten-free by happenstance, and almost painfully adorable.

CANDIED ORANGE PEEL
1 medium orange
½ cup water
⅓ cup granulated sugar

ORANGE-ALMOND CAKES
Cooking spray
4 eggs
1 cup plus 2 tablespoons granulated sugar
2 cups blanched almond meal
1 teaspoon baking powder
2 tablespoons water
¾ cup sliced almonds
1 tablespoon confectioners' sugar, for dusting

NOTE: Blanched almond meal has a texture like flour and a creamy color. It can be tricky to measure depending on how much it's settled, so if you have a kitchen scale, measure out 225 grams (half a 450-gram package) for this recipe. I like the product from Bob's Red Mill.

You can also make one 8-inch square cake — it may need a few minutes longer to bake.

4 (5¾- BY 3¼-INCH) LOAVES

1. **Make the candied orange peel:** Peel all the zest off the orange in thick strips with a good vegetable peeler. (It's okay if there's still some white pith attached.) Combine the zest, water, and sugar in a small saucepan and bring to a boil over high heat. Reduce heat and cook the orange peels at a strong simmer until soft and curling, about 45 minutes. Transfer the peels to a cooling rack set over a plate with a slotted spoon and let cool at least 1 hour.

2. **Make the cakes:** Preheat the oven to 350°F. Spray four 5¾- by 3¼-inch loaf pans with the cooking spray and set aside.

3. Combine the eggs, granulated sugar, almond meal, baking powder, and water in a food processor. Add the orange peel and process until the mixture is completely blended and there are no longer large chunks of orange peel, about 1 minute.

4. Divide the batter among the prepared pans. Sprinkle with the sliced almonds, and bake for 30 to 35 minutes, or until puffed and golden. (The edges should just be starting to pull away from the pans.)

5. Run a small knife around the edges of the pans immediately, then let the cakes cool in the pans. When cool, remove the cakes from the pans (unless you're giving the pans themselves as part of a gift; disposable cake pans are great for this recipe) and dust them with the confectioners' sugar.

Recipe from LIZ LaMONTE, NORTHWEST WILD FOODS

Northwest Wild Foods' Blackberry Bars

Northwest Wild Foods does what we all wish we had time to do each summer; they comb the slopes of the Olympic Mountains for berries — tiny blackberries, red and blue huckleberries, wild mountain blueberries — and pack them away for a years' worth of enjoyment in jams that are only lightly sweetened to let the real flavors shine through. Liz LaMonte's husband called her mother for this recipe, which puts the company's blackberry jam front and center, but confused sticks of butter with cups. Liz knew the dough was extra buttery the second she started the mixer, but the family decided this version was actually better.

1½ cups (3 sticks) unsalted butter, softened

1 cup packed light brown sugar

1½ cups unbleached all-purpose flour

1½ cups quick-cooking oats

½ teaspoon salt

1 (8-ounce) jar blackberry jam

2 DOZEN (2-INCH) BARS

1. Cream the butter and brown sugar together on medium speed for 1 minute in a stand mixer fitted with the paddle attachment. Scrape down the sides of the bowl and the paddle; then add the flour, oats, and salt, and mix on low speed until well blended, scraping the sides of the bowl down as necessary.

2. Transfer about ¾ cup of the mixture to a small bowl, cover, and refrigerate. Dump the remaining mixture into a 9- by 13-inch baking pan, and pat or spread it into an even layer, roughly ½ inch thick. (An offset spatula works best for this, because the dough is quite soft, but hands will do.) Refrigerate the pan and the extra dough for about 1½ hours, or until firm enough to crumble instead of smearing when you handle it.

3. Preheat the oven to 400°F. Spread the jam in a thin layer over the chilled crust, then scatter small crumbles of the leftover dough evenly over the jam. Bake for 25 minutes, or until the jam is bubbling and the topping is golden brown. Let cool completely in the pan, then cut into squares and serve. The cooled bars can be stored in a sealed container for up to 3 days.

Anjou's Lemon Cream Shortbread Bars

Nestled among the Wenatchee Valley's fruit orchards between Leavenworth and Wenatchee, Anjou is known for serving great coffee, and for making homemade breads and pastries done with a twist on classic French technique. Their cinnamon rolls, for example, are made from perfectly flaky croissant dough. Their lemon bars are made with an immodest amount of butter — and once you've tasted them, any other kind just won't do the trick.

These bars — really a smooth, tart, lemon cream sandwiched between thick shortbread cookie-crust layers — are part of what gives Anjou its delicious reputation.

Although they can be made in one day, it's best to count on a full night to refrigerate the completed bars; they're easier to cut when completely chilled.

LEMON CREAM

1 cup granulated sugar

Zest of 2 large lemons, grated

4 eggs, at room temperature, beaten

¾ cup lemon juice (from 4 large lemons)

1¼ cups (2½ sticks) unsalted butter, diced and softened

SHORTBREAD CRUST

1 pound (4 sticks) cold unsalted butter, cubed

½ teaspoon kosher salt

1 cup granulated sugar

4½ cups unbleached all-purpose flour

Confectioners' sugar, for dusting

16 SQUARES

1. **Make the lemon cream:** Blend the granulated sugar and lemon zest together with your fingertips in the work bowl of a double boiler (or in a heat-resistant bowl that fits over a saucepan filled with 1 inch of simmering water without touching the water), until the mixture looks like damp sand. Whisk in the eggs until the mixture is a bit thicker than when it started, about 1 minute, then whisk in the lemon juice.

2. Place the bowl over simmering water and cook, whisking continuously to keep the eggs from scrambling, until the cream thickens and reaches 180°F on an instant-read thermometer. As you cook the cream, adjusting the temperature as necessary to keep the water at a bare simmer, notice that at first the cream is light and foamy. The bubbles will get larger, and finally, as the cream starts to thicken, you'll notice the whisk will begin leaving tracks in the lemon cream. (The tracks mean it's almost ready.) When the cream is ready (it may take up to 10 minutes), transfer it to a stand mixer fitted with the whisk attachment or a bowl large enough to use with an immersion (stick) blender. Let the cream cool to 140°F, about 15 minutes, while you make the crust.

3. Preheat the oven to 350°F.

4. **Make the crust:** Cream the butter and salt on low speed in a stand mixer fitted with the paddle attachment, until softened, 2 to 3 minutes. Add the granulated sugar, increase speed to medium, and mix until the mixture is light and fluffy, 3 to 4 minutes, scraping down the sides of the bowl as needed. With the mixer on low, add the flour in three separate additions, turning the mixer off between each addition, then mixing just until no white parts remain.

5. Scoop about one-third of the dough out onto a clean work surface, gather it into a ball, and press it into a disc. Wrap the disc in plastic wrap and chill until firm, about 1 hour.

6. Dump the remaining dough into an 8-inch square baking pan and use your hands to pat it into an even layer. Bake the crust for about 20 minutes, or until the edges are lightly browned. Remove and cool to room temperature, or until the rest of the dough is firm enough to grate.

7. Beat the lemon cream with the stand mixer or an immersion blender on medium speed while adding the butter, a few pieces at a time. When all the butter has been incorporated, continue beating the cream until pale and thick, 3 to 4 minutes longer.

8. Transfer the lemon cream to a large, shallow container, cover the surface directly with plastic wrap, and let chill until the crust is finished baking and the chilled dough is firm.

9. Pour the chilled lemon cream over the baked crust, spreading it into a smooth, even layer, then use the large holes on a box grater to grate the chilled dough directly over the lemon cream in a roughly even layer. (The dough will come almost to the top of the pan, but there's no need to pat it down.) Bake for 30 to 35 minutes, or until the shortbread topping is firm and just barely beginning to brown. (The lemon cream will remain soft under the top crust.)

10. Let the bars cool to room temperature, chill for 4 hours (or preferably overnight), dust liberally with confectioners' sugar, then cut and serve.

LEARNING THE ART OF THE PIE

SOMEONE ONCE DESCRIBED Kate McDermott to me as the MacGyver of pie — with the right tools, she can fiddle with any crust until it's perfectly flaky. Maybe it's an innate gift. (We can't all be born pie heroes, can we?) Maybe there are secrets she'll never tell. Or maybe she's just made so many thousands of pies that she's found a crust that works perfectly, every single time. Lucky for us, she loves to teach. I signed up for a class.

McDermott has kind eyes, a quick smile, and soft hands (one benefit of years of working with butter). At Art of the Pie, the series of pie-making classes McDermott first offered in Seattle and now teaches around the world, she teaches that pie is primarily about three things: love, music, and intuition. But first and foremost, the pie is about the crust.

Kate McDermott

McDermott only has one rule in her pie-making classes, and that's to keep all the ingredients well chilled at all times. She starts her crusts by taking her mixing bowl and her flour out of the freezer, and then quickly blends them with a mixture of pure Irish butter and leaf lard, the smooth, clean fat rendered from around a pig's kidneys. She uses the leaf lard regardless of the type of pie she's making; it doesn't have much of a scent, but it insinuates itself between layers of moist flour in just the right way, resulting in a flaky, shattery crust that beats any combination of butter, margarine, and shortening. She likes to say that the hardest part of the class is getting the lid off the plastic tub of lard; while she gives measurements to students, her own are made in teacups and handfuls and soup spoons. For a baker, this woman is awfully laid-back. There are no furrowed brows; the soundtrack to *The Big Chill* blares.

Once the crust is divided into two parts, wrapped neatly or not so neatly, and retired to the refrigerator to rest, McDermott starts in on the fruit. She talks about fruit the way most of us talk about the weather; deciding what goes into any given pie is more a matter of fate and happenstance than of personal decision. Fruit that's growing together is happy together, she says, and each time she teaches, she buys whatever looks best and makes pie that fits the fruit, depending on how tart or sweet it is. She squeezes and tastes first, always before reaching for a knife, then she piles the fruit up whole into the day's pie plate, making a mound,

rounded but not mountainous, that looks like it'll settle down into a nice pie shape that's not too drippy.

Here's where the love comes in. Each time McDermott rolls out a crust, she dedicates it to someone, or something. Whether it's an apple pie for happiness or a blackberry pie for a late friend, each disc of dough carries with it an intention. McDermott insists that no pie is complete without a little love, and after rolling mine out with thoughts of my uncle's battle with cancer, I'm convinced that perhaps a tear or two makes every pie better.

Once the crust is properly chilled, filled, fluted, and glazed with egg wash, and then always chilled again, a pie can go into the oven. She waits for the scent of freshly baked pie to waft through her kitchen — a sign that the pie's about 80 percent there, she says — and for the crust to get a nice golden hue. Then, McDermott listens to her intuition. More precisely, she listens to the pies.

She wants to hear the crust sizzle, and she wants to hear the filling *whump*. Toward the end of the baking time, she slides the rack out of the oven, to listen to the sound a pie's liquid makes as it cooks. When the rhythm changes from soft, rapid ripples to larger, bass-toned bubblings, or *whumps*, the filling is cooked, and the pie's ready to come out. She calls it the secret of the sizzle-whump.

Fortunately, McDermott's terrible at keeping actual secrets. Over the course of a class, she promises to share her tips on everything pie — how to prevent air pockets in apple pie, how to flute a lattice-top crust, how to cool a pie (on the kind of jar racks used for canning), and how long to wait before serving them (overnight, if possible, so the filling has a chance to set). And at the end, over a slice of the pie she's prepared for us ahead of time and a glass of champagne, she spills it all, with that smile and a big enough dose of palpable encouragement to send me straight back to the kitchen when I get home.

Recipe from KATE McDERMOTT, ART OF THE PIE

Free-Form Pear Crostata

Made with the crust that pie expert Kate McDermott has made famous in Seattle and food magazines nationwide, this simple, rustic tart uses butter as well as leaf lard, and also works with any stone fruit — just use one to two tablespoons more flour if the fruit is super juicy.

Look for leaf lard at farmers' markets; although it doesn't taste meaty, it's made from the fat that surrounds a pig's kidneys and is often sold by pork producers.

1 recipe Kate's Pie Dough (recipe follows)

2 medium firm-ripe red-skinned pears, unpeeled, cored, and sliced lengthwise into ¾-inch-thick wedges

3 tablespoons light brown sugar

1 tablespoon unbleached all-purpose flour

½ teaspoon ground cinnamon

⅛ teaspoon kosher salt

1 egg white whisked with 1 tablespoon water (for the egg wash)

2 tablespoons granulated sugar (for sprinkling crust, optional)

1 tablespoon unsalted butter, cut into small pieces

1 tablespoon honey mixed with 1 teaspoon boiling water (optional)

1 (8-INCH) TART

1. Make the pie dough and let chill for at least 1 hour. While it chills, mix the pears, brown sugar, flour, cinnamon, and salt together in a medium bowl.

2. Line a baking sheet with parchment paper or a silicone baking mat.

3. Place the chilled dough on a well-floured board and sprinkle additional flour on top. Thump the disk with a floured rolling pin several times. Roll the crust out in all directions, working from the center outward, until it's about 10 inches in diameter (a little more or less won't hurt). Use a small, sharp knife to trim about ¼ inch off around the edges, if desired. (This isn't necessary, but it will allow you to show off the gorgeous layers in your crust.)

4. Gently transfer the crust to the prepared baking sheet and dump the fruit filling (emphasis on dump, this is not an exact process) onto the center, leaving a roughly 2-inch border around the edges. Working with slightly wet hands to encourage the dough to stick together, fold the dough up and around the fruit, overlapping it and pinching it together where necessary — it's more important to work quickly than to work precisely. Transfer the baking sheet and the tart to the refrigerator and chill until the crust is firm again, about 1 hour.

5. Preheat the oven to 425°F. Brush the crust with the egg wash, sprinkle it with granulated sugar, if desired, then dot the pears with the butter. Bake the tart for 20 minutes, then reduce

the oven temperature to 375°F and continue baking for 40 to 45 minutes longer, or until the crust is golden brown and the filling is thick and makes soft popping noises. As soon as the tart comes out of the oven, brush it with the honey mixture, if desired. Allow the tart to cool completely on the baking sheet, then carefully transfer it to a serving plate and slice.

Kate's Pie Dough

- 1¼ cups unbleached all-purpose flour (King Arthur's unbleached white flour is recommended), plus more for rolling
- 4 tablespoons leaf lard, cut into various small pieces, pea to walnut size
- 4 tablespoons salted or unsalted Irish butter, cut into various small pieces, pea to walnut size
- ¼ teaspoon kosher salt
- 3–5 tablespoons ice water

NOTE: McDermott always chills all ingredients and implements, right down to the flour and the mixing bowl used, before starting her crusts.

1 (9-INCH) PIECRUST, UNBAKED

1. Stir the flour, lard, butter, and salt together in a very large cold mixing bowl to coat the fats with the flour. Blend the mixture together with clean hands until it looks like coarse meal with some lumps in it. (The lumps make flaky pies.)

2. Sprinkle about 1½ tablespoons of ice water over the mixture and stir lightly and quickly with a fork. Add another tablespoon of the water, mix, then add another tablespoon and mix again. Squeeze a handful of the dough together; you're looking for dough that clumps together. If it doesn't stay together, continue adding water in ½ tablespoon increments until the dough adheres to itself.

3. Transfer the dough to a piece of waxed paper or plastic wrap (you can leave any excess flour in the bottom of the bowl) and pat it into a chubby disk about 4 inches in diameter. Chill the dough for at least 1 hour or up to 3 days before baking as desired.

Puyallup Fair Rosy Peach Pie

Since its inception in 1900, the Puyallup Fair has held various cooking and baking contests; in 2011, the "culinary arts" had 41 divisions, including quick breads, confections, and, of course, pies. Kimberly Arnold can't remember exactly when she began entering the baking contests at the fair — maybe the mid-'90s, when her oldest kids started doing 4-H. In the years since, she's entered almost every category, including cloverleaf dinner rolls, scones, cakes, fudge, and biscotti. In 2011, she won the fair's peach pie–baking contest with this recipe, which snuggles peaches and raspberries under a pecan-flecked crumb topping.

1 (9-INCH) PIE

PIE CRUST

- 1½ cups unbleached all-purpose flour, plus more for rolling
- 1½ teaspoons granulated sugar
- ½ teaspoon salt
- 4 tablespoons cold unsalted butter, cut into 8 pieces
- ¼ cup cold shortening
- ¼ cup plus 1–2 tablespoons ice water

PEACH-RASPBERRY FILLING

- ½ cup granulated sugar
- ¼ cup cornstarch
- ¼ teaspoon ground nutmeg
- ¼ teaspoon ground cinnamon
- 4 cups peeled, sliced ripe peaches (about 2 pounds, or 4 large peaches)
- 2 cups frozen raspberries, defrosted
- Juice of 1 small lemon (about 2 tablespoons)

1. **Make the crust:** Blend the flour, granulated sugar, and salt with a whisk in a mixing bowl. Add the butter and shortening, and using a pastry cutter or your fingertips, blend the ingredients until the butter is the size of small peas. Add the ¼ cup of water a little at a time, using a large fork to stir the ingredients together as you add it. Add the additional 1 to 2 tablespoons of water as needed, stirring until very little loose flour remains on the bottom of the bowl and the dough clumps together when you squeeze it between your fingertips. Gently pack the dough into a flat disc, wrap it in plastic wrap, and refrigerate it for at least 30 minutes or overnight.

2. **Make the filling:** Combine the granulated sugar, cornstarch, nutmeg, and cinnamon in a large bowl. Add the peaches, 1 cup of the raspberries, and lemon juice, and stir to blend. Mash the remaining cup of raspberries in a separate bowl, then strain the juice into the fruit mixture, discarding the pulp. Stir the juice into the rest of the fruit, and set the filling aside.

3. **Make the topping:** Pulse the flour, pecans, butter, brown sugar, and salt in a food processor until well blended and uniform, about twenty 1-second pulses.

4. Preheat the oven to 400°F.

TOPPING

- ¾ cup unbleached all-purpose flour
- ¾ cup toasted pecans
- 6 tablespoons cold unsalted butter, cut into 6 pieces
- ½ cup firmly packed light brown sugar
- ¼ teaspoon kosher salt

5. When the crust has chilled, roll it out to a roughly 10-inch circle on a lightly floured work surface with a floured rolling pin, and place it in a pie plate, crimping the edges with your fingers or a fork. Stir and add the filling, place the pie pan on a baking sheet (to catch any drips), and bake for 30 minutes, or until the crust is just barely beginning to brown. Scatter the topping over all of the fruit, spreading it all the way to the edges of the pie. Decrease the oven temperature to 375°F and bake 30 to 35 minutes longer, or until the topping is browned and the filling is bubbling. Let cool for 1 to 2 hours before serving.

Summer Cherry Goat's Milk Frozen Yogurt

In the span of a few short years, Molly Moon's Homemade Ice Cream blossomed from a one-woman show (yes, her real name is Molly Moon) to a Seattle institution. Some of her flavors, like Vivace coffee and Theo chocolate, capitalize on Seattle-made ingredients and are available year-round. Others, like this sweet mixture of just-off-the-tree cherries and fresh goat's milk yogurt, are only available seasonally. Be sure to cool the compote completely before adding it to the frozen yogurt — otherwise you'll end up with yogurt soup.

ABOUT 1 QUART

CHERRY COMPOTE

- 1 pound fresh cherries, pitted
- ¾ cup sugar
- Juice of 1 small lemon (about 2 tablespoons)

FROZEN YOGURT BASE

- 2½ cups goat's milk yogurt
- ½ cup sugar
- ½ cup honey
- 1 tablespoon vanilla extract

NOTE: This recipe doesn't take much work, but it's best to start the night before you plan to serve it. I make the compote and yogurt base at night, then whirl it in the ice cream maker the next morning and serve it later that day.

1. **Make the compote:** The night before you plan to serve the frozen yogurt, combine the cherries, sugar, and lemon juice in a small nonreactive saucepan. Bring the mixture to a simmer over high heat, then adjust the heat and cook at a strong simmer, stirring occasionally, until the liquid has thickened considerably, about 20 minutes. Transfer the compote to a shallow bowl and refrigerate until completely chilled, 2 to 3 hours, or overnight.

2. **Make the frozen yogurt base:** Combine the yogurt, sugar, honey, and vanilla in a large bowl, whisking until the sugar and honey are completely dissolved. Cover and refrigerate until completely chilled, at least 1 hour, or overnight.

3. Pour the yogurt base into an ice cream maker and freeze according to the manufacturer's instructions. Spoon about one-quarter of the frozen yogurt into a freezer-safe container, then scoop about one-third of the cherry compote over the yogurt, spreading it out in an even layer. Repeat with the remaining ingredients, layering the yogurt and compote and ending with yogurt. Cover tightly and freeze until firm, at least 4 hours, then serve.

Two-Pound Espresso Brownies

If there's one Washington brand that rings across the globe, it's Starbucks, the coffee company with more than 17,000 stores in more than 50 countries around the world. The company popularized the concept of espresso drinks in America, and in Seattle, where it was founded, coffee-drinking culture still defines the city's personality. It's a mistake, though, to ignore the rest of the state's roasting and brewing scene. Take Batdorf & Bronson coffee roasters, in the state capital, Olympia: from their single-origin beans to their espresso blends, they take coffee seriously, and they do it well. Stop in at their tasting room to learn the difference between beans from the best growing regions of Latin America, Indonesia, and Africa. And should you have a bit of coffee left over, grind it up, and use it in these dark, sweet treats, which depend on a pound each of butter and chocolate and a hefty helping of ground espresso beans for their rich flavor.

There's nothing like a hot brownie, but the texture of these actually improves and goes from cakey to chewy when you refrigerate them overnight.

1 pound (4 sticks) unsalted butter, plus more for buttering the pan

1 pound (16 ounces) bittersweet chocolate

¼ cup lightly packed, very finely ground espresso beans

1 cup granulated sugar

1 cup packed dark brown sugar

6 eggs

1 tablespoon vanilla extract

½ teaspoon salt

1¾ cups bread flour

2 DOZEN BROWNIES

1. Preheat the oven to 350°F. Butter a 9- by 13-inch baking pan and set aside.

2. Chop the chocolate into small pieces with a large serrated knife and transfer it to a heatproof mixing bowl. Melt the butter in a small saucepan over medium heat until bubbly. Remove the pan from the heat and let rest for 2 minutes, then pour the butter over the chocolate and whisk until completely smooth. Add the ground espresso beans, and whisk again until smooth.

3. Meanwhile, beat the granulated sugar, brown sugar, and eggs together for 1 minute on medium speed in a stand mixer fitted with the paddle attachment. Scrape down the sides of the bowl, add the vanilla and salt, and beat again to combine. Add the melted chocolate-butter mixture on low speed in a slow, steady stream, mixing until the batter is uniform in color.

4. Remove the bowl from the mixer, sift the flour on top of the batter, and fold the flour in by hand until no white streaks remain. Pour the batter into the pan.

5. Bake the brownies for 40 to 50 minutes, or until puffed and just cracking and a toothpick inserted into the center comes out with a few moist crumbs attached. Cool to room temperature, cover loosely with foil, and refrigerate overnight. Store the brownies in an airtight container, for up to 3 days.

THEO CHOCOLATE: GOING FROM BEAN TO BAR

SEATTLE'S THEO CHOCOLATE bills itself as the only "organic, fair trade, bean-to-bar chocolate factory in the United States." Like the chocolate they sell at their factory and at stores nationwide, that moniker can be a mouthful, which is why some focus on simpler facts: Chocolate grows on trees very far away. Theo buys cacao beans — grown in football-shaped pods — only from the best growers, brings them to Seattle, and forms them into the chocolate bars stamped by a company named for cacao's Latin designation, *Theobroma cacao*.

The process of making chocolate begins in the fields. First, pods are removed from the trees individually, by hand, at their optimum ripeness. Workers scoop raw cacao beans out of the pods, then ferment them for up to 9 days to develop their flavor. Next, the beans are laid out on mats to dry under the sun for about 7 days, during which they shrink in size by about half. The dried beans are then delivered to chocolate factories like Theo, where the process of going from bean to bar continues.

When the beans arrive at the Seattle factory, they're sorted, then roasted in large rotating ovens at 210°F to 290°F, for about 2 hours. The outer shells are removed, which leaves the nib, the hard center that eventually becomes actual chocolate. (At this point, in the absence of sugar, the chocolate still tastes bitter, but the nibs can be used in recipes, imparting a flavor all their own — see Cocoa Nib Cookies, page 222). These nibs are crushed and ground into a paste that is then sweetened with sugar, cocoa butter, vanilla, and sometimes milk.

By now, the chocolate has the right basic flavor, but not its signature silky texture, so it's sent to a conching machine. Here, the chocolate mixture is mixed and mashed between large steel rollers, a process that can take up to 6 days. As a result of conching, the chocolate develops a much smoother and mellower flavor.

Before being packaged, the chocolate is tempered and poured into molds for bars — and that's when we get to swoon.

221

Cocoa Nib Cookies

If you're looking for a great loaf of bread, drive an hour or so north of Seattle, toward Bellingham, and hang a left a few miles after Burlington. Go until you almost reach the water, to the little artists' enclave of Edison, where the number of bakeries per capita must exceed that of even the most well-fed French towns. The shining glory of Edison's main street is Breadfarm, whose hand-formed loaves rely on locally grown grains and produce for their flavor. Go with a picnic in mind, and make sure you browse the collection of cookies, where flavors like chocolate-ginger and cocoa nib put your old chocolate chip recipe to shame.

For this cookie recipe, Breadfarm uses cocoa nibs, which are unsweetened, crushed cocoa beans, from Seattle's Theo Chocolate (see Recipe Contributors and Suppliers, page 274).

1⅓ cups plus 1 tablespoon unbleached all-purpose flour

⅔ cup cocoa powder

¼ teaspoon ground cinnamon

½ teaspoon kosher salt

1 cup (2 sticks) unsalted butter, softened

½ cup granulated sugar

1 tablespoon chilled brewed coffee

⅓ cup cocoa nibs

2 egg whites, whisked to blend, for washing dough

¼ cup demerara or turbinado sugar, for topping

2 DOZEN (2-INCH) COOKIES

1. Sift the flour, cocoa powder, cinnamon, and salt into a medium bowl, whisk to combine, and set aside.

2. Beat the butter and granulated sugar on high speed in a stand mixer fitted with the paddle attachment (or using an electric mixer) until pale and fluffy, about 5 minutes. Add the coffee and mix on low speed to combine. Add the flour mixture in three additions on low speed, mixing between each addition just until the dry ingredients are incorporated and scraping down the sides of the bowl when necessary. Fold in the cocoa nibs gently by hand.

3. Divide the dough into two equal parts, and place each on a roughly 15-inch square piece of waxed paper. Roll each piece of dough into a log roughly 1½ inches in diameter and 6 inches long. Wrap the logs in the waxed paper (plastic wrap also works) and chill until firm, at least 3 hours or overnight. (The dough can be made up to this point and refrigerated up to 2 weeks before baking.)

4. Preheat the oven to 350°F. Line two baking sheets with parchment paper or silicone baking mats and set aside.

5. Remove the logs from the refrigerator, brush them both on all sides with the egg white, and sprinkle the outsides with about 3 tablespoons of demerara sugar. Slice the logs into ½-inch rounds, and arrange the cookies about 1 inch apart on the baking sheets. (The cookies won't spread much.) Sprinkle the tops of the cookies with the remaining demerara sugar (you don't need to use the egg wash here), and bake for 15 to 20 minutes, rotating the baking sheets halfway through, until the cookies are firm to the touch.

6. Let the cookies cool completely on the baking sheets (really, wait!) before serving. Store the cookies at room temperature in an airtight container up to 1 week.

PAIRING WINE AND CHOCOLATE

At Petits Noirs, the chocolatier nestled into the old purple house in Walla Walla wine country, co-owner James Boulanger says there's no such thing as a bad pairing. "There are no rules," he says. "There's just what you like." That said, he certainly has his favorites. He loves how salt on chocolate tames the tannins in some wines and extends the finish in most, and how the fresh fruit in his fig truffles lets the sanguine, meaty flavor of a local cabernet settle a bit. Is it a risk to pick up a chocolate bar with your bottle of wine for dessert? Sure, he says. But if you can find components in a chocolate that enhance or contrast with the wine in an interesting way, you've picked the right bar. ★

Dark Chocolate Cake
with Figs, Fennel, and Pistachios

Ask any wine lover what they like to pair with chocolate and odds are good they'll wrinkle their nose; in many places, there's an unwritten taboo against combining cacao in any form with anything but a sweet wine. But some, like James Boulanger and Lan Wong, the chocolatiers behind Walla Walla's Petits Noirs, believe rules are meant to be broken. Inspired by one of their chocolate *boutons* accented with dried Calimyrna fig, toasted pistachio, and fennel seeds, this deeply chocolaty, elegant cake is the confection to have around if you expect the wine to flow long after dinner ends.

CAKE

- ½ cup (1 stick) unsalted butter, cut into 16 pieces, plus extra for greasing the pan
- 6 ounces chopped bittersweet chocolate (65–75 percent cacao)
- 1 teaspoon vanilla extract
- ¼ teaspoon salt
- 3 eggs, at room temperature
- ¾ cup sugar
- ¼ cup unbleached all-purpose flour
- 6 dried Calimyrna figs, stems removed and finely chopped

TOPPING

- 4 ounces chopped bittersweet chocolate (65–75 percent cacao)
- ⅓ cup plus 1 tablespoon heavy cream
- ½ cup toasted pistachios, finely chopped
- 2 teaspoons toasted fennel seeds, finely chopped
- Large-flake sea salt, for sprinkling

NOTE: If you have a double boiler, use it to melt the chocolate.

🍥 *Pair with Ellanelle Wine Company's 2008 cabernet sauvignon.*

8–10 SERVINGS

1. **Make the cake:** Preheat the oven to 375°F. Butter an 8-inch round cake pan. Line the bottom of the pan with a round of waxed paper or parchment paper, and butter the paper.

2. Melt the butter and the chocolate in a small saucepan over very low heat, stirring constantly. When the mixture is almost smooth, stir in the vanilla and salt and set aside.

3. Beat the eggs and sugar on medium speed in a stand mixer fitted with the paddle attachment until thick, about 3 minutes. Blend in the chocolate mixture. Add the flour, mixing in brief pulses, just until no white spots remain. Gently fold in the figs by hand. Pour the batter into the prepared pan and smooth out the top with a spatula.

4. Bake the cake for 25 to 35 minutes, or until a toothpick inserted into the center comes out clean. Let cool for about 5 minutes. Invert the cake onto a serving plate, remove the paper, and let cool for about 10 minutes.

5. **Make the topping:** While the cake cools, combine the chocolate and the cream in a small saucepan, and stir constantly over very low heat until melted and smooth. Spread the ganache over the top of the cake with a flat spatula or knife, letting it drip down the sides a bit, if desired. Sprinkle the pistachios, fennel, and salt to taste over the warm ganache, and let cool for at least 10 minutes to let the frosting set up. To store the cake, let it cool completely, then cover and keep at room temperature for up to 3 days.

Honeyed Panna Cottas

Sweetened with honey and stabilized with a wisp of gelatin, this elegant dessert comes together in under 15 minutes. If you like, serve it with plenty of chopped fresh fruit and a drizzle of honey or with macerated strawberries (page 250) or Homemade Bourbon Butterscotch Sauce (page 261).

Corky Luster, the beekeeper and honey expert behind Ballard Bee Company, recommends using an amber or dark honey for this recipe — something with good cinnamon and molasses notes, if possible.

¼ cup cold water

2 teaspoons unflavored gelatin (from 1 envelope)

2 cups heavy cream

1 cup whole milk

½ cup high-quality honey

Seeds from ½ vanilla bean, split

SPECIAL EQUIPMENT: 6 small ramekins, custard cups, or wine glasses

6 SERVINGS

1. Pour the water into a small heatproof bowl, and sprinkle the gelatin on top. Let the mixture stand until the gelatin thickens, so it looks like pale applesauce. Bring about an inch of water to a simmer in a shallow saucepan over medium heat, and place the bowl containing the gelatin into the water. Stir until the gelatin dissolves and the liquid becomes clear, then remove the bowl from the simmering water and set aside.

2. Combine the cream, milk, honey, and vanilla bean seeds in a small saucepan and cook over medium-high heat, stirring occasionally, just until the cream bubbles around the edges. Stir in the gelatin mixture, then pour the mixture into six 8-ounce ramekins, custard cups, or wine glasses.

3. Cover the panna cottas with plastic wrap and chill until firm, preferably overnight. Serve chilled or at room temperature.

Top Pot Doughnut Bread Pudding

Seattle's Top Pot Doughnuts is known for its eccentric signage, excellent coffee, creative doughnut names, and of course for its doughnuts. Satisfy your craving with a stop at any of its Seattle locations; when you're done with Double Troubles and Pink Feather Boas and Valley Girl Lemons, bring home some simple glazed raised rings and make bread pudding. Because some of bread pudding's typical ingredients are already found in the doughnuts, this dessert is quick to make.

Of course, if you do want to make Top Pot's actual doughnuts, their cookbook, *Top Pot Hand-Forged Doughnuts: Secrets and Recipes for the Home Baker*, is the best place to start; this recipe is from that book, which I wrote in conjunction with Top Pot's owners, Mark and Michael Klebeck.

BREAD PUDDING

Butter, for the pan

6 cups (1-inch) cubes leftover raised doughnuts (about 4 whole)

4 eggs

2 tablespoons dark rum, or ½ teaspoon rum extract

½ teaspoon ground cinnamon

¼ cup granulated sugar

1 teaspoon vanilla extract

1 cup whole milk

¾ cup heavy cream

ICING

1 cup confectioners' sugar, sifted

1 teaspoon vanilla extract

1½ tablespoons hot water

6 SERVINGS

1. **Make the bread pudding:** Preheat the oven to 350°F. Grease a 9- by 5-inch loaf pan with the butter, and fill with the cubed leftover doughnuts. Set aside.

2. Whisk the eggs, rum, cinnamon, granulated sugar, and vanilla together in a mixing bowl until well blended. Add the milk and cream, whisk to blend, and pour over the doughnuts, turning the top pieces so that all of the doughnuts are soaked in the wet mixture.

3. Bake for 45 to 50 minutes, or until browned on top and firm in the center. Let cool for 10 minutes in the pan.

4. **Make the icing:** While the pudding cools, whisk the confectioner's sugar, vanilla, and hot water until smooth.

5. Serve the pudding still warm, drizzled with the icing.

HOW TOP POT DOUGHNUTS GOT ITS NAME

The way Mark and Michael Klebeck tell it, there were a lot of accidents involved in opening Seattle's Top Pot Doughnuts, the city's go-to spot for fried and frosted treats. They'd salvaged a sign that read "TOPSPOT" from a defunct Chinese restaurant and planned to use their sign for their Capitol Hill bakery and coffee shop — until, driving with the sign on the highway one day, the "S" fell off, leaving the brothers with "Top Pot." Rather than fixing the sign, they replaced the letter with a coffee pot, and Top Pot Doughnuts was born. My favorite? King's Rings, the maple-glazed raised doughnuts Top Pot loads with chunks of bacon and sells every January, for Elvis's birthday. ★

Rosemary Apple Crisp

Washington State harvests about 10 *billion* apples each year. Many of them are the varieties you've heard of — Red Delicious, Granny Smith, Fuji, and Gala. But increasingly, small Washington growers' penchant for heirloom varieties is being translated to farmers' market tables. Today, apples with names like Gravenstein, Cox's Orange Pippin, Bramley's Seedling, and Spitzenberg are making their way into pies and crisps at home. This rosemary-scented version of a traditional apple crisp is still clearly on the sweet side; talk to your apple producer and ask for a tart, flavorful apple that holds up well when baked, such as one of the above heirloom varieties. If the grocery store is your only option, choose a mix of Pink Lady, Honeycrisp, and Granny Smith.

6-8 SERVINGS

FILLING

- 2½ pounds tart apples (about 6 medium), peeled, cored, and chopped into ¾-inch pieces
- ¼ cup granulated sugar
- 1 tablespoon chopped fresh rosemary
- 1 tablespoon cornstarch
- Juice of 1 small lemon (about 2 tablespoons)

TOPPING

- 1¼ cup old-fashioned oats
- ¾ cup sliced almonds
- ½ cup firmly packed light brown sugar
- 2 teaspoons finely chopped fresh rosemary
- ¼ teaspoon kosher salt
- 5 tablespoons unsalted butter, melted

1. Preheat the oven to 350°F.

2. **Make the filling:** Stir together the apples, granulated sugar, rosemary, cornstarch, and lemon juice in a large bowl. Dump the mixture into an 8-inch square (or similar) baking pan and bake for 30 minutes.

3. **Make the topping:** Meanwhile, stir together the oats, almonds, brown sugar, rosemary, and salt in the same bowl. Drizzle the butter on top, and stir until the ingredients are evenly moist.

4. After the filling has baked for 30 minutes, scatter the topping over the apples and bake for 35 to 45 minutes longer, until well browned and bubbling at the edges. Let cool for 10 minutes, then serve warm.

Hot Cakes' Original S'mores Cookies
with Smoked Chocolate

After a stint at Seattle's Canlis restaurant and years as the renegade head chocolatier behind Theo Chocolate, when the Seattle company was first recognized for its delicately balanced (and sometimes outlandishly creative) flavors, Autumn Martin set out on her own with a company called Hot Cakes. She was most famous for her take-and-bake molten chocolate cakes, which she sold mainly at farmers' markets, until she opened Hot Cakes Molten Chocolate Cakery, where her reputation for fun new creations grew. Try these cookies, which rely on home-smoked chocolate chips for real fireside flavor.

According to Martin, her Girl Scout troop, #1492, was the one credited with the invention of the timeless ooey-gooey, sweet, sticky backyard dessert, the s'more. To memorialize it in a much more transportable cookie, she converts her backyard smoker into a cold-smoker, which keeps the chocolate in its solid form while still allowing it to absorb plenty of smoke flavor. The result? Chocolate taken to a whole new, delicious level. You can make the cookies without smoking the chocolate chips, of course, but I can't promise you'll have camping flashbacks if you don't.

2¼ cups pastry flour

1 cup whole-wheat flour

½ teaspoon baking soda

½ teaspoon baking powder

1 teaspoon salt

1 cup (2 sticks) unsalted butter, softened

1 cup firmly packed dark brown sugar

⅔ cup granulated sugar

2 eggs

8 ounces (1½ cups) Cold-Smoked Chocolate Chips (page 232)

1 cup mini marshmallows

ABOUT 18 LARGE COOKIES

1. Preheat the oven to 375°F. Line two baking sheets with parchment paper.

2. Whisk together the pastry flour, whole-wheat flour, baking soda, baking powder, and salt in a medium bowl.

3. Cream the butter, brown sugar, and granulated sugar on low speed in a stand mixer fitted with the paddle attachment (or using an electric mixer) until the mixture is a few shades lighter and appears fluffy, about 3 minutes. Scrape down the bowl and paddle to ensure all of the sugar and butter has been thoroughly creamed, and mix again.

4. Add the eggs, one at a time, mixing after each addition. Mix briefly on low speed until the batter looks uniformly smooth.

5. Add the dry ingredients in three stages, mixing on low speed after each addition just until no white remains, scraping the sides of the bowl down when necessary. Add the smoked chocolate chips, and stir by hand until they are evenly dispersed throughout the batter.

6. Scoop the batter onto the prepared sheets in pucks about 3 inches apart (roughly six per sheet) using a 2-ounce ice cream scoop or a ¼-cup measure. If using an ice cream scoop, pat the cookies down just a bit so they are flat on the top. Gently press about four mini marshmallows into the top of each cookie, spacing them evenly.

7. Bake the cookies for about 20 minutes, rotating the sheets halfway through, or until the edges are light golden brown and the marshmallows are toasted. (The centers will still be slightly gooey when they come out of the oven, which gives them a chewy texture. If you like your cookies a bit more crisp, leave them in the oven for a few minutes longer.)

8. Cool the cookies for at least 7 minutes before transferring them to the counter or a rack to continue cooling. Repeat with the remaining dough. Store cooled cookies at room temperature in an airtight container.

NOTE: Organic sugar has residual molasses in the crystal, making it darker in color and richer in flavor. The sugar Hot Cakes uses is almost black and is super-moist. Seek out the darkest brown sugar you can find and use an organic cane sugar, if you can — it gives the cookies more molasses flavor and a chewier texture.

If you're a fan of oatmeal cookies, stir 1½ cups old-fashioned oats into the dry ingredients as you make the cookies.

Hot Cakes' Original S'mores Cookies (continued)

DIY: Cold-Smoked Chocolate Chips

Done by trapping smoking wood chips in a box with chocolate chips, this nifty smoking process doesn't melt the chocolate — it just imbues it with rich, smoky flavor. It takes about 3 hours. (The kind of box a pair of women's boots comes in works perfectly, but feel free to improvise — as long as the box closes tightly, it should work.)

12 cups alder-wood chips

8 ounces (1½ cups) chocolate chips

SPECIAL EQUIPMENT: 3 small foil pans, a gas or charcoal grill, and large flat box with a lid

8 OUNCES DARK CHOCOLATE CHIPS

1. Divide the wood chips between two of the small foil pans, add water to completely cover the chips in each pan, and set them aside to soak for 1 hour.

2. Heat a grill over high heat (about 500°F). Drain the wood chips in one pan and place them back in the foil pan, dripping wet. (Leave the wood chips in the other pan to continue soaking.) Place the drained pan on the grilling grate, close the grill lid, and roast the wood chips until they begin to smoke and smolder, stirring them every 10 minutes or so.

3. Meanwhile, place the chocolate chips in the third foil pan, and place the pan in a box large enough to fit two pans side by side and still close tightly. Place the box on concrete, grass, or another fireproof surface.

4. After 40 minutes to 1 hour, when the wood chips on the grill have blackened and are smoking profusely, quickly transfer the pan to the box with the chocolate chips. Close the box and smoke the chocolate chips until the wood stops smoking, about 30 minutes. (It's best to keep the lid closed for this entire process.)

5. While the chocolate smokes, repeat the draining and blackening process with the second batch of wood chips. Replace the first pan of wood chips with the second, giving the chocolate chips a second round of smoke.

6. When the wood has stopped smoking, use the chocolate chips immediately, because they lose their smoky flavor over time. (Try adding them to banana bread or using them in mole sauce!)

Ten-Minute Yogurt Cake

Grace Harbor Farms, up in Custer, an hour or so north of Seattle, makes cream-topped whole milk yogurt from gorgeous Guernsey cows. It makes a great dessert on its own, but stirred into a batter, it gives moisture and tang the way sour cream does. If you're up for an unpretentious slice of cake, try this simple one-layer number — there's enough sugar to make it taste like a treat, but not so much that you can't eat it for breakfast. Serve each slice with a dollop of extra yogurt.

Cooking spray, for the pan

2 eggs

1 cup sugar

1 cup plain whole milk yogurt

½ cup (1 stick) unsalted butter, melted

2 teaspoons vanilla extract

1½ cups unbleached all-purpose flour

1 tablespoon baking powder

½ teaspoon salt

1 (8-INCH) CAKE

1. Preheat the oven to 350°F. Grease an 8-inch round pan with the cooking spray.

2. Whisk the eggs and sugar until blended in a large bowl. Whisk together the yogurt, melted butter, and vanilla in a small bowl, then whisk it into the egg mixture.

3. Whisk together the flour, baking powder, and salt in a separate bowl. Fold the dry mixture into the wet ingredients until all the flour has been incorporated. Pour the batter into the prepared pan and smooth out the top with a spatula.

4. Bake for 35 to 40 minutes, or until the cake is puffed, golden, and beginning to brown at the edges. Let cool for 10 minutes in the pan, then carefully transfer the cake to a serving platter, and serve warm.

11
BREAKFAST
& BRUNCH

Adapted from THE TURTLEBACK FARM INN COOKBOOK

Cinnamon Toast Pudding with Vanilla Sour Cream

Bill and Susan Fletcher, the owners of Orcas Island's Turtleback Farm Inn, are impossibly cute. After a stay in one of their well-appointed rooms — ask for a spot in the orchard house, which looks out over apple trees and grazing sheep — you might see them pedaling into town on bikes for the inn's supplies. This is one of their guests' favorite breakfasts, adapted from the inn's own cookbook.

6 tablespoons unsalted butter, softened

8 (½-inch-thick) slices artisanal sourdough bread

¾ cup applesauce (preferably homemade)

½ cup plus 1 tablespoon sugar

2 teaspoons ground cinnamon

1 teaspoon ground nutmeg

6 eggs

3 cups whole milk

2½ teaspoons vanilla extract

1 cup sour cream

8 SERVINGS

1. Preheat the oven to 350°F. Grease a 9- by 13-inch baking dish with about ½ tablespoon of the butter and set aside.

2. Toast the bread until light brown, then spread it all on both sides with the remaining butter. Cut each piece into quarters, and arrange the bread on the bottom of the prepared pan. Smear the applesauce in an even layer over the bread.

3. Blend ½ cup of the sugar, cinnamon, and nutmeg in a small bowl. Sprinkle the sugar mixture in an even layer over the applesauce.

4. Whisk the eggs, milk, and 1½ teaspoons of the vanilla to blend in a mixing bowl. Pour the liquid over the ingredients in the pan and bake for 30 to 35 minutes, or until puffed and nicely browned.

5. While the pudding bakes, stir the remaining teaspoon vanilla, the remaining tablespoon sugar, and the sour cream together. Serve the pudding hot, topped with dollops of the vanilla sour cream.

Oddfellows' Polenta Breakfast Cake

There are few, if any, Seattle restaurants that encapsulate the city's quirky personality as well as Oddfellows, the Capitol Hill café located (not surprisingly) in a sprawling old Oddfellows hall. All morning, you'll find freelancers and musicians perched on stools you surely recognize from high school shop class, typing away next to their Americanos and baked eggs with spinach and ham. Lunch brings a slightly more social crowd, typically tattooed and pierced; consistently good people-watching is paired with incredible sandwiches and salads. At dinner, there's table service and affordable, intelligent comfort food that makes Oddfellows as much a food-lovers' haven as it is a date destination.

And all day long, hidden in the pastry counter by the cash register, you'll find this simple, gorgeous cake, my favorite of all the things they make, especially when I can eat it for breakfast. The secret to its moisture? A good dose of almond flour, and a soaking syrup made with lemon juice and brown sugar. This recipe is good for two 9- by 5-inch loaf pans — do not substitute 8- by 4-inch pans, because they're not quite big enough.

Butter and flour, for greasing the pans

2¼ cups granulated sugar

1⅔ cups unbleached all-purpose flour

1½ cups fine cornmeal

1 cup almond flour

2 teaspoons baking powder

1 teaspoon kosher salt

1¾ cups (3½ sticks) unsalted butter, melted

6 eggs

1 tablespoon vanilla extract

1 cup firmly packed light brown sugar

½ cup lemon juice (from 3 large lemons)

2 (9- BY 5-INCH) LOAVES

1. Preheat the oven to 350°F. Butter and flour two 9- by 5-inch loaf pans, and set aside.

2. Whisk together the granulated sugar, flour, cornmeal, almond flour, baking powder, and salt in a medium bowl. Pour the melted butter into a large bowl, then whisk in the eggs, one at a time. Stir in the vanilla, then add the dry ingredients to the butter and egg mixture, stirring until no lumps remain.

3. Divide the batter between the prepared pans, and bake for 50 to 60 minutes, or until the cakes are golden on top and firm in the center.

4. A few minutes before pulling the cakes out, combine the brown sugar and lemon juice in a small saucepan. Bring to a simmer over high heat, and cook until the brown sugar has dissolved completely, 1 to 2 minutes. When the cakes come out, pour the syrup on top of the cakes (with the cakes still in the pan). Let the cakes sit and soak the syrup up for about 15 minutes. Run a small knife around the edges of each pan, and remove the cakes. Serve warm or at room temperature.

Quick Cinnamon Twisps

In 1994, Katie Bristol opened Cinnamon Twisp Bakery in the Methow Valley with a group of friends. Years on, much has changed about the town of Twisp, and about the bakery's ownership, but Bristol's team is still producing their trademark cinnamon twisps — twirls of puffy whole-wheat dough doused with honey and hazelnuts. This version uses a ready-made dough for an easy approximation of the real (secret) recipe that hits the spot when you can't drive to Twisp.

1¼ cups toasted hazelnuts (skins removed), finely chopped

½ cup firmly packed light brown sugar

2 teaspoons ground cinnamon

½ cup (1 stick) unsalted butter

¼ cup honey

2 sheets ready-bake puff pastry (from a 17-ounce package), thawed overnight in the refrigerator

Unbleached all-purpose flour, for dusting

8 LARGE TWISTS

1. Preheat the oven to 425°F. Line two baking sheets with parchment paper or silicone baking mats and set aside.

2. Stir about two-thirds of the hazelnuts, the brown sugar, and the cinnamon together in a small bowl. Set aside.

3. Melt the butter in a small saucepan over low heat. Stir in the honey and set aside.

4. Spread one sheet of the puff pastry out on a clean working surface lightly dusted with flour. Brush it with a thin layer of the honey butter (you won't use it all), then sprinkle half the brown sugar mixture over the entire sheet. Top with the second sheet of puff pastry, then spread the remaining brown sugar mixture over the second sheet. Gently roll the nuts and sugar into the puff pastry using a rolling pin (or a smooth drinking glass) — the goal is to encourage the sugar to stick, not to roll the pastry out.

5. Cut the dough into eight strips the long way, each a bit more than an inch wide, then cut once in the other direction so you have 16 long rectangles. Pinch two rectangles together at one short end, holding them closed with the thumb and index finger of one hand. Twist the end of each of the two rectangles around a few times with your other hand, then pinch the two pieces together at the other end so they stick together. Place the folded twist on one baking sheet, and repeat with the remaining dough, placing four twists on each of the baking sheets. Scoop any stray nuts up off your work surface and sprinkle them onto the twists.

6. Bake the twists for 20 minutes, rotating the pans after about 15 minutes, halfway through the total baking time. Decrease the heat to 350°F and bake for 10 minutes longer, or until the twists are puffed and golden brown.

7. Remove the twists from the oven and transfer them immediately to a cooling rack. Reheat the remaining honey butter, stirring until smooth, then brush it liberally all over the twists. Sprinkle the remaining hazelnuts over the twists, then lightly brush again with the honey butter. Let the twists cool for 5 minutes before serving.

Recipe from GAVIN STEPHENSON, THE FAIRMONT OLYMPIC HOTEL

The Fairmont's Rooftop Honey-Pepper Bacon

Walking into the Fairmont hotel in downtown Seattle, you might pick up a swanky hotel vibe — outrageously fancy cars, impossibly attentive staff, and a high-end restaurant — that makes you wish you'd paid more attention to your grandmother's admonishments about table manners. But take note: there's nothing old-fashioned about what's going on up on the roof. Since 2011, the Fairmont has been keeping bees up there to churn out the honey the hotel uses on its menus. This bacon, from chef Gavin Stephenson, is utterly simple to make but tastes like a more laborious treat.

1 pound thick-cut applewood-smoked bacon
⅓ cup high-quality honey
Cracked black pepper

4–6 SERVINGS

1. Preheat the oven to 350°F. Line a large, rimmed baking sheet with foil.

2. Arrange the bacon on the foil in one layer, then drizzle with the honey and season evenly with cracked pepper. Bake for 18 to 20 minutes, or until the bacon is crisp. Drain the bacon for 1 to 2 minutes on paper towels, then transfer to a plate and serve immediately.

Honey–Cottage Cheese Pancakes

The flavor of these fluffy pancakes, inspired by Adrift restaurant in Anacortes, comes from replacing sugar with honey, so use a high-quality honey. Note that the pancakes really do take 4 to 6 minutes per side, so plan for patience. Better yet, have two or three pans going at once.

6 SERVINGS

3 cups unbleached all-purpose flour

1 tablespoon baking powder

1 teaspoon baking soda

¼ teaspoon salt

2 cups (16 ounces) cottage cheese

½ cup high-quality honey, warmed

1¼ cups milk

3 eggs

¼ cup vegetable oil

1 teaspoon vanilla extract

4 tablespoons butter, for greasing the pan

1. Whisk the flour, baking powder, baking soda, and salt together in a large bowl. Whisk the cottage cheese, honey, and milk together in a medium bowl, then whisk in the eggs, oil, and vanilla. Add the wet ingredients to the dry ingredients, and stir gently until just blended.

2. Heat a large nonstick skillet or cast-iron griddle over medium-low heat. Grease the skillet with 1 teaspoon of the butter, then drop the batter by scant ¼ cupfuls into the pan at least 2 inches apart. (The pancakes will spread slowly as they cook.) Cook the pancakes until browned on both sides and nicely puffed in the center, 4 to 6 minutes per side. Repeat with the remaining butter and pancake batter, and serve piping hot.

BUSY AS A BEE

THE REASON CORKY LUSTER likes beekeeping changes every time someone asks him. Sometimes it's that he loves meeting people. Sometimes it's that he loves working with bees — his "girls," he calls them. Some days, it's that his little honey and beekeeping supply firm, Ballard Bee Company, is replenishing the bee population in the Seattle area, giving the city a stable environmental platform uncommon in urban spaces.

"The world doesn't need another Kohler toilet," says Corky, who used to be a house remodeler. "When I started this, I really believed in why I was doing it. I wanted to do my part to help bee colony populations, and I wanted to give people choices about their food sources."

In the few short years since he started his business, Luster has gone from having a few beehives in his own yard to caring for about 120 hives across the city and at small local farms. Some are "hosted" by families who might not have the time or experience to beekeep, and some, including the hives on top of restaurants like Bastille Café & Bar (page 72) and hotels like The Fairmont (page 239), are managed by Luster in conjunction with chefs.

"The interesting part of watching my clients learn to beekeep is that having a hive brings people into the food system. Instead of just watching it and going to the farmers' market to buy things, they begin to actually participate," says Luster. Each year in Seattle, there's a waiting list for hosting hives.

Strangers to honey harvesting always ask about the sting factor. Of course, even though they're not food-driven like wasps, bees do sting. Luster estimates he gets stung from ten to a hundred times a day — but he wouldn't have it any other way. It's how the bees communicate. He works without gloves, which enables him to handle the bees lightly while judging their temperaments. "It rarely happens, but you can't have an aggressive hive in an urban environment," he says. If he hears or sees that a hive is agitated, he moves the hive to a less populated space, like one of the many farms he works with just outside Seattle.

"It's tedious work," he admits. But when he sees his honey being used by restaurants like Ivar's, a steadfast Seattle staple not particularly known for its use of local ingredients, he's encouraged. "I'm making a bigger impact than I ever imagined I could."

You'll recognize Ballard Bee Company's honey by their label, which looks like it was pulled directly from the periodic table of elements — something Luster says represents the elemental, medicinal nature of honey. For more information, see Recipe Contributors and Suppliers, page 274.

Pimped Root Vegetable Hash

If there's one restaurant to hit in Bellingham, it's The Little Cheerful, a funky spot with an extensive hot sauce collection, great eggs Benedict with crab, and an irrepressible sense of humor. They'll "pimp" their hash browns if you'd like, which means smothered with cheese and grilled onions.

You can use any root vegetables for my version — consider potatoes, carrots, or beets. Just aim for a total of about two pounds raw vegetables and cook them until they're all a bit shy of al dente. If hash isn't hash to you without meat, sprinkle a ½ pound of cooked, chopped bacon onto the vegetables before you add the onions and cheese.

1 pound parsnips, peeled and cut into ½-inch pieces

1 pound sweet potatoes, peeled and cut into ½-inch pieces

2 tablespoons extra-virgin olive oil

1 large onion, chopped

Salt

Freshly ground black pepper

8 ounces cheddar cheese, shredded (2 cups)

4–6 SERVINGS

1. Preheat the oven to 400°F.

2. Combine the parsnips and sweet potatoes in a medium saucepan and add cold water to cover. Bring to a simmer and cook until both vegetables are firm-tender (just shy of al dente), about 10 minutes. Drain the vegetables and set aside.

3. Meanwhile, heat 1 tablespoon of the oil over medium-high heat in a large ovenproof skillet (such as cast iron). Add the onions, salt and pepper to taste, and cook, stirring occasionally, until soft and charred in places, about 15 minutes. Transfer the onions to a bowl.

4. Add the remaining tablespoon of oil to the pan. When hot, add the vegetables and cook until browned in spots, turning just once or twice, about 10 minutes. (If you fiddle with the vegetables too much, they'll stick, so seriously, hands off.)

5. Spread the onions over the vegetables, then top with the cheese, and bake for 5 to 10 minutes, or until the cheese is completely melted and beginning to bubble. Serve hot.

Portage Bay Cafe's Banana Pancakes

I know you. You're the kind of person who sees "vegan pancakes" on a menu and skips right over them. At least, you did before someone with a T-shirt reading "Eat Like You Give a Damn" explained how the sweetness of hemp milk and ripe bananas, combined with rice flour and a little brown sugar, makes these pancakes perfect fodder for fresh fruit or a smear of homemade chocolate-hazelnut butter. Before you tried them, even though you were sure a pancake couldn't be great without eggs or regular flour. Before you admitted that although Portage Bay Cafe is a popular Seattle brunch spot because of the rest of its stellar pancake menu, you really like these best.

2¼ cups white rice flour (such as Bob's Red Mill's)

¼ cup firmly packed light brown sugar

1½ tablespoons baking powder

⅛ teaspoon freshly grated nutmeg

⅛ teaspoon ground cinnamon

2½ large ripe bananas

2 cups hemp milk

2 tablespoons canola oil, plus more for pan or pancake griddle

8 (6-INCH) PANCAKES

1. Whisk the flour, brown sugar, baking powder, nutmeg, and cinnamon together in a large bowl. Whirl the bananas together with about ½ cup of the hemp milk in a food processor until smooth. With the machine running, add the remaining 1½ cups hemp milk and the oil to the banana mixture. Pour the wet ingredients into the dry ingredients and mix until smooth.

2. Preheat a nonstick griddle or nonstick pan over medium heat. When hot, brush the surface with a thin layer of oil, and cook ½ cup of batter at a time, until toasted on each side and puffed in the center, 2 to 3 minutes per side. Serve immediately.

Deep-Dish Walla Walla Onion Quiche

Nestled into the rolling hills in Walla Walla wine country, Abeja is both a winery and a boutique bed-and-breakfast. The name, Spanish for "honeybees," reflects a commitment to sustainable farming practices and a deep appreciation for the mostly Latino work crew. As a winery, it's a bit unusual because the gorgeous tasting room isn't open to the public. But if you join their wine club or, better yet, stay in one of the well-appointed rooms, you can schedule a tasting at your convenience and enjoy breakfast in the herb garden in the morning.

This quiche, one of Abeja's breakfast staples, is the kind of dish that will keep getting you invited to potlucks. It does take a few days to make, because it's imperative that you blind bake the crust and let the quiche rest a night in the refrigerator, so the custardlike filling sets up — but once it's made, it's highly transportable. Mary Besbris, the inn's cook, suggests making the crust the first day, baking it alone and then with the filling in it the second day, and serving the quiche on the third day, straight out of the refrigerator. In fact, I like it best cold.

1 recipe Kate's Pie Dough (page 215), or pastry for a 9-inch piecrust

2 thick-cut slices bacon, finely chopped

2 medium Walla Walla sweet onions

1⅓ cup heavy cream, warmed

1⅓ cup whole milk, warmed

4 eggs

½ teaspoon kosher salt

⅛ teaspoon freshly ground white pepper

Pinch freshly grated nutmeg

10 ounces Gruyere cheese, shredded (⅔ cup)

8 SERVINGS

1. Roll the chilled crust into a 12-inch circle between two layers of parchment paper. Peel one side of the paper off, and transfer the crust to a 9-inch round pan, paper side up, pressing the dough up and over the sides of the pan so it hangs over the edges by about ½ inch. Freeze the dough until firm, at least 20 minutes. (You can do this up to 1 day ahead.)

2. Preheat the oven to 400°F. Fill the crust (on top of the paper) with raw beans or pie weights, and bake 15 to 20 minutes, until just beginning to brown. (This is called blind baking.) Set aside to cool. (You can turn the oven off.)

3. While the crust bakes, cook the bacon in a large skillet over medium heat until crisp, about 10 minutes. Transfer the bacon to a paper towel–lined plate and set aside. Peel and halve the onions, and cut into ¼-inch slices. Add the onions to the pan with the bacon fat, and cook over medium-low heat, stirring occasionally, until dark brown, 45 to 60 minutes. Set aside.

4. When the onions are done cooking, preheat the oven to 350°F.

5. Whirl the cream, milk, eggs, salt, pepper, and nutmeg in a blender until light and fluffy. Scatter half the bacon, onions, and cheese on the bottom of the crust. Pour half the egg mixture in. Add the remaining bacon, onions, and cheese, then enough of the remaining egg mixture to bring the filling to about ¼ inch from the top of the crust.

6. Bake the quiche on the middle rack of the oven for 45 to 55 minutes, or until the quiche is set. (It may still jiggle a bit, but it should jiggle as one piece, instead of just in the center.) Remove from the oven, cool to room temperature, then refrigerate, covered, overnight.

7. Serve the quiche cold, in slices, or rewarm individual slices in a 300°F oven for 30 minutes before serving.

Certified organic Walla walla onions $3.00 bunch

THAT'S ONE SWEET ONION

Since a French soldier brought this particular onion's ancestor to Walla Walla more than a century ago, it's been cultivated for the sweetness that has helped earned its stature as the Washington State Vegetable. From the sweet onion sausage produced at a little take-out counter called Onion World to locally made sweet onion jam, the Walla Walla region is an onion lover's paradise. ★

Cherry Wood Herb-baked Eggs

Pepper Fewel likes to say, as her father used to, that the outside of a horse does wonders for the inside of a person. That might be why a stay at her Cherry Wood Bed Breakfast and Barn in the wine country just east of Yakima doesn't feel like staying at any other bed-and-breakfast. Of course, it might also be that your bed is inside a posh little teepee overlooking the area's orchards and vineyards and a stable of 30 well-mannered rescue horses. Or it could be the wine from the previous day's tasting ride. Or it could be these eggs, inspired by the ones Fewel makes to order each morning, flecked with herbs from her gardens and served piping hot under a fresh western sky. Yes, it must be the eggs.

In place of the thyme and rosemary, you can use any combination of finely chopped herbs — Fewel often adds parsley, chives, or sage.

1 tablespoon unsalted butter

2 tablespoons heavy cream

4 eggs

1 small garlic clove, finely chopped

1 teaspoon finely chopped fresh thyme

1 teaspoon finely chopped fresh rosemary

Freshly ground black pepper

2 tablespoons grated Parmesan cheese

2 SERVINGS

1. Preheat the oven to 375°F.

2. Combine ½ tablespoon of the butter and 1 tablespoon of the cream in each of two (16-ounce) ramekins or small ovenproof bowls. Place the ramekins on the middle rack of the oven and bake for 5 minutes, or until the butter has melted and the cream is beginning to bubble.

3. Crack two eggs into each ramekin, and top with the garlic, thyme, rosemary, and pepper to taste. Sprinkle with the Parmesan, and bake for 10 to 15 minutes, or until the whites are slightly puffed and firm and the yolks have just clouded over (more or less depending on how well cooked you like your eggs). Serve immediately.

Wild Ginger Steamed Beef Dumplings

In 1989, Rick and Ann Yoder opened Wild Ginger in downtown Seattle. At the time, mixing Southeast Asian cuisines was considered novel; they offered traditional, authentic dishes from Vietnam to China, Cambodia to Malaysia. As in Asia, their chefs make fresh coconut milk, sambals, egg noodles, and oyster sauce from scratch. In 2010, the restaurant's Bellevue location started offering a dim sum brunch, proving yet again that the Yoders' team could transport cooking techniques learned abroad right back to Seattle.

DUMPLINGS

- 1 pound ground beef
- ¾ teaspoon kosher salt
- ½ tablespoon sugar
- 1 tablespoon potato starch
- ¼ cup finely chopped pork fat
- 1 teaspoon gingerroot juice, from about 1 inch gingerroot, finely chopped
- ¾ teaspoon sesame oil
- ⅛ teaspoon five-spice powder
- ½ cup packed chopped fresh cilantro
- ¼ pound jicama, peeled and finely chopped

DIPPING SAUCE

- ¼ cup soy sauce
- 2 teaspoons sesame oil

NOTE: For the pork fat, consider cutting about ¾ inch off the fatty ends of every piece of a 12-ounce package of unsmoked bacon. If you have access to dried lemon or orange peel, soak, drain, and mince a pinch of it, and add it to the mixture along with the potato starch.

SPECIAL EQUIPMENT: Bamboo steamer

ABOUT 2 DOZEN DUMPLINGS

1. **Make the dumplings:** Purée the beef, salt, and sugar together in a food processor until finely puréed, about 1 minute — don't walk away, because the machine may walk around the counter a bit. Once the meat is smooth, add the potato starch and purée again for about 30 seconds. Add the pork fat, ginger juice, sesame oil, and five-spice powder, and whirl again for about 30 seconds longer to ensure the ingredients are fully combined. Stir in the cilantro and jicama by hand.

2. Refrigerate the mixture, covered, until cold, about 2 hours or overnight. Fashion the mixture into 1-inch balls using a 1-inch old-fashioned ice cream scoop or wet hands, and place on a plastic wrap–lined plate. (Dip your hands frequently into a bowl of cold water to keep the mixture from sticking.)

3. Place the finished dumplings into a bamboo steamer. (Depending on the size of your steamer, you may need to work in batches.) Fill a wok or skillet with enough water to come about ½ inch up the side of the bottom of your steamer, and bring the water to a simmer over high heat. Place the steamer over the water and steam the dumplings for about 12 minutes, until no longer pink in the center.

4. **Make the sauce:** While the dumplings are steaming, stir the soy sauce and sesame oil together in a small bowl. Serve the dumplings hot with the dipping sauce on the side.

Kabocha-Buttermilk Bundt Cake

Every fall at the University District Farmers Market in Seattle, shoppers ogle the winter squash. Ranging from the expected oranges and yellows to vibrant reds, greens, and even bluish hues, the variety is stunning — but for baking, I go for kabocha squash almost every time. Green or orange skinned, kabocha squash has a rich, yellowy flesh that mashes up soft and smooth (like canned pumpkin) when it's cooked. Stirred into a stunning bundt cake made with emmer flour from the Methow Valley, it's the best way to capture a Washington fall in a cake. Yes, it's a cake. But it's best for breakfast.

You can leave the cake simply glazed, or top it with a flurry of toasted hazelnuts or toasted coconut right when the glaze goes on. This cake can also be made ahead, wrapped in foil and plastic, and frozen up to 1 month. Glaze after defrosting at room temperature.

CAKE

10–12 SERVINGS

- 1 cup (2 sticks) unsalted butter, softened, plus more for pan
- 1½ cups unbleached all-purpose flour
- 1 cup emmer flour or whole-wheat flour
- 2 teaspoons baking powder
- 1 teaspoon baking soda
- ¼ teaspoon salt
- 1 cup granulated sugar
- 2 eggs
- 1 cup buttermilk
- ¼ cup honey
- 2 teaspoons vanilla extract
- 1½ packed cups mashed kabocha squash (from 1 small squash)
- ¼ cup chopped toasted nuts (pecans, walnuts, or hazelnuts) or toasted sweetened coconut flakes (optional)

SPECIAL EQUIPMENT: 12-cup bundt cake pan or 10-inch tube pan

1. **Make the cake:** Preheat the oven to 350°F. Generously (and carefully) butter the bundt cake pan, and set aside.

2. Whisk the flour, emmer flour, baking powder, baking soda, and salt together in a bowl, and set aside.

3. Whip the butter and granulated sugar together on medium speed in a stand mixer fitted with the paddle attachment (or use an electric hand mixer) until light, 3 to 4 minutes. Add the eggs one at a time, scraping down the sides of the bowl and mixing between additions.

4. Stir the buttermilk, honey, and vanilla together in a bowl. With the machine on low, alternate adding the dry and wet mixtures — first some of the flour, then some of the milk, then flour, milk again, and finally flour. When just mixed, add the squash, and mix on low until uniform in color.

5. Transfer the batter to the prepared bundt cake pan, smooth the top, and bake (I find it easier to transfer if it's on a baking sheet) for 40 to 45 minutes, or until a toothpick inserted into the center comes out with just a few crumbs, and the top springs back when touched lightly. Let the cake cool 10 minutes in the pan, then carefully invert it onto a serving platter.

GLAZE

¾ cup confectioners' sugar
1 tablespoon honey
1 teaspoon vanilla extract
1 tablespoon buttermilk or water

NOTE: To roast the squash, slice the squash roughly in half and remove the seeds with an ice cream scoop. Roast cut side down on a parchment- or silicone-lined baking sheet (no need to oil it) at 400°F for about 1 hour, or until the skin is easy to poke with a fork. (Timing will depend on the size and age of the squash.) Let the squash cool, peel away the skin and any other tough pieces, and mash it like you would potatoes, until smooth.

If you're afraid of cutting the squash, you can also put the entire thing — stem and all — into the oven, and bake it a bit longer. Just be sure to scoop out the seeds and stringy stuff before you mash the flesh. Stir any leftover mashed squash into oatmeal or risotto.

6. Make the glaze: When the cake is cool to the touch (after about an hour), whisk the confectioners' sugar, honey, vanilla, and buttermilk together until smooth, adding water if necessary to make a thick, barely pourable glaze. Drizzle the glaze (or pour it right out of the bowl) along the crown of the cake, allowing it to ooze down the inside and outside of the cake. Sprinkle the nuts over the glaze, if desired. Once the glaze has dried, the cake keeps well, covered in plastic wrap at room temperature, for up to 3 days.

Masa-Thyme Scones with Macerated Strawberries

In early summer, buying strawberries at Seattle markets requires more decision-making than you might expect. But taste through the varieties week after week, from Shuksans to Hoods to Rainiers to Quinaults, and you'll probably develop a favorite. Each year, devotees to the delicate, sweet Shuksan variety traipse to a farm in the Skagit Valley to pick the first crop, which will keep (off the vine) for a maximum of about a day. The best solution to using a trunkful of berries is, of course, to make jam, followed by shortcake.

Served with lightly sweetened fresh whipped cream, this version of strawberry shortcake has a hint of the garden. Based on photographer Lara Ferroni's house recipe, these scones are almost a relative of cornbread — they're tender but not too fragile.

6 SCONES

SCONES

- ¾ cup unbleached all-purpose flour
- ½ cup masa harina (fine corn flour)
- ½ cup whole-wheat pastry flour
- ⅓ cup plus 1 tablespoon sugar
- 1 tablespoon chopped fresh thyme
- 1 tablespoon baking powder
- ½ teaspoon kosher salt
- 1 cup plus 2 tablespoons heavy cream

STRAWBERRIES

- 2 pints small ripe strawberries, hulled and sliced
- 2 tablespoons sugar
- 2 teaspoons finely chopped fresh thyme

1. **Make the scones:** Preheat the oven to 350°F. Line a baking sheet with parchment paper or a silicone baking mat and set aside.

2. Whisk the all-purpose flour, masa harina, pastry flour, ⅓ cup of the sugar, thyme, baking powder, and salt together in a large mixing bowl.

3. Whisk 1 cup of the cream on high speed in a stand mixer fitted with the whisk attachment (or using an electric mixer) until soft peaks form when you pull the whisk out of the cream. Gently fold half the cream into the flour mixture, then mix in the other half, taking care to incorporate the flour at the bottom of the bowl.

4. Lightly flour a work surface, then carefully pour the mixture out onto the surface. (The dough will probably be a bit wet still with dry bits of flour here and there.) Flour your hands, and carefully shape the dough into a 3- by 8-inch rectangle, about 1 inch thick. Fold the dough in half once or twice, gently kneading and patting it back together until it becomes moldable (but not folding any more than necessary). Reshape the dough into the rectangle.

5. Cut the rectangle into thirds with a small, sharp knife, then cut each smaller piece into two triangles. Carefully transfer the scones to the prepared baking sheet, placing them very close together but not quite touching so that each edge is only about ¼ inch from its neighbor. Brush the scones with the remaining 2 tablespoons cream, then sprinkle with the remaining tablespoon sugar.

6. Bake for 15 to 18 minutes, until lightly browned and firm to the touch. Cool for 5 minutes on the pan, then carefully transfer to a wire rack until ready to serve.

7. **Make the strawberries:** Combine the berries, sugar, and thyme in a bowl and let sit until the berries begin to give up their juices, about 10 minutes or up to 1 hour. Serve the scones slightly warm, if possible, with the berries and fresh whipped cream.

Recipe from ERIN MCPHERSON KOLAR, TINY'S ORGANIC

Tiny's Pluot Muffins

Walking across Greg McPherson's East Wenatchee fruit and vegetable farm is like following a toddler through a toy store; the only thing that makes him more excited than the apple he's telling you about is the pluot in the next row over. "Try this one," he says, picking up his favorite. "It's called a Flavor Grenade."

His place, Tiny's Organic, grows eight varieties of pluots, which are a cross between a plum and an apricot. This particular kind has the sunset blush and smooth skin of a nectarine, the texture of a plum that's not quite ripe, and the sweetness of a ripe apricot. They're delicious eaten out of hand or stirred into muffins. This recipe is from McPherson's daughter Erin, who runs the vegetable side of the farm.

12 MUFFINS

Cooking spray

1½ cups plus 1 tablespoon unbleached all-purpose flour

½ teaspoon salt

¼ teaspoon baking soda

2 small, ripe pluots, cut into ½-inch pieces (about 1 cup chopped fruit)

½ cup (1 stick) unsalted butter, softened

1 cup granulated sugar

½ teaspoon vanilla extract

2 eggs

⅓ cup plain yogurt

¼ cup firmly packed light brown sugar

NOTE: For gluten-free muffins, substitute gluten-free all-purpose baking flour for the all-purpose flour and increase the baking soda to ½ teaspoon. Fill the muffin cups only two-thirds full and bake as directed. (The recipe will make about 15 muffins.)

1. Preheat the oven to 350°F. Grease a 12-cup muffin pan with cooking spray.

2. Whisk 1½ cups of the flour, salt, and baking soda to blend in a medium bowl.

3. Toss the pluots and the remaining tablespoon flour in a small bowl.

4. Whip the butter and granulated sugar on medium speed in a stand mixer fitted with the paddle attachment (or using an electric mixer) until light and fluffy, about 2 minutes. Stir in the vanilla. Add the eggs one at a time, scraping down the sides of the bowl between additions. With the machine on low speed, add half the dry ingredients, then the yogurt, then the remaining dry ingredients, mixing just until no white spots remain. Gently fold the pluots in by hand.

5. Divide the batter between the muffin cups. (You'll fill each almost to the top.) Sprinkle the brown sugar evenly over the muffins, and bake for 25 to 30 minutes, or until lightly browned and firm in the center. Let the muffins cool in the pan for 10 minutes before serving or cool to room temperature on a cooling rack.

12
SNACKS, DRINKS & PUT-UPS

Buttery Baked Soft Pretzels

Tucked into a corner of Leavenworth, the so-cute-it-hurts Bavarian town located just east of the Cascade Mountains on Route 2, you'll find München Haus, an unabashedly German joint that serves its brats and currywursts with housemade cider sauerkraut, a long line of mustards, and, always, a smile. Even in the winter, my husband and I like to sit in the heated *biergarten* under Hofbräuhaus umbrellas, drinking draft pints from Icicle Brewing Company, which the deceptively young-looking proprietress, Pamela Brulotte, also owns with her husband. No matter which wurst we order, there are always buttery, salty soft pretzels, which Brulotte says München Haus serves by the thousands in the summer. Serve these, my own slightly less traditional version, with cheese sauce and German mustard, like Brulotte does.

8 PRETZELS

1½ cups warm water (about 105°F)

1 package active dry yeast
(2½ teaspoons)

2 tablespoons firmly packed light brown sugar

4 cups unbleached all-purpose flour, plus more for kneading and forming

1 teaspoon kosher salt

Vegetable oil or cooking spray, for greasing the baking sheets

⅓ cup baking soda

Pretzel salt

4 tablespoons unsalted butter, melted

1. Combine the water, yeast, and brown sugar on low speed in a stand mixer fitted with the paddle attachment, just until blended. Let the mixture sit until good and foamy, about 10 minutes.

2. Meanwhile, whisk the flour and kosher salt together in a medium bowl. With the machine on low speed, add the yeast mixture little by little, mixing with the paddle until the dough cleans the side of the bowl and adding more flour if necessary. (The dough shouldn't stick to the sides of the bowl as it mixes, but it's okay if it sticks to the bottom.) Switch to the dough hook and knead the dough on medium-low speed until smooth and elastic, about 5 minutes. Remove the hook from the dough, cover the bowl with plastic wrap, and set aside to rise for 30 minutes.

3. Preheat the oven to 425°F. Line two baking sheets with parchment paper, brush the paper with oil or spray with cooking spray, and set aside.

4. Fill a large deep pot, roughly 10 inches in diameter, with about 2 inches of water, and bring to a boil.

5. While the water heats, form the pretzels: Transfer the dough to a lightly floured work surface, and use a large knife to cut it into 8 roughly equal sections. Working with one piece

at a time, roll, pull, and/or twist each lump of dough into a roughly 24-inch-long rope. Form each rope into a pretzel, twisting the dough over itself twice in the center and pressing the ends gently into the bottom loop of dough to adhere. (You can add more flour as needed to keep the dough from sticking to the counter, but you want the dough to remain tacky enough to stick to itself while the pretzels boil and bake.) Place the pretzel on one of the prepared sheets, and repeat with the remaining dough.

6. When the water boils, add the baking soda (the water will bubble up), and stir until completely dissolved. Working with two pretzels at a time, cook the pretzels at a simmer for 30 seconds on each side, transferring them to and from the water and back to the sheets with a wide slotted spatula. (This process helps the pretzels brown.) Take care to drain the pretzels completely before setting them back on the sheets.

7. Sprinkle the boiled pretzels with pretzel salt, and bake for 25 to 30 minutes, rotating the sheets halfway through baking, or until deep golden brown. Brush the hot pretzels immediately (and quite liberally) with melted butter, and serve piping hot.

Pamela Brulotte

Recipe from AMY PENNINGTON

Pickled Asparagus with Orange, Mint, and Allspice

This pickle recipe uses a soft champagne vinegar, and rather than spiking the brine with the usual vegetable pickle suspects — garlic and chiles — it uses a brine scented delicately with allspice and infused with mint. A strip of orange peel lends a subtle citrus note to each jar. Use the minted asparagus on a green salad such as the Wood Sorrel, Fava Bean, and Asparagus Salad with Green Garlic Drizzle (page 62) or as a side dish with grilled chicken or fish.

4 PINTS

5 pounds asparagus, trimmed (about 2½ pounds after trimming)

5 cups champagne vinegar

1 tablespoon sugar

1 teaspoon salt

1 cup packed fresh mint leaves, plus 4 whole sprigs

8 (½- by 3-inch) strips orange zest

4 teaspoons whole allspice berries

NOTE: Use a vegetable peeler to remove just the orange part of the orange's peel. (You don't want to include the white pith.)

SPECIAL EQUIPMENT: 4 pint-sized canning jars and lids

1. Trim the asparagus to fit into a pint jar; each stalk should be about 3½ inches tall.

2. Combine the vinegar, sugar, and salt in a small saucepan and bring to a boil. Remove the pan from the heat, add the mint leaves, and let cool to room temperature.

3. Pack the pint jars with the trimmed asparagus, fitting in as many spears as possible. Add two orange peels, one mint sprig, and 1 teaspoon of allspice to each jar.

4. Strain the mint out of the vinegar, then return the vinegar to the stove and bring to a boil over high heat. Pour about 1 cup of vinegar into each jar, allowing ½ inch at the top of each jar for headspace, but making sure the tips of the asparagus are covered. Wipe rims, add lids, and process jars in a water bath according to the canning jars' manufacturers' instructions for 10 minutes once the water returns to a boil. Allow to cool on the counter overnight. Check seals; store at room temperature.

Preserved Meyer Lemons

Meyer lemons are sweeter than regular lemons, which means that once they're preserved — packed in salt and left to pickle over the course of a few months — they lend a lovely sweet-salty note to anything they grace. Use them in picnic's Kale Salad (page 100), Steamed Dungeness Crab Legs with Preserved Meyer Lemon Aioli (page 188), or in your favorite North African–inspired dishes.

6 Meyer lemons
2 cups kosher salt

6 PRESERVED LEMONS

SPECIAL EQUIPMENT: 2 pint-sized canning jars and lids

1. Wash the lemons well. Slice the stem end off each lemon with a serrated knife. Starting from the blossom (smooth) end, slice each lemon into quarters lengthwise, stopping about ¼ inch from the bottom, so the lemon stays intact.

2. Place three lemons in each of two pint-sized canning jars, pouring about ⅓ cup salt over each lemon as you add it, stuffing salt between the slices of each fruit.

3. Screw the lids on the jars and refrigerate the lemons for 3 months, giving the jars a gentle shake about once a week. (They'll slowly release their liquid and turn the salt into a brine.) The lemons will keep indefinitely in the refrigerator, packed in brine. To use, rinse lightly, if desired. The brine also makes a delicious addition to salad dressings.

Caramelized Strawberry-Rhubarb Jam

Here's a jam that takes instant gratification into account. Start with a trip to the farmers' market. Buy a flat of strawberries. Eat a pint right there in the sun, chatting with friends, and down another pint on the way home — if you're on a bike, congratulations. (You must be a Seattleite.) Now you have four pints left, which you'll roast in the oven with bits of fresh rhubarb until they've both caramelized into a deep, brownish burgundy. It's easier than regular jam because there's no stirring involved, but the result, with its sweet, deep flavor, is even more toast-worthy.

4 pints small, ripe strawberries, hulled
½ pound rhubarb, chopped
½ cup sugar
 Juice of 1 large lemon (about 3 tablespoons)

1 PINT

1. Preheat the oven to 350°F.

2. Combine the strawberries, rhubarb, sugar, and lemon juice in a large roasting pan. Mash about 25 times with a potato masher, until all the large chunks of fruit are gone, then roast for 1 to 1½ hours, stirring once halfway through, or until the fruit has melted into a jam and no liquid runs down the pan when you tip it sideways.

3. Store the jam in small jars in the refrigerator for up to 2 weeks.

Rosemary-roasted Hazelnuts

Bar snacks are a dime a dozen, but it's rare to come across something that's simultaneously salty, oily, nutty, hot, *and* grown locally. Made by simply roasting Washington DuChilly hazelnuts — the variety with thin skin that doesn't have to be scrubbed off — with great olive oil, chopped fresh rosemary, and sea salt, these are our state's Marcona almonds.

This recipe doubles and triples beautifully, if you're serving larger crowds.

MAKES 1 CUP

1 cup dry-roasted DuChilly hazelnuts

2 teaspoons extra-virgin olive oil

1 teaspoon finely chopped fresh rosemary

¼–½ teaspoon sea salt

1. Preheat the oven to 400°F.

2. Mix the hazelnuts and the oil in a small ovenproof dish. Sprinkle the rosemary on top, then roast for 10 minutes, or until fragrant and toasted. Toss with salt to taste, and serve warm.

Homemade Bourbon Butterscotch Sauce

Delancey, the Ballard pizza joint owned by Brandon Pettit and Molly Wizenberg, is of course known for its pizza. But its clientele loved the accoutrements so much — warm chocolate chip cookies with sea salt, perfect pickles, salads with homemade cheeses — that the couple opened a community kitchen, The Pantry at Delancey, in the back with friends. Available for group dinners and private events, The Pantry also offers extremely popular cooking classes. With titles like "How to Be a Pie Ninja" and "Cook Like an Egyptian," it's no wonder.

This butterscotch sauce, from their "Homemade Holiday Gifts" class, is a great staple for your refrigerator. Drizzle it over ice cream and a Two-Pound Espresso Brownie (page 220), Top Pot Doughnut Bread Pudding (page 228), Honeyed Panna Cotta (page 226), or just directly into your mouth.

½ vanilla bean

2 cups firmly packed light brown sugar

½ cup (1 stick) unsalted butter

1½ cups heavy cream

2 teaspoons kosher salt

3 tablespoons bourbon

1 tablespoon water

Juice of 1 small lemon (about 1 tablespoon)

ABOUT 4 CUPS

1. Split the vanilla bean lengthwise with a small, sharp knife. Scrape the seeds into a medium bowl with the back of the knife, add the brown sugar, and rub the seeds and sugar together with your fingers to distribute the seeds evenly and break up any clumps. (Reserve the vanilla bean pod.)

2. Melt the butter in a medium saucepan over medium-low heat. When melted, add the brown sugar mixture, and stir to moisten all the sugar completely. Cook, stirring occasionally, until the sugar begins to caramelize, 5 to 10 minutes. (It should stop looking granular and start looking more like taffy.)

3. Whisk in the cream, the vanilla bean pod, and the salt; increase the heat to medium; and cook at a low boil, stirring occasionally, until the sauce has turned a full shade darker, 10 to 15 minutes longer. Remove the pan from the heat, remove the vanilla bean, and stir in the bourbon, water, and lemon juice.

4. Serve the sauce warm, or cool to room temperature, pour into jars, and store in the refrigerator for up to 1 week. Reheat the sauce gently in a small pan before serving.

WOODINVILLE WHISKEY CO.

"WHEN WE SET UP SHOP in Washington, it wasn't because we couldn't find a map to Kentucky," Orlin Sorensen is fond of saying. When he founded Woodinville Whiskey Co. in 2009, shortly after Washington State legalized craft distilling, he didn't want to re-create Kentucky bourbon. He wanted to make whiskeys using Northwestern ingredients, focusing both on aged bourbons and on the unaged "white" whiskeys that are typically used as base mixers in cocktails. "When you look at whiskey produced on a massive scale, you don't see the same quality [as you do with small-batch producers]," says Sorensen. "Look at small producers of other products — coffee and microbrewed beers. The little guys are making the best end products."

Woodinville Whiskey Co.'s aged whiskeys are still too young to determine for sure whether they'll beat the old Kentucky standbys. But Sorensen thinks that the combination of constant experimentation with new barreling techniques, training from the industry's best whiskey distillers, and unique combinations of Northwestern ingredients will soon land their products at the top.

For information on their products and their Woodinville tasting room, see Recipe Contributors and Suppliers, page 274. And you might put a few bottles in the basement, just in case.

Barrel-Aged White Manhattan

Across Seattle, aged cocktails are gaining popularity. They're just what they sound like: cocktails, often classics, made in big batches and then mellowed for a few weeks in a secure vessel. Many bars use oak barrels from Woodinville Whiskey Co., where distillers Orlin Sorensen and Brett Carlile make unaged (clear!) whiskey, bourbon whiskey, rye whiskey, vodka, and the aging kits home cocktailing enthusiasts are now using to age their own drinks at home. The result? A drink with more tannin and a hint of oak. And more to talk about, naturally.

5½ cups unaged whiskey (such as Headlong White Dog Whiskey)

2 cups Dolin Blanc Vermouth

⅔ cup Benedictine

1 ounce orange bitters (such as Regan's Orange Bitters No. 6)

Lemon or orange peel twists, for garnish

SPECIAL EQUIPMENT: 2-liter oak aging barrel

2 LITERS

1. First, seal the barrel: Fill the barrel with hot water and place in a sink or outdoors. Top off the barrel two to three times a day until it no longer leaks. (This may take a day or two.)

2. Combine the whiskey, vermouth, Benedictine, and bitters in a large bowl or pitcher, pour the liquid into the barrel, and insert the bung. Store at room temperature, shaking the barrel gently each day.

3. Age the cocktail for 2 to 6 weeks, depending on the desired results, tasting frequently. (The ingredients will gain flavor both from the oak and from sitting together over time.) Once the cocktail has achieved a flavor you like, empty the barrel through a small mesh strainer and funnel into empty bottles.

4. To serve, stir 3 ounces of the cocktail with ice and strain into a cocktail glass, or pour over fresh ice into an old-fashioned glass. Finish with a lemon or orange twist.

Pickled Beets with Clove and Star Anise

One year, my friend Hannah decided she'd can something every month of the year, both to save money and to extend (and appreciate) each season during the other seasons. In January in Washington, that meant beets. Here's my latest version (inspired by Hannah's monthly practice), spiced with clove and whole star anise. (Put the spices on the outside of the beets, if you want the jars to look gorgeous.)

Eat the beets right out of the refrigerator as a snack, serve them as an appetizer at room temperature, toss them into a salad, or reheat them in their liquid and serve them as a side dish.

2½ pounds fist-sized beets (about 8 medium), peeled, halved, and cut into ½-inch-thick slices

12 whole black peppercorns

7 whole cloves

5 star anise

2 allspice berries

⅓ cup firmly packed light brown sugar

2 cups water

1¾ cup apple cider vinegar

2 teaspoons kosher salt

NOTE: If you'd like to can the beets, follow the jar manufacturer's directions for canning shelf-stable vegetables before the beets cool.

SPECIAL EQUIPMENT: 3 pint-sized canning jars and lids

3 PINTS

1. Combine the beets, peppercorns, cloves, star anise, allspice berries, brown sugar, water, vinegar, and salt in a large saucepan. Bring to a simmer and cook, covered, until the beets are just fork-tender, about 25 minutes. Set the pot aside, covered, and allow the beets to cool to room temperature.

2. Transfer the beets to three pint-sized canning jars using tongs or a big slotted spoon. Top with the liquid and spices, cover, and refrigerate for up to 3 weeks.

Homemade Grilled Green Hot Sauce

Visit Tonnemaker Hill Farm in the late summer or early fall or peruse one of the central Washington farm's stands in Seattle, and you'll see swathes of color — the bins are full of red, yellow, purple, and green peppers, with names like Joe Parker, Golden Dagger, Big Bomb, and Kung Pao. They would all make excellent choices for homemade hot sauce, but this version of the traditional egg and taco topper, made with more common varieties, is still plenty hot.

It's no mistake that there's no peeling or seeding involved; the process is meant to be simple. You can refrigerate the prepared sauce up to 2 months, or can it properly to render it shelf-stable.

1 pound Hatch chile pepperss (about 10)

¾ pound poblano peppers (about 4)

¼ pound jalapeños (about 4)

1 pound tomatillos (about 8), husks removed and rinsed

2 tablespoons canola or other neutral oil

½ teaspoon kosher salt

1½ cups white vinegar

ABOUT 4 CUPS

1. Prepare a medium fire (350°F to 450°F) in a gas or charcoal grill.

2. Mix the Hatch chiles, poblanos, jalapeños, tomatillos, and oil together in a large bowl until all the vegetables are coated with a thin layer of oil. Transfer them to the grill's grates, allowing any excess oil to drip back into the bowl first. Wipe the bowl out. Grill the vegetables, turning three or four times, until the vegetables are charred and tender and the peppers have puffy skins, about 15 minutes.

3. Transfer the vegetables back to the bowl. When they're cool enough to handle, remove the stems from all the peppers. Combine the peppers and tomatillos in a food processor. Whirl until finely puréed, then add the salt and vinegar, and purée again. Taste for seasoning, then pour the sauce into bottles or small jars and refrigerate between uses for up to 2 months.

Recipe from KATHY CASEY FOOD STUDIOS — LIQUID KITCHEN

Cherry Mojitos for a Crowd

Before female star chefs were the norm, and before bartenders were chefs, and before Seattle really blossomed as a food town, there was Kathy Casey. Restaurant owner, cookbook author, TV personality, and food writer, Casey still seems to be all things to the food world here. Today, she's most well known for making creative cocktails like these cherry mojitos, which are a great way to celebrate Washington's cherry bounty when you're done eating them out of hand.

Pick a sweet variety of cherries, such as Bing or Lambert, for this recipe. Garnish the drinks with additional mint sprigs, and cherries with the stem still on.

3 cups pitted fresh sweet cherries (about 1½ pounds)

1½ packed cups fresh mint sprigs

2 cups sugar

3 cups Bacardi Limón rum

2 cups fresh lime juice

¼ cup clear cherry liqueur (such as Maraska maraschino)

Ice, for serving

2 (10-ounce) bottles soda water

NOTE: You can make the cherry-rum mixture up to 3 days in advance and keep it refrigerated — the flavors will actually improve.

8 COCKTAILS

1. Combine the cherries, mint, sugar, rum, lime juice, and liqueur in a large nonreactive container, such as a glass pitcher. Stir well to dissolve the sugar. Cover and refrigerate overnight.

2. For each serving, fill a large rocks glass or tumbler with ice and measure in 6 ounces (¾ cup) of the rum mixture, making sure to get a few cherries into each glass. Top with 2 ounces (¼ cup) of the soda. Stir, then garnish with extra mint and a cherry, if desired.

Pickled Red Onions with Mustard Seeds

Since you'll be slicing 5 pounds of onions here, consider borrowing a mandoline slicer, which makes the process go much, much faster, and moving the whole operation outdoors, which cuts down on the eye stinging. The onions are ready to eat right when they cool because they're softened ahead in the vinegar brine, but you'll have extra brine left over. Instead of throwing it away, use it to make refrigerator pickles: Bring it back to a boil and pour it over fresh, clean baby carrots, green or yellow wax beans, or cooked, sliced beets, and refrigerate for a few days before eating.

This recipe makes enough for 8 pints pickled onions, but you can use whatever combination of large and small jars works for you and your canning setup.

2 cups sugar

2 tablespoons kosher salt

10 cups apple cider vinegar

5 pounds red onions, cut into $\frac{1}{8}$-inch slices with the grain

¼ cup mustard seeds

24 whole black peppercorns

SPECIAL EQUIPMENT: 8 pint-sized canning jars and lids

8 PINTS

1. Combine the sugar, salt, and vinegar in a large pot, and bring to a simmer, stirring occasionally as the sugar dissolves. Place the onions in a large bowl (or two smaller ones), pour the vinegar mixture over the top, and let sit for 30 minutes, stirring occasionally.

2. Put 1½ teaspoons mustard seeds and 3 peppercorns in each canning jar. When the onions have softened and turned bright pink, stuff the jars full. Add the brine until it comes to ¼ inch from the rim. Wipe rims, add lids, and process jars in a water bath according to the canning jars' manufacturers' instructions for 10 minutes once the water returns to a boil. Allow to cool on the counter overnight. Check seals; store at room temperature.

DIY: FRESH-HOPPED ALE

THE SAME GROWING CONDITIONS that make Washington's Yakima Valley perfect for grapes make it ideal for growing hop bines (technically, they're bines, not vines), whose flowers contribute to a beer's flavor, bitterness, aroma, and stability. Driving across Interstate 90, you'll see huge swathes of land — called hop yards — covered by what looks like a grid of two-by-fours linked with nets or strings for the hops to climb.

Yakima accounts for about three-fourths of the country's hop production. Every first Saturday in October, the town hosts the Fresh Hop Ale Festival, with beers made with fresh hops instead of the dried ones that are more commonly used. The amateur fresh-hopped homebrew contest is always a favorite.

My husband and I grow Hallertau and Centennial hops in our backyard. (Contrary to its reputation, Seattle is often a very dry place during the growing season.) Each year, after a few sunny days in a row, right around Labor Day, we harvest them with friends and incorporate them into a pale ale that we drink around Halloween.

If you have access to fresh hops, and are familiar with beer brewing, try using the continuous hopping method with 1 pound of Hallertau hops and 1 pound of Centennial hops. Choose a recipe for a pale ale; strong or typically hoppy beers (or beers that are overwhelmingly malty) often overwhelm the delicate flavor of fresh hops. It's also important that you use the hops within 24 hours of picking, when the flowers, or "cones," still have most of their moisture. (This is why fresh hopping is also referred to as wet hopping.) Add a handful of each type of hop every five minutes during the boiling process instead of using dried hops.

The result is an ale with floral or spicy tones that changes from year to year, the same way the flavor of any other crop does — a good surprise come Halloween when the rains have arrived, and your warmth comes not from the sun, but from a pint.

Recipe from LARS RINGSRUD, SNOWDRIFT CIDER CO.

Snowdrift Cider's Shrub Steppe

Peter and Lars Ringsrud's cider business started as a fun hobby, with a 100-year-old hand-cranked press. Now the father-son team produces more than 1,500 cases a year and has leapt to the forefront of Washington's growing hard cider industry. Every fall, they host a family apple-picking party. On the steppes of East Wenatchee, people gather, young and old, to pack cider apples into huge wooden bins, relishing the way the valley's hot summers and cold, snowy winters give the apples the aromatics needed for great ciders.

Technically, a shrub is a mixture of fruit, vinegar, and sugar, often cooked and used as a syrup to sweeten cocktails, like this one, made with cider and rum.

If the only cider you can find comes in a six-pack, you should probably look harder (or pick up the phone and call Snowdrift) before making this cocktail.

6 COCKTAILS

SHRUB SYRUP

- 1 small ripe nectarine, pitted and diced
- 1 cup sugar
- ½ cup roughly chopped fresh oregano
- ¼ cup raisins
- 1½ teaspoons ground allspice
- ¼ cup balsamic vinegar
- 1 teaspoon vanilla extract

COCKTAIL

- 2 (750 mL or similar) bottles chilled craft cider (dry or semidry)
- 6 ounces dark rum
- 6 ounces shrub syrup

1. **Make the shrub syrup:** Combine the nectarine, sugar, oregano, raisins, allspice, vinegar, and vanilla together in a bowl, and mash until well blended. Cover with plastic wrap, and refrigerate overnight.

2. Before serving, strain the syrup through a fine-mesh sieve, discarding the solids.

3. **Make the cocktail:** Fill each of six large glasses with about 6 ounces (¾ cup) of the cider. Combine the rum and 6 ounces of the syrup in a cocktail shaker filled with ice, shake to chill, and pour about 2 ounces (¼ cup) of the mixture gently into the center of each glass so that the darker shrub mixture settles on the bottom. Serve immediately.

Asian Pears with Toasted Goat Cheese and Sweet Buttered Walnuts

Although Asian pears taste quite distinct from the European varieties we're more familiar with today, they both originated in the steppes of Asia. Wade Bennett, the sometimes eccentric (but always knowledgeable) farmer behind Rockridge Orchards, an Enumclaw-based outfit whose goods are sold at many Seattle-area farmers' markets, is my Asian pear expert. When ripe, Asian pears are not quite soft, which means they're perfect for snacking with a little slice of cheese, or the way Bennett taught me to eat them, broiled with goat cheese and topped with simple honey- and butter-candied walnuts. The pears get good and warm but still somehow manage to stay crisp. This snack can be prepared in advance, then reheated for 5 minutes in a 350°F oven before serving — just take care to watch the nuts, because they burn quickly.

2 tablespoons unsalted butter

2 tablespoons honey, plus more for drizzling

3 cups walnut halves

2 Asian pears (such as Hosui)

4 ounces goat cheese, crumbled

NOTE: If you can't find Asian pears, you can substitute crisp Anjou pears.

4–8 SERVINGS

1. Preheat the oven to 400°F.

2. Melt the butter over medium heat in a small ovenproof pan. Add the honey, stirring until it dissolves into the butter, then add the walnuts, stirring gently, so that the liquid coats all parts of every nut.

3. Transfer the pan to the oven and roast the nuts for 10 to 15 minutes, or until fragrant, stirring two or three times. Pour the nuts onto a cooling rack set over a piece of aluminum foil, and let cool.

4. Set the oven to broil. Slice the pears into ½-inch rounds across the core, so you get about four even slices from each piece of fruit. Pick out and discard any seeds. Place the slices directly on a baking sheet and scatter the crumbled goat cheese onto them. Broil the pears about 4 inches from the broiling unit for a few minutes, rotating the pan halfway through, or until the goat cheese is toasted and the pears are sizzling.

5. Transfer the pears to plates, top each with a few walnuts (you'll have some leftover for snacking), and serve immediately, drizzled with additional honey.

NOT JUST ANY PEAR

VISIT ROCKRIDGE ORCHARDS' FARM STORE in Enumclaw, located in the shadow of Mt. Rainier, in early fall and you might find owner Wade Bennett taking a visitor on a pear-tasting tour that sounds more like a stop at a high-end winery. "Try this one," he'll say, handing over a round, mottled Asian pear called Ichiban. "It tastes like butterscotch." But instead of the flighty, nuanced flavor you might expect, the crisp, taut-skinned pear explodes in your mouth like butterscotch candy. The next one, Chojuro, tastes not just like rum, but like *drinking* rum. And on he goes, from Kosui and Hosui to Nijisseiki pears, with flavors from brandy to vanilla to melon, and none of them shy.

Bennett says that the area's volcanic soil and water contribute to the sweetness of the fruit he grows — mainly apples, which he makes into ciders and wines, but also pears and other fruit, as well as a few unusual crops like bamboo shoots, tea leaves, and ginger. "You can't grow non-sweet fruit here," he asserts, comparing the natural sugar levels found in Washington fruit to the always-tart flavors in, say, Vermont apples. "It's a curse and a blessing." Clearly, for his Asian pears, it's a blessing.

Recipe Contributors & Suppliers

Below is a list of recipe contributors, restaurants, wineries, farms, producers, cheesemakers, inns, and events that appear in *Dishing Up Washington*. The list is divided by region.

GREATER PUGET SOUND (EXCLUDING SEATTLE)

Batdorf & Bronson
(multiple locations)
www.batdorfcoffee.com

Café Juanita
9702 Northeast 120th Place
Kirkland, WA 98034
425-823-1505
www.cafejuanita.com
  Spicy Roasted Cauliflower with Cumin, Lime, and Pine Nuts, 84

Chateau Ste. Michelle
14111 Northeast 145th Street
Woodinville, WA 98072
425-488-1133
www.ste-michelle.com

The Hardware Store
17601 Vashon Highway Southwest
Vashon, WA 98070
206-463-1800
www.thsrestaurant.com
  Hardware Store Fried Chicken, 140

The Herbfarm
14590 Northeast 145th Street
Woodinville, WA 98072
425-485-5300
www.theherbfarm.com
  Crisp Spring Chicken with Oysters and Nettle Sauce, 128

Hitchcock Restaurant
133 Winslow Way East
Bainbridge Island, WA 98110
206-201-3789
http://hitchcockrestaurant.com
  Roasted Bone Marrow with Huckleberry and Sweet Onion Mostarda, 170

The Inn at Langley
400 First Street
Langley, WA 98260
360-221-3033
www.innatlangley.com
  Sunchoke Purée with Sautéed Radishes and Rosemary Oil, 46

Island Spring Organics
206-463-9848
www.islandspring.com

JM Cellars
14404 137th Place Northeast
Woodinville, WA 98072
206-522-4823
www.jmcellars.com

Kurtwood Farms
kurt@kurtwoodfarms.com
www.kurtwoodfarms.com

La Boucherie at Sea Breeze Farm
17635 100th Avenue Southwest
Vashon, WA 98070
206-567-4628
www.seabreezefarm.net
  Sea Breeze Farm's Pork Rib Ragu, 142

Stokesberry Sustainable Farm
7429 85th Lane Southeast
Olympia, WA 98513
www.stokesberrysustainablefarm.com

Tatanka Take-Out
4915 North Pearl Street
Ruston, WA 98407
253-752-8778

Trellis Restaurant at the Heathman Hotel
220 Kirkland Avenue
Kirkland, WA 98033
425-284-5900
www.trellisrestaurant.net
  Wild Salmon with Sweet Corn Salad and Lemon-Herb Vinaigrette, 76
  Barrel-Aged White Manhattan, 263

Woodinville Whiskey Co.
16110 Woodinville Redmond Road Northeast, Suite 3
Woodinville, WA 98072
425-486-1199
www.woodinvillewhiskeyco.com

NORTH CASCADE MOUNTAINS

Bluebird Grain Farms
888-232-0331
www.bluebirdgrainfarms.com

Cinnamon Twisp Bakery
116 North Glover Street
Twisp, WA 98856
509-997-5030
www.cinnamontwisp.com

Glover Street Market
124 North Glover Street
Twisp, WA 98856
509-997-1320
www.gloverstreetmarket.com
  Glover Street Chicken Curry Stew, 136

NORTHEAST WASHINGTON

Billy's Gardens
800-417-6387
www.billysgardens.com

Dry Fly Distilling
1003 East Trent Avenue #200
Spokane, WA 99202
509-489-2112
www.dryflydistilling.com

Olsen Farms
1900-C Rocky Creek Road
Colville, WA 98114
509-685-1548
www.olsenfarms.com
  Olsen Family Potato Soup, 40

Quilceda Farm
2317 158th Street Northwest
Marysville, WA 98271
360-652-3231
www.quilcedafarm.com

NORTHWESTERN WASHINGTON

Adrift
510 Commercial Avenue
Anacortes, WA 98221
360-588-0653
www.adriftrestaurant.com

Breadfarm
5766 Cains Court
Edison, WA 98232
360-766-4065
www.breadfarm.com
  Cocoa Nib Cookies, 222

Fishing Vessel *St. Jude*
Bellevue, Washington
425-378-0680
www.tunatuna.com

Full Circle Farm
31904 Northeast 8th Street
Carnation, WA 98014
866-328-9355
www.fullcircle.com

Golden Glen Creamery
15098 Field Road
Bow, WA 98232
360-766-6455
www.goldenglencreamery.com

Grace Harbor Farms
2347 Birch Bay Lynden Road
Custer, WA 98240
360-366-4151
www.graceharborfarms.com

Holmquist Hazelnut Orchards
9821 Holmquist Road
Lynden, WA 98264
800-720-0895
www.holmquisthazelnuts.com

Little Cheerful
133 East Holly Street
Bellingham, WA 98225
360-738-8824
www.littlecheerful.com

Northwest Wild Foods
12535 Pulver Road
Burlington, WA 98233
360-757-7940
www.nwwildfoods.com
  Northwest Wild Foods' Blackberry Bars, 209

Skagit River Ranch
28778 Utopia Road
Sedro Woolley, WA 98284
360-856-0722
www.skagitriverranch.com
  Skagit River Ranch Pot Roast, 164

Taylor Shellfish Farms
(multiple locations)
www.taylorshellfishfarms.com
  Melrose Mussels, 183

OLYMPIC PENINSULA

Mt. Townsend Creamery
(multiple locations)
www.mttownsendcreamery.com
  Camp Fire Grits, 91

Mystery Bay Farm
360-385-3309
www.mysterybayfarm.com

Nash's Organic Produce
1865 East Anderson Road
Sequim, WA 98382
360-683-4642
www.nashsorganicproduce.com

Pane d'Amore
(multiple locations)
www.panedamore.com
    Baby Orange-Almond Cakes,
    208

Phocas Farms
343 Robinson Road
Port Angeles, WA 98362
360-457-2917

Port Angeles Farmers Market
Corner of Front and Lincoln
    Streets
Port Angeles, WA
http://farmersmarketportangeles.com

Sammie Shack
1440 F Street
Port Townsend, WA 98368
360-379-5463
    Chetzamelta Sandwiches, 112

Some Like It Hott
360-531-1410
www.aldersmoked.com

SAN JUAN ISLANDS

Allium
310 East Main Street
Eastsound, WA 98245
360-376-4904
www.alliumonorcas.com
    Saffron Clam Chowder, 14

Buck Bay Shellfish Farm
77 EJ Young Road
Olga, WA 98279
360-376-5280

Jones Family Farms
1934 Mud Bay Road
Lopez Island, WA 98261
360-468-0533
www.jffarms.com

Turtleback Farm Inn
1981 Crow Valley Road
Eastsound, WA 98245
800-376-4914
www.turtlebackinn.com
    Cinnamon Toast Pudding with
    Vanilla Sour Cream, 236

Willows Inn
2579 West Shore Drive
Lummi Island, WA 98262
360-758-2620
www.willows-inn.com

SEATTLE

Anchovies & Olives
1550 15th Avenue
Seattle, WA 98122
206-838-8080
*www.ethanstowellrestaurants.com/
anchoviesandolives*

Art of the Pie
www.artofthepie.com
    Free-Form Pear Crostata, 214

Ba Bar
550 12th Avenue
Seattle, WA 98122
206-328-2030
http://babarseattle.com

Baguette Box
(multiple locations)
www.baguettebox.com

Ballard Bee Company
206-459-4131
www.ballardbeecompany.com

Ballard Farmers Market
Seattle Farmers Market
    Association
Ballard Avenue Northwest
Seattle, WA 98107
*http://ballardfarmersmarket.
    wordpress.com*
    Saffron available occasionally
    from Phocas Farms

bar ferd'nand
1531 Melrose Avenue
Seattle, WA 98122
206-623-5882
www.ferdinandthebar.com

Bastille Café & Bar
5307 Ballard Avenue Northwest
Seattle, WA 98107
206-453-5014
http://bastilleseattle.com
    Roasted Beet Salad with
    Pickled Currants, Preserved
    Lemon, Chèvre, and
    "Rooftop" Arugula, 72

Blueacre Seafood
1700 7th Avenue
Seattle, WA 98101
206-659-0737
www.blueacreseafood.com
    Green Curry Mussels, 187

Brave Horse Tavern
310 Terry Avenue North
Seattle, WA 98109
206-971-0717
www.bravehorsetavern.com
    Brave Horse Tavern's Deviled
    Eggs, 26

Cafe Flora
2901 East Madison Street
Seattle, WA 98112
206-325-9100
www.cafeflora.com
    Lentil-Pecan Pâté, 24

Cafe Lago
2305 24th Avenue East
Seattle, WA 98112
206-329-8005
www.cafelago.com
    Cafe Lago's City of Seattle
    Eggplant, 99

The Calf & Kid
1531 Melrose Avenue
Seattle, WA 98122
206-467-5447
www.calfandkid.com

Canlis
2576 Aurora Avenue North
Seattle, WA 98109
206-283-3313
www.canlis.com
    Watermelon Gazpacho, 52

Carmelita
7314 Greenwood Avenue North
Seattle, WA 98103
206-706-7703
www.carmelita.net

**Copperleaf Restaurant at
    Cedarbrook Lodge**
18525 36th Avenue South
Seattle, WA 98188
206-214-4282
*www.cedarbrooklodge.com/
    copperleaf_restaurant.php*
    Warm Foraged Mushroom
    Salad with Arugula,
    Fingerling Potatoes, and
    Bacon, 63

The Corson Building
5609 Corson Avenue South
Seattle, WA 98108
206-762-3330
www.thecorsonbuilding.com

Delancey
1415 Northwest 70th Street
Seattle, WA 98117
206-838-1960
www.delanceyseattle.com

El Gaucho
(multiple locations)
www.elgaucho.com
    El Gaucho's Mashed Potatoes,
    86

emmer&rye
1825 Queen Anne Avenue
    North
Seattle, WA 98109
206-282-0680
www.emmerandrye.com
    Spicy Beef and Lamb Stew
    with Emmer and Rye, 50

**The Fairmont Olympic
    Hotel**
411 University Street
Seattle, WA 98101
888-363-5022
www.fairmont.com/seattle
    The Fairmont's Rooftop
    Honey-Pepper Bacon, 239

Foraged and Found Edibles
866-951-1031
(multiple locations)
www.foragedandfoundedibles.com

Go Go Green Garden
206-571-5646
www.gogogreengarden.com

Golden Beetle
1744 Northwest Market Street
Seattle, WA 98107
206-706-2977
http://golden-beetle.com
    Persian Cucumber Salad with
    Labne, 70
    DIY: Homemade Labne, 71

Grounder's Garlic Fries
(multiple locations at Safeco
    Field)
1250 First Avenue South
Seattle, WA 98134
http://mariners.mlb.com/sea/ballpark

**Hot Cakes Molten
    Chocolate Cakery**
(multiple locations)
www.getyourhotcakes.com
    Hot Cakes' Original S'mores
    Cookies with Smoked
    Chocolate, 230

How to Cook a Wolf
2208 Queen Anne Avenue
    North
Seattle, WA 98109
206-838-8090
*www.ethanstowellrestaurants.com/
howtocookawolf*

Joule Restaurant
3506 Stone Way North
Seattle, WA 98103
206-632-1913
www.joulerestaurant.com

**Kathy Casey Food Studios
— Liquid Kitchen**
5130 Ballard Avenue Northwest
Seattle, WA 98107
206-784-7840
www.kathycasey.com
  Pale Ale Oven-Roasted
    Clams, 196
  Cherry Mojitos for a Crowd,
    266

La Carta de Oaxaca
5431 Ballard Avenue Northwest
Seattle, WA 98107
206-782-8722
www.lacartadeoaxaca.com

Loki Fish Company
(multiple locations)
206-937-1048
www.lokifish.com

Luc
2800 East Madison Street
Seattle, WA 98112
206-328-6645
http://thechefinthehat.com/luc
  Seared Duck with White
    Beans, Fresh Figs, and
    Huckleberry Gastrique, 127

**Madison Park
  Conservatory**
1927 43rd Avenue East
Seattle, WA 98112
206-324-9701
http://madisonparkconservatory.com
  Roasted Cornish Game
    Hens with Parsnips and
    Bergamot-poached Prunes,
    132

Mama Lil's Peppers
(multiple locations)
www.mamalils.com

**Ma'ono Fried Chicken &
  Whisky**
4437 California Avenue
  Southwest
Seattle, WA 98116
206-935-1075
http://maono.springhillnorthwest.
  com
  Chicken-fried Veal
    Sweetbreads, 173

Matt's in the Market
94 Pike Street, Suite 32
Seattle, WA 98101
206-467-7909
www.mattsinthemarket.com

Melrose Market
1501–1535 Melrose Avenue
Seattle, WA 98122
www.melrosemarketseattle.com

**Molly Moon's Homemade
  Ice Cream**
(multiple locations)
www.mollymoonsicecream.com
  Summer Cherry Goat's Milk
    Frozen Yogurt, 218

Monsoon Restaurants
(multiple locations)
www.monsoonrestaurants.com
  Saigon Chicken Salad, 138

**Neighborhood Farmers
  Market Alliance**
www.seattlefarmersmarkets.org

Oddfellows Cafe + Bar
1525 10th Avenue
Seattle, WA 98122
206-325-0807
www.oddfellowscafe.com
  Oddfellows' Polenta
    Breakfast Cake, 237

The Pantry at Delancey
1417 Northwest 70th Street
Seattle, WA 98117
206-436-1064
http://thepantryatdelancey.com
  Homemade Bourbon
    Butterscotch Sauce, 261

**Paseo Carribean
  Restaurant**
(multiple locations)
www.paseoseattle.com

PCC Natural Markets
(multiple locations)
www.pccnaturalmarkets.com

picnic
6801 Greenwood Avenue North
Seattle, WA 98103
206-453-5867
www.picnicseattle.com
  picnic's Kale Salad, 100
  Preserved Meyer Lemons, 258

Pike Place Fish Market
86 Pike Place
Seattle, WA 98101
800-542-7732
www.pikeplacefish.com

Pike Place Market
Pike Place and 1st Avenue
www.pikeplacemarket.org

Poppy
622 Broadway East
Seattle, WA 98102
206-324-1108
http://poppyseattle.com
  Grilled Asparagus with Fried
    Sage and Lemon, 94

Portage Bay Cafe
(multiple locations)
www.portagebaycafe.com
  Portage Bay Cafe's Banana
    Pancakes, 243

Rain Shadow Meats
1531 Melrose Avenue
Seattle, WA 98122
206-467-6328
www.rainshadowmeats.com
  Rain Shadow Meats' Italian
    Sausage & Meatballs, 144

Red Mill Burgers
(multiple locations)
www.redmillburgers.com

Revel
403 North 36th Street
Seattle, WA 98103
206-547-2040
www.revelseattle.com
  Zucchini Pancakes with
    Blossoms and Basil, 113

RN74
1433 4th Avenue
Seattle, WA 98101
206-456-7474
http://michaelmina.net/restaurants/
  locations/rnwa.php
  RN74 Beef Bourguignon, 166

Rover's
2808 East Madison Street
Seattle, WA 98112
206-325-7442
http://thechefinthehat.com/rovers

Salumi Cured Meats
309 3rd Avenue South
Seattle, WA 98104
206-621-8772
www.salumicuredmeats.com
  Spaghetti with Guanciale alla
    Armandino, 154

**Seattle Farmers Market
  Association**
www.seattlefarmersmarket
  association.wordpress.com

Serious Pie
(multiple locations)
http://tomdouglas.com
  Yukon Gold Potato Pizza
    with Rosemary and Olive
    Oil, 109

Sitka & Spruce
1531 Melrose Avenue
Seattle, WA 98122
206-324-0662
www.sitkaandspruce.com
  Cider-battered Puget
    Sound Silver Smelt with
    Homemade Garlic Aioli, 198

**SkyCity at the Space
  Needle**
400 Broad Street
Seattle, WA 98109
800-937-9582
www.spaceneedle.com/restaurant

Spinasse
1531 14th Avenue
Seattle, WA 98122
206-251-7673
www.spinasse.com
  Hunter's-style Rabbit with
    Wild Mushrooms and
    Tomato, 163

Staple & Fancy
4739 Ballard Avenue Northwest
Seattle, WA 98107
206-789-1200
www.ethanstowellrestaurants.com/
  stapleandfancy
  Geoduck Crudo with Celery,
    Lime, Chiles, and Radish, 22

Tavolàta
2323 2nd Avenue
Seattle, WA 98121
206-838-8008
www.ethanstowellrestaurants.com/
  tavolata

Theo Chocolate
3400 Phinney Avenue North
Seattle, WA 98103
206-632-5100
www.theochocolate.com

Tilth Restaurant
1141 North 45th Street
Seattle, WA 98103
206-633-0801
www.tilthrestaurant.com

Top Pot Doughnuts
(multiple locations)
www.toppotdoughnuts.com

Uwajimaya
(multiple locations)
www.uwajimaya.com

Veraci Pizza
500 Northwest Market Street
Seattle, WA 98107
206-525-1813
www.veracipizza.com

Volunteer Park Cafe
1501 17th Avenue East
Seattle, WA 98112
206-328-3155
www.alwaysfreshgoodness.com
Roasted Fall Mushroom
Bruschetta, 18

The Walrus and the Carpenter
4743 Ballard Avenue Northwest
Seattle, WA 98107
206-395-9227
http://thewalrusbar.com

Wild Ginger
(multiple locations)
www.wildginger.net
Wild Ginger Steamed Beef
Dumplings, 247

Wild Salmon Seafood Market
888-222-3474
(multiple locations)
http://wildsalmonseafood.com

SOUTH CASCADE MOUNTAINS

Rockridge Orchards & Cidery
40709 264th Avenue Southeast
Enumclaw, WA 98022
360-802-6800
http://rockridgeorchards.com

Summit House Restaurant at Crystal Mountain Resort
33914 Crystal Mountain Boulevard
Crystal Mountain, WA 98022
888-754-6199
www.crystalmountainresort.com

WALLA WALLA AND SOUTHEAST WASHINGTON

àMaurice Cellars
178 Vineyard Lane
Walla Walla, WA 99362
509-522-5444
www.amaurice.com

Blue Valley Meats
1162 West Pine Street
Walla Walla, WA 99362
509-876-4700
www.bluevalleymeats.com

Brasserie Four
4 East Main Street
Walla Walla, WA 99362
509-529-2011
www.brasseriefour.com

Charles Smith Wines
35 South Spokane Street
Walla Walla, WA 99362
509-526-5230
www.charlessmithwines.com

Ellanelle Wine Company
541-938-3743
http://ellanelle.com

Gramercy Cellars
635 North 13th Avenue
Walla Walla, WA 99362
509-876-2427
https://gramercycellars.com

The Inn at Abeja
2014 Mill Creek Road
Walla Walla, WA 99362
509-522-1234
www.abeja.net
Deep-Dish Walla Walla Onion
Quiche, 244

Kerloo Cellars
16 North 2nd Avenue
Walla Walla, WA 99362
206-349-0641
www.kerloocellars.com

Onion World
2 South 1st Avenue
Walla Walla, WA 99362
509-522-2541
www.onionworld.com

Petits Noirs
622 South Main Street
Milton Freewater, OR 97862
541-938-7118
www.petitsnoirs.com

WENATCHEE VALLEY AND THE CENTRAL CASCADE MOUNTAINS

Alpine Lakes Sheep Cheese
509-548-5786
www.alpinelakescheese.com

Anjou Bakery
3898 Old Monitor Highway
Cashmere, WA 98815
509-782-4360
www.anjoubakery.com
Anjou's Lemon Cream
Shortbread Bars, 210

Icicle Brewing Company
935 Front Street
Leavenworth, WA 98826
509-548-2739
www.iciclebrewing.com

München Haus
709 Front Street
Leavenworth, WA 98826
509-548-1158
www.munchenhaus.com

Sleeping Lady Mountain Resort
7375 Icicle Road
Leavenworth, WA 98826
800-574-2123
www.sleepinglady.com
Caesar Salad with Roasted
Onion, Preserved Lemon,
and Bacon, 64

Snowdrift Cider Co.
227 Ward Street
East Wenatchee, WA 98802
509-630-3507
http://snowdriftcider.com
Snowdrift Cider's Shrub
Steppe, 270

Tiny's Organic
509-264-3973
www.tinysorganic.com
Tiny's Pluot Muffins, 252

YAKIMA VALLEY AND CENTRAL WASHINGTON

Alvarez Organic Farms
300 Murray Road
Mabton, WA 98935
509-830-5242
www.alvarezorganicfarms.com

AprèsVin
509-531-1293
www.apresvin.com

Cherry Wood Bed Breakfast and Barn
3271 Roza Drive
Zillah, WA 98953
509-829-3500
www.cherrywoodbbandb.com

Chinook Wines
220 Wittkopf Loop
Prosser, WA 99350
509-786-2725
www.chinookwines.com

Gilbert Cellars
5 North Front Street
Yakima, WA 98901
509-249-9049
www.gilbertcellars.com
Gilbert Cellars' Bacon-
wrapped Dates, 31

Maison Bleue Winery
357 Port Avenue, Studio D
Prosser, WA 99350
www.mbwinery.com

MOJAVE at Desert Wind Winery
2258 Wine Country Road
Prosser, WA 99350
509-786-7277
www.desertwindwinery.com
Tenderloin Steaks with Syrah-
glazed Wild Mushrooms,
160

Rodeo City Bar-B-Q
204 North Main Street
Ellensburg, WA 98926
509-962-2727
www.rodeocitybarbq.com
Grilled Chicken with Rodeo
City Bar-B-Q Rub, 123

Syncline Wine Cellars
111 Balch Road
Lyle, WA 98635
509-365-4361
www.synclinewine.com

Tonnemaker Hill Farm
4122 West Lake Sammamish
Parkway Southeast
Bellevue, WA 98008
206-660-7287
www.tonnemaker.com

Twede's Café
137 West North Bend Way
North Bend, WA 98045
425-831-5511
www.twedescafe.com
Twede's Special Hot Wings,
125

Windfall Winery / Kestrel Vinters
2890 Lee Road
Prosser, WA 99350
509-786-2675
www.kestrelwines.com

A Menu for Every Occasion

Welcome-to-the-Northwest Seafood Supper

Northwest Crab Chowder, 55

Creamy Razor Clam Linguine with Parsley and Chives, 192

Mixed Greens with Apricot-Tomme Toasts, 68

Hot Cakes' Original S'mores Cookies with Smoked Chocolate, 230

Big Night In with Your Honey

Marinated Goat Cheese with Honey and Hazelnuts, 28

Roasted Chicken with Honey-glazed Shallots, 119

Caesar Salad with Roasted Onion, Preserved Lemon, and Bacon, 64

Honeyed Panna Cottas, 226

Brunch at Home

Cherry Wood Herb-baked Eggs, 246

Pimped Root Vegetable Hash, 242

The Fairmont's Rooftop Honey-Pepper Bacon, 239

Kabocha-Buttermilk Bundt Cake, 248

Fancy Fall Birthday Dinner

Barrel-Aged White Manhattans, 263

Gilbert Cellars' Bacon-wrapped Dates, 31

Cream of Wild Mushroom Stew with Sage and Sherry, 44

Roasted Cornish Game Hens with Parsnips and Bergamot-poached Prunes, 132

Free-Form Pear Crostata, 214

Food for the Man Cave

Brave Horse Tavern's Deviled Eggs, 26

Buttermilk-battered Corn Dogs, 168

Garlic Fries, 102

Ice cream with Homemade Bourbon Butterscotch Sauce, 261

Holiday Feast

Cider-brined Turkey with Rosemary and Thyme, 120

El Gaucho's Mashed Potatoes, 86

Roasted Carrots with Mustard and Dill, 78

Seattle Winter Market Salad, 60

Dark Chocolate Cake with Figs, Fennel, and Pistachios, 225

LIGHTISH SUMMER SHOWER LUNCHEON

PICNIC PERFECT

MEXICAN NIGHT

WINTER DINNER PARTY

Quickish Pork Posole

INDEX

Reprint Permissions

page 207, Jon Rowley, "The Art of Eating an Oyster," The Beautiful Taste, December 7,
2010, http://jonrowley.com/2010/12/07/art-of-eating-an-oyster/

page 228, recipe from Mark and Michael Klebeck with Jess Thomson, *Top Pot Hand-Forged
Doughnuts: Secrets and Recipes for the Home Baker*, Chronicle Books, 2011.

Explore the Bounty of Storey's Dishing Up Series

With authentic recipes and profiles of local artisans, chefs, and farmers, each book explores the region's bounty so you can prepare your favorites at home. Now, you can travel without leaving your kitchen!

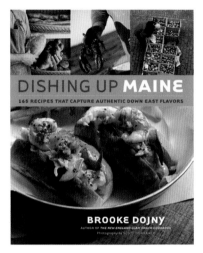

Dishing Up Maine, by Brooke Dojny. 288 pages. Paper. ISBN 978-1-58017-841-9.

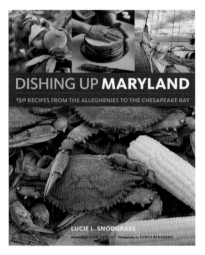

Dishing Up Maryland, by Lucie L. Snodgrass. 288 pages. Paper. ISBN 978-1-60342-527-8.

Dishing Up Oregon, by Ashley Gartland. 288 pages. Paper. ISBN 978-1-60342-566-7.

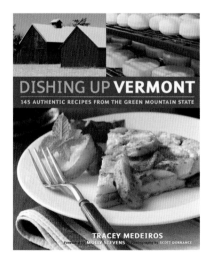

Dishing Up Vermont, by Tracey Medeiros. 288 pages. Paper. ISBN 978-1-60342-025-9.

These and other books from Storey Publishing are available wherever quality books are sold or by calling 1-800-441-5700. Visit us at *www.storey.com*.